Eight Tens @ Eight Festival

A Smith and Kraus Book
Published by Smith and Kraus, Inc.
177 Lyme Road, Hanover, NH 03755
www.SmithKraus.com

Copyright © 2001 by Smith and Kraus
All rights reserved

Manufactured in the United States of America

Cover and Text Design by Julia Hill Gignoux, Freedom Hill Design

First Edition: June 2001
10 9 8 7 6 5 4 3 2 1

CAUTION: Professionals and amateurs are hereby warned that the plays represented in this book are subject to a royalty. They are fully protected under the copyright laws of the United States of America, and of all countries covered by the International Copyright Union (including the Dominion of Canada and the rest of the British Commonwealth), and of all countries covered by the Pan-American Copyright Convention and the Universal Copyright Convention, and of all countries with which the United States has reciprocal copyright relations. All rights, including professional, amateur, motion picture, recitation, lecturing, public reading, radio broadcasting, television, video or sound taping, all other forms of mechanical or electronic reproduction such as CD-ROM and CD-I, information storage and retrieval systems and photocopying, and the rights of translation into foreign languages, are strictly reserved. Particular emphasis is laid upon the question of public readings, permission for which must be secured from the Author's agent in writing. Pages 201–203 are an extension of this copyright page.

Library of Congress Cataloguing-in-Publication Data

Eight Tens @ Eight Festival : thirty one-acts from the Santa Cruz Festivals I–VI /
edited by Wilma Marcus Chandler and John Howie Patterson. —1st ed.
p. cm. — (Contemporary playwrights series)
ISBN 1-57525-242-2
1. One-act plays, American. 2. American drama—20th century. I. Title: Eight Tens at Eight Festival. II. Chandler, Wilma Marcus. III. Patterson, John Howie. IV. Series.

PS627.O53 E39 2001
812'.04108054—dc21

Library of Congress Control Number: 2001032088

Eight TENS @ Eight *Festival*

THIRTY 10-MINUTE PLAYS FROM THE
SANTA CRUZ FESTIVALS I-VI

edited by
Wilma Marcus Chandler
and
John Howie Patterson

CONTEMPORARY PLAYWRIGHTS SERIES

Smith and Kraus, Inc.

In memory of Edith Cooper, Normann Pesenti, and Gloria Plume
and
dedicated to the loyal audiences of the
Santa Cruz Actors' Theatre

ACKNOWLEDGMENTS

The Ten Minute Festival could never happen without the help of countless numbers of stalwart souls who work and volunteer year after year to bring these plays to light.

We would like to thank the many writers and editors who have served on the play-judging committees over the years, the playwrights who have provided, at this counting, over 350 plays from which to select, the scores of directors who have allowed the plays to flourish, the hundreds of actors who have rehearsed for weeks, months (only to sit backstage for hours during the festival and then go on for ten minutes!!!) and most especially to the shift crews and board operators who make the final difference between what might be a lumbering evening of eternal set changes, and the magic, lightning-quick switches that have become the trademark of these shows. Eight plays (or nine, or ten) in one night are either a nightmare or a wondrous dream!

Most of all we wish to thank: William "Skip" Epperson, Donna Teague, David Eisley, Mark Hopkins and Dohn Grube for being the amazing set designers that they are, and our all-knowing and always faithful Lena Mason, the Festival Production Coordinator and Stage Manager who, over the years, has remained calm and glorious through many a rough sea.

CONTENTS

INTRODUCTION vii

ANCESTOR by Sam Patterson 1
APRIL SHOWERS by Philip Slater 8
ASHES by Claire Braz-Valentine 14
THE ATOMIC PINEAPPLE by David A. Sullivan 21
DINNER by Richard Markgraf 31
ETAINE AND ETAIRE by Karen Villeneuve 36
FRIED CHICKEN, HOT OR COLD by Ann MacGregor Gibb 41
HABITS by Steve "Spike" Wong 48
THE HARD CEL by Philip Pearce 54
ID by Kyle Wood 62
LOVE AND DEATH by Kathryn Chetkovich 71
MATCHING COLORS by Edith Cooper 77
MRS. SCHEINBAUM by Frank Hilmes 84
MY HIGHER POWER by Melissa Klein 89
NOCTURNE, WITH APPLES by Scott Munson 94
PARCHEESIED by John Howie Patterson 103
PAY PHONE by Wilma Marcus Chandler 110
THE PERM by Dale Elizabeth Attias 117
POETRY READING by John Chandler 124
THE RAIN ARE FALLIN by Richard Bennett 130
RETROGRADE by Doug Brook 135
SAN FRANCISCO FEVER by Anne Adams 142
SIMÓN MALDONADO'S EPIPHANY by Juan Duarte 149
SLINGIN' HASH AT THE LOWLIFE BAR AND GRILL by Susan Forrest . 154
SNACK TIME by Eric Elliot 162
SOUP by John Howie Patterson 168
THERAPY IN THE PARK by Doug Hanvey 174
TURNING INTO MOTHER by Elaine Clark McCarthy 181
UNDERPANTS by Wilma Marcus Chandler 188
ZEN GRAVY by Sharon Bandy 194

COPYRIGHT STATEMENTS 201

INTRODUCTION

The Santa Cruz Actors' Theatre has been a driving force in contemporary theatre here in the Monterey Bay Area for over fifteen years.

Long-committed to bringing new writers together with fine actors, directors and designers in projects that expand the theatre-going public's appreciation for the living art of the stage, we continue to offer full productions, staged readings by emerging playwrights and classes, residencies, and festivals of various kinds throughout the year.

The Ten Minute Festival, known as Eight Tens @ Eight, began seven years ago as a writing project for local authors in our creative and culturally diverse community, and has grown and blossomed beyond expectation to now encompass the whole West Coast.

Each January our five-week run of the winning plays is a guaranteed sell-out with audiences eager to see and argue over which plays were enjoyable, which were "little jewels" and which ones were gratefully only ten minutes long.

This collection brings together thirty of the winning plays. We hope you will find them inspiring and entertaining.

Wilma Marcus Chandler
Artistic Director, Eight Tens @ Eight Festival

John Howie Patterson
Manager, Santa Cruz Actors' Theatre

Santa Cruz, California
December, 2000

ANCESTOR
by Sam Patterson

FIRST PERFORMANCE
January 1996

ORIGINAL CAST

Millicent	Johanna Bochner
Sid	Mikki Adams
Jane	April Vogensen
Directed by	Mary Kay Gamel
Sets by	William "Skip" Epperson

CHARACTERS

MILLICENT: About thirty-eight years old. Obsessive about ancestors, blood lines.
SID: Millicent's brother, about thirty-four years old.
JANE: Engaged to marry Sid.

SCENE
Millicent's apartment in an exclusive suburb of New York City.

TIME
Present.

SETTING
The set is an elegant living room. It's a hot summer's day. Shades are drawn to keep out the heat. The soft drone of an air-conditioner can be heard. Sofa, chairs are covered with bed sheets.

ANCESTOR

At rise: Doorbell chimes. Millicent enters stage right and crosses to front door, center stage. She's wearing a hostess gown. She opens door to reveal couple who are obviously suffering from the heat. Jane is wearing shorts and a halter. Sid is wearing an unbuttoned short sleeved shirt with shirttail hanging out over shorts. He's carrying a small suitcase. He mops brow with handkerchief as he enters.

MILLICENT: You poor darlings. You're absolutely melting.

SID: *(Placing suitcase on floor.)* It must be a hundred and ten in the shade.

JANE: *(Taking deep breath.)* Air-conditioning. I love it.

MILLICENT: This abominable heat wave! Ten days . . . unrelenting . . . How can you stand to live in an apartment without air-conditioning!

JANE: Thanks for saving our lives for this weekend.

MILLICENT: When Sid called and told me how hot it was in the city, how could I not ask you to come out. *(Pause.)* Did I tell you Jack is away? On assignment?

JANE: Sid's promised we'll move to an air-conditioned place when—

MILLICENT: When what Sid? When the cows come home!

SID: When we save up enough for a security deposit.

JANE: *When* we get married. In the Fall. Right, Sid?

MILLICENT: In the meantime you fry, you poor darling.

(Sid looks at sofa, picks at sheet to register annoyance, then sits.)

MILLICENT: *(Noticing his annoyance.)* I think the sheets make the room seem cooler, don't you?

SID: Not to mention, it keeps me from sweating all over the expensive fabric.

MILLICENT: Sid.

SID: Where is Jack anyway?

MILLICENT: *(Pause.)* Washington, I think.

SID: You don't know where he is?

MILLICENT: Of course I know where Jack is. I said Washington, didn't I? *(Beat.)* Fry like two eggs on the sidewalk. You could get heatstroke. *(Pause.)* Remember Sid . . . when Daddy fried an egg on the sidewalk right in front of the house on Benefield Street?

SID: You're making that up.

MILLICENT: You were ten and I was. . . *(Pause.)* Well never mind. *(Beat.)* Won't you let me lend you the money?

SID: Money for what?

MILLICENT: For the security deposit. You could get Jane off the lower East Side.
SID: I think I told you before. Our building's not wired for air-conditioning.
JANE: I don't mind the lower East Side.
MILLICENT: You can't raise children on the lower East Side.
SID: We don't have any children.
MILLICENT: I know you don't. You're not even married yet.
SID: We could have a child even though we're not married.
MILLICENT: But you wouldn't.
SID: *(Sid looks knowingly at Jane.)* We might.
MILLICENT: *(Surveying room, then to Jane.)* I'm afraid you're going to have to sleep out here.
SID: As long as it's cool.
JANE: It'll do fine.
SID: I'm not going to budge from this room until Monday morning.
MILLICENT: I'm old fashioned, I guess. The two of you sleeping in the same bed. Well sofa bed. As it turns out.
SID: Which is quite different from a regular bed. Anyway we've been living together for the past six months.
MILLICENT: What you do in town is no concern of mine. But out here in the suburbs. In the confines of my own home.
SID: We're getting married in six months. For Christ's sake.
MILLICENT: Sid . . . Please don't take the Lord's name in vain. *(Long pause.)* I made us a batch of ice tea. How about it?
JANE: Just what I was wishing for.
MILLICENT: You must get over your shyness with me, Jane . . . If you wish for ice tea, you should just come right out with it. If you're going to be my sister-in-law.
SID: It's just Jane's way of being polite.
MILLICENT: But I could make some iced coffee. I have some cokes in the fridge.
JANE: I really would like iced tea.
MILLICENT: Well all right. But only if you're sure. *(Beat.)* Sid can tell you I'm rather famous for my iced tea.
SID: How many ways are there to make ice tea?
MILLICENT: I fix it the same way Momma did. First bring the water just to the boiling point. Not a moment beyond. I use the loose tea leaves. From a mail-order house in San Francisco. Then . . .
JANE: Can I help?
MILLICENT: No. You *may* not. Everything's all ready. You two just sit quietly and cool off.

(Millicent exits.)

SID: *(Looking after Millicent, then lowering his voice.)* It didn't take her long to bring up money.

JANE: Sid! She might hear you. Your sister seems generous to a fault.

SID: Generous, my ass.

JANE: I don't think you know your sister very well.

SID: She never misses an opportunity to point out my lack of ability to earn big bucks. Like Jack does.

JANE: Maybe she just wants to share.

SID: I grew up with her, not you.

JANE: I've seen this kind of situation before. You'll always be her little brother. You may as well just accept that.

SID: What are you? A psychologist?

JANE: Perhaps you're just a wee bit oversensitive.

SID: Baloney.

JANE: Jealous?

SID: Of what!

JANE: *(Indicating room.)* Of all this for one thing. And the central air-conditioning.

SID: *(Shaking head violently.)* No! I hate all this stuff from Bloomingdale's. I feel like a mannequin in a display window.

JANE: Jack's position maybe. His money.

SID: I'm not jealous.

JANE: Me thinks the gentleman doth protest too much.

(Millicent enters with tray of iced teas, places on coffee table.)

MILLICENT: Protest what?

SID: Nothing. Jane just likes to quote Shakespeare. No reason.

MILLICENT: *(Handing a glass of tea to Jane.)* I adore Shakespeare. When we were growing up . . . remember, Sid? Mother used to read us Shakespeare.

SID: You have the most remarkable memory.

MILLICENT: *(Ignoring his jab.)* Mother could have been an actress if she'd had certain advantages.

SID: I seem to remember her reading books like "Amarilly of Clothesline Alley."

MILLICENT: Oh she took all the parts. Read them out with such feeling. *(Pause, then assumes regal pose.)* Out! Out! Damned spot!

SID: Oh yeah. I remember now.

MILLICENT: Of course you remember.

SID: That's when old Lady Macbeth puts her dog, Spot, out for the night.

(Sid laughs, Jane joins in.)

(Millicent scowls, then smiles.)

MILLICENT: Don't laugh at Sid's chestnuts or you'll spoil him, Jane. *(Pause.)* That's what we can do. After you're cooled off a bit, we can read one of Shakespeare's tomes.
(Millicent goes to bookshelf, looks for book.)

MILLICENT: I bought several copies of Hamlet when we did a reading for the Tuesday Club.

SID: But I brought a puzzle to work on.
(Sid gets up, retrieves puzzle box from suitcase, and holds it up for Millicent to see. It's a picture of Mona Lisa.)

SID: See? Mona Lisa. I found it in the closet when I went to get the suitcase.

MILLICENT: Mona Lisa. *(Millicent goes to coffee table, looks at box.)* I'm sure I gave you Mona Lisa for Christmas . . . two . . . three years ago?

SID: Maybe. I don't remember.

MILLICENT: There's a lot you don't remember.

SID: 1000 pieces. It should carry us through the whole weekend.

JANE: You know I've been wanting to ask you who the gentleman is over the mantle piece.

SID: Your guess is as good as . . .

MILLICENT: The ancestor! *(Glaring at Sid.)* Our great great grandfather Duncan Gordon. Usually I just plainly refer to him as "the ancestor."

SID: Come on, Millicent. Jane's going to be family. You know darn good and well.

JANE: He's certainly handsome.

MILLICENT: My last hope.

SID: *(Shrugs as if giving up.)* Ok to use the coffee table to work the puzzle? *(Dumps puzzle pieces on table.)*

MILLICENT: *(Brightly.)* Careful not to scratch the finish. *(To Jane.)* My little ace in the hole.

SID: *(Arranging puzzle pieces.)* I'm starting the puzzle. How about it! Jane?

MILLICENT: Right now I'm afraid I'm up a blind alley. But I've got to keep going. He's my last chance to make it to the Daughters.

SID: *(Holding up two puzzle pieces.)* Here's a good sized portion of her lip.

MILLICENT: You see . . . the courthouse in Waxsaw County, S.C., burned to the ground in 1809. Most of the records were lost. Including a record of Duncan Gordon having fought in the War of Independence. If I can prove my case . . . *(To Sid.)* You could join the Sons of the Revolution. And of course, your children. And so on.

SID: *(Putting another piece of the puzzle in place.)* Ah. The mystery of that provocative smile. If we only knew what it meant. Like she knows some big joke on the whole world.

MILLICENT: *(To Jane.)* I do know Duncan Gordon left a young widow. I have proof of her existence. It's all so fascinating. Elizabeth Gordon moved to Trenton, New Jersey, to be near the cemetery where Duncan is buried. I went there myself. It was eerie. Something led me straight to Duncan's grave.

SID: I read somewhere . . . some art historian claims . . .

JANE: Then your portrait of Duncan.

SID: The Mona Lisa is, in fact, Da Vinci's self-portrait. In drag. But would he do that? What earthly reason.

JANE: *(To Sid.)* He was a notorious homosexual. Everyone knows that.

MILLICENT: *(Frowning.)* Everyone knows what! What are you saying?

SID: She's not talking about your precious Duncan.

JANE: What! Oh heaven's no. *(Burst of laughter.)* I meant Leonardo. You thought I meant your ancestor?

MILLICENT: You asked about Duncan's portrait.

SID: Ah. The tip of her nose.

MILLICENT: While doing my research, I uncovered a cousin.

SID: Under what rock?

MILLICENT: *(Tersely.)* Sid . . . you never met her. She's a third or fourth cousin on Daddy's side. When she died, she left the portrait to me. *(Pause.)* And your family . . . Jane?

JANE: Johnny's-come-lately, I'm afraid. I'm only third generation Irish, German, Swedish stock.

MILLICENT: Of course you need only to prove that one of your parent's ancestors go back to the Revolution for your children to be eligible.

JANE: That would have to be you, Sid.

SID: A bunch of snobs. Who gives a damn if you had an ancestor in the Revolutionary War or not. I wouldn't want any children of mine to . . .

MILLICENT: If you're referring to the Merricks. They are atypical. There are many lovely people involved here. They do a lot of good work that no one ever hears about.

JANE: They wouldn't let Marion Anderson sing in Constitution Hall just because she had skin of a different color.

MILLICENT: But that was such a big to-do over nothing. I had it all explained to me. They say Eleanor Roosevelt was at the bottom of things. Used the situation to contrive. *(Pause.)* I made some tomato sandwiches to eat later.

SID: With Vidalia onion?

MILLICENT: Of course. I made them as soon as I knew you were coming. With no crusts. Just the way Momma used to do. I pressed them flat and put a damp tea towel over them so they will be good and mushy.

SID: Listen. If you two don't stop yapping and help me, we'll never get the puzzle done by Sunday night. *(Holding up box.)* Look at all this intricate detail in the background. You know how difficult that is to figure out! I bet most people never even notice it. There's a road curving around. That little dark spot could be some peasant with a big bundle on his back. And a bridge on the right. Spikey mountains in the distance. An icy cold lake! Who know what's happening in the part we can't see. Hiding there in the shadows.
(Blackout.)

END OF PLAY

APRIL SHOWERS
by Philip Slater

FIRST PERFORMANCE
January 2000

ORIGINAL CAST

    Forkman/George . . . . .Richard Lockie
    Forkboy/Bobby . . . . .Jeff Bean
    Shirley . . . . .Celandine Orescan
    Knife/Walter . . . . .Derek Eselius
    Spoon #1 . . . . .Crystal Bettancourt
    Spoon #2 . . . . .Sara Bickford
    Directed by . . . . .Sebastian DeFrancesco
    Sets by . . . . .Mark Hopkins

APRIL SHOWERS

A man, medium height, with a hat shaped like the tines of a fork, stands in the second stage right section of a four-section bin about waist-high. He stands stiffly, his body tilted back against the upper stage right corner.

FORKMAN: I hate being the first one, all alone in the dark. So quiet. The way my voice echoes in here. Ah, they're coming at last — I hope they don't put one of those stuck-up knives in with me . . .
(The lights go out suddenly. The sound of a dishwasher being opened.)
Hey! Who are you? You're new, aren't you?
(The sound of a dishwasher closing. Lights up again. A shorter, younger man wearing a hat with shorter tines has appeared in the next section, stage left.)
FORKBOY: I'm Bobby. They just brought me from the store. What is this place?
FORKMAN: You'll find out soon enough.
BOBBY: What's that supposed to mean?
FORKMAN: It's a little unnerving the first time it happens . . .
BOBBY: What?! Tell me!
FORKMAN: Relax, boy, I'll show you the ropes. Here they come again . . .
(Lights go out again, sound of a dishwasher being opened.)
Pay no attention to those people. We don't mingle . . .
(Sound of a dishwasher closing. Lights come up again. In the far left section of the bin are two women with spoon hats. They talk quietly to each other, standing close together in the same stiff position as the others, tilting left.)
FORKMAN: Besides, they're . . . *(He whispers to the Bobby.)*
BOBBY: Wow!
FORKMAN: It's a big world, Bobby. Unfortunately you won't get to see much of it. You little fellas only get used on special occasions.
BOBBY: How do you know that?
FORKMAN: Oh, I've been around. I've travelled, boy. I went to a potluck once.
BOBBY: Wow! Uh . . . what is that, exactly?
FORKMAN: It's dangerous. You go to a completely strange place with all kinds of weird food and sometimes they forget about you and you never get home again! Kind of like a picnic.
BOBBY: A pic . . . ?
FORKMAN: I know a guy who got taken to a picnic and was completely forgotten. He spent years all alone in a soft green place and when he got back home no one recognized him. He was all dark and weird-looking and they never used him anymore, except to pry open lids.

BOBBY: That's awful!

FORKMAN: Life's an adventure, boy. You should have been here before they got health conscious. Eggs, cheese, you name it! Stuck to you like . . . *(Lights go out again, sound of a dishwasher being opened.)* Oh, great. Him. I should have warned you about those . . . Oh! Hi, Shirley!

(Sound of a dishwasher closing. Lights up again. A tall knife man is standing stiffly, tilted upper stage right, in the far right bin. He wears a pointed hat. A Forkwoman, medium height, is in the Forkman's bin, tilted upper stage right. The Forkman is still tilted upper stage left.)

SHIRLEY: Hi, George.

GEORGE: How have you been? You look really . . .

SHIRLEY: Down.

GEORGE: Sorry to hear that.

SHIRLEY: I hit bottom.

GEORGE: I hate it when that happens.

BOBBY: What?

GEORGE: Being on the bottom. You lie there week after week with everyone on top of you.

SHIRLEY: You feel so weighed down. It's so depressing . . .

GEORGE: Especially when you've got a bent one right on top of you! Pressing down on all the wrong places! Like that poor devil that fell in the disposal. God, he was scratchy! Sometimes I wish I was in one of those fancy places where every fork is exactly the same. But then I wouldn't have ever met you, Shirley! The sunshine of my . . .

SHIRLEY: The load begins to get lighter and you think, "Hurray! I'm going to be taken out! At last!" And then, BANG, the whole lot are back on top of you again! If they hadn't had that dinner party last weekend I'd be there still.

GEORGE: You'd think they'd have the decency to rotate us, not just grab whoever happens to be on top ...

SHIRLEY: And the way they throw us in any which way . . . Remember the time they threw a knife in our room? Wasn't that awful? *(To the knife.)* No offense.

KNIFE: None taken. It was the worst day of my life.

SHIRLEY: We all felt so uncomfortable. We didn't know what to say to each other . . . *(Whispering to George.)* So afraid of making a faux pas in front of him. And having him make some pointed rejoinder. They can be so cutting, you know . . .

(A clicking is heard as the machine is turned on.)

GEORGE: Hang on! Here we go!
BOBBY: What?! What's this? What's happening? Can I get in with you?
(He tilts over to George's side, but George has already slid over so he's pressed up against Shirley.)
GEORGE: Better stay put, boy! It's gonna get pretty wild around here!
(To Shirley, putting his arms around her.)
You O.K., honey?
(A sudden sound of rushing water and machinery as the machine starts up. All the characters blink their eyes and hunch over a little as if they were being deluged with water, and they shout to be heard.)
BOBBY: But what about me?! What about me?!
(As George continues to ignore him he tilts himself with great difficulty over toward the two spoons, who now slowly shift upper stage right and each put an arm around him.)
SPOON 1: Buck up, boy! Won't last long!
SPOON 2: I know it's awfully scary the first time . . .
SPOON 1: My first time — almost bent myself!
SPOON 2: I was so scared — if I'd been carrying anything I would have spilled it, I was shaking so much . . .
SPOON 1: I had to hold her, keep her from rattling.
SPOON 2: If she hadn't been here I don't know what I would have done. But you get used to it.
GEORGE: Hang on to me, baby! I'll keep you dry!
(Shirley pushes him away so that he slides over, tilting upper stage left.)
SHIRLEY: Stop that, George! If I don't get clean, they'll put me back and make me go through it all over again! Wait till we get home!
GEORGE: But what if they don't put us together?
SHIRLEY: Go fork yourself, George!
GEORGE: Come on, honey, don't get your tines all twisted, you know I'd do anything for you! I'm just excited to see you, is all!
(A lull in the noise, sound of water emptying out. They all straighten up and stop blinking. George and Shirley talk quietly.)
BOBBY: What? What now?
SPOON 1: We're on the short cycle.
BOBBY: What's that mean?
SPOON 2: It means it's going to get really, really hot in here.
BOBBY: Why do the other forks hate you?
SPOON 1: Jealous, that's all.

SPOON 2: It's because we nest so perfectly together. Each one fitting so deliciously on top of the other . . .

(They demonstrate.)

BOBBY: We fit pretty well, too, not as tight, maybe . . .

SPOON 1: The big ones get bent out of shape with use. Tines get crooked. Don't nest well. It's a hard life.

SPOON 2: Oh, it's so hot! I hate this part!

(Spoon 1 fans her.)

BOBBY: It's worse than the water!

SHIRLEY: It doesn't last forever, thank God.

SPOON 2: It's hard for him. It all seems so terrifying the first time.

SHIRLEY: I remember my first time. I thought I was melting.

GEORGE: It can happen! I saw a knife and fork melt once! They were all white and they just turned into blobs!

KNIFE: Plastic. We're made of sterner stuff.

SHIRLEY: Speak for yourself. My tines are starting to sag.

GEORGE: You still look like a million dollars, honey!

BOBBY: I feel like I'm suffocating!

KNIFE: Just remember, son, you're stainless.

SPOON 2: I hope I don't wind up on top again, I'm ready for a rest.

SHIRLEY: Once I was the first one out five times in a row! I was exhausted!

SPOON 1: Don't know why the fools can't rotate us. Obviously don't know the first thing about maintenance.

GEORGE: I was just saying that very same thing to Shirley here . . .

SPOON 1: What about you, big fella?

KNIFE: Well, we don't nest like you folks. They just toss us in, helter-skelter. All in a jumble — never know who's going to be out first . . .

GEORGE: Then how come you act so superior?

KNIFE: Well, after all, we are a bit sharper than you chaps . . .

SHIRLEY: If we didn't hold the meat, you couldn't cut it!

KNIFE: I'm quite aware of that fact, and if I've never expressed my gratitude I can only apologize for an unforgivable lapse in courtesy. We do appreciate it, I assure you.

GEORGE: So what makes you think you're better than us?

KNIFE: Well it's just that . . . I don't mean to sound prudish, but . . . you folks are always . . . entering people's mouths! That just seems so . . . well, I don't know how to say it . . .

SPOON 1: Go on, big fella, spit it out!

KNIFE: Well it just seems rather . . . disgusting!

SHIRLEY: You've never been in a mouth?
KNIFE: Never!
GEORGE: I find that hard to believe, Walter.
WALTER: You think I'm lying? I never lie! I've always prided myself on being completely upright! Integrity is my watchword! And . . . stop looking at me that way!
SPOON 1: Come on, big fella, *never?*
WALTER: No! Not . . . not really . . . I mean . . . Oh . . . all right! Just . . . just once. I was . . . I was very young, you understand . . .
SPOON 2: Walter, it's not your fault! You didn't have any control over it . . .
SHIRLEY: What happened? Tell us!
WALTER: It was . . . peanut butter! He was . . . holding me in his hand, using me to scoop it out and spread it on a cracker, and then . . . at the end . . . he just suddenly . . . he just suddenly . . . put me in his mouth! It was so utterly odious and repulsive! I don't know how you people stand it all the time!
SPOON 1: Come on, Walter, fess up. You enjoyed it, didn't you.
WALTER: Of course not!
SPOON 1: Not even a little bit?
WALTER: No! NO! How could you say such a . . .
SPOON 1: Walter?
WALTER: Oh. God. Yes. Yes, I did! That was the most shameful part!
(A click as the cycle ends.)
GEORGE: Buck up, Walter! We've all been there!
SPOON 1: Join the crowd. We're all just flatware, after all.
SPOON 2: In a way being in a mouth is a little like . . . you know . . . the old days? You know what I mean? The softness . . .
SHIRLEY: Oh! Yes! Ohh! That was so nice! Lying there all peaceful in that soapy water. Caressed by a soft sponge . . .
BOBBY: What? What was?
GEORGE: Something you'll never know, boy. Unless this thing breaks down.
SPOON 1: Getting washed by hand.
SPOON 2: Will we ever have it again?
(All except Bobby sigh dreamily.)
SHIRLEY: Oh, well, at least it's getting cooler . . .
(The lights slowly fade.)

END OF PLAY

ASHES
by Claire Braz-Valentine

FIRST PERFORMANCE
January 1996

ORIGINAL CAST

Joseph ....Robert Johnson
Annie ....Patti Fitchen
Directed by ....Karen Magaldi-Ungar
Sets by ....William "Skip" Epperson

CHARACTERS
ANNIE
JOSEPH: Annie's brother.

NOTES
Ashes is a play with two characters: Joseph and Annie, adult brother and sister. The play takes place in the living room of their deceased father, Timothy O'Malley. They have just returned from their father's memorial service. Although they have suffered a terrible childhood, they have learned to cope between themselves even though they appear to have not learned to communicate with each other. Joseph is the quieter of the two and the peacemaker. Annie is more animated and, although she appears to be more outward, depends greatly on Joseph. They have a great love for each other and during the play reenact the ways in which they loved each other as children to solve issues and settle problems. This is a game they play. This is how they cope. This is how they love each other.

SETTING
Living room. Couch. Side table with bottles of liquor. Chair.

TIME
Present. Evening.

ASHES

Joseph enters sadly, stands for minute, thinks quietly. He walks to the mantel, picks up a photo of an older man who looks like him, and almost breaks down.

JOSEPH: God, Daddy . . . I'm sure going to miss you. I really never thought I'd feel this way, but I do.
(From outside, we hear Annie stomping her feet and yelling.)
ANNIE: Oh shit! Bull shit! Cow shit!
(Annie stands at the doorway, wiping her feet.)
ANNIE: Well, this is just perfect. I return from our father's memorial service and walk right into a pile of fresh cow shit. How appropriate! That really stinks, literally and figuratively. Why didn't he ever keep those damn cows fenced in? They're always wandering around the place like they're some damn dignitaries in search of a bathroom. Daddy paid about as much attention to his animals as he did to us, Joseph. *(Loud.)* I said there's cow shit on the front walk, Joseph!
(Annie comes in and slams the door.)
JOSEPH: We'll have to sell the cows now, Annie.
ANNIE: What's this WE business? What do you expect me to do? Put a cow in my car with my kids and drive it home to the city? Take it up in the elevator to my apartment? Take it on walks through the city with a For-Sale sign around its neck? Where I live, Joseph, people don't buy cows, at least not with the fur still on them.
JOSEPH: Don't get so dramatic. And stop acting childish. We've got to put up an ad at the Farmer's Co-op, make a few phone calls to some of Daddy's friends, that's all. Simple. And it's hide not fur.
(Annie takes off some of her clothes.)
ANNIE: Hide, leather, fur. No difference. I don't eat them. I don't sell them! Jesus! It's hot in here.
JOSEPH: Barbara kept it warm. He was always cold . . . at the end, the last few months.
ANNIE: Oh . . . I didn't know that. *(Awkward.)* So . . . I'm probably having a fucking hot flash. I bet I'm starting menopause. Isn't that a bitch? You always did get the breaks, no periods, no childbirth. All you got were pimples and you still turn out gorgeous. Where is that damn thermostat?
(Annie finds thermostat, turns it down. Throws things in a pile on a chair.)
(Joseph picks up a few of Annie's things.)

JOSEPH: You're dressed like a nun again! Every time you want to escape something you dress like a nun. Even down to the beads. It's all right, Annie. Everything's going to be all right.

ANNIE: I know that. And I am not dressed like a nun! I just couldn't decide what things to wear, so I wore everything black I owned.

JOSEPH: You are too dressed like a nun. Sometimes I really think you should have become one. There was a time when you wanted to. THAT would have been interesting!

ANNIE: Oh, right! We've got enough guilt in our lives from twelve years of Catholic school, thanks. Anyway I haven't been to Church in years . . . until today at least. Isn't that something . . . he lived such a hell-raising life and then everyone has to go to Church to say good bye to him. I knew he was really dead then, because if he wasn't he would have died laughing looking at all of us acting so pious.

JOSEPH: Speak for yourself. I take my family to church every Sunday.

ANNIE: I know you do, Joseph. You were always better than I.

(Annie looks out the window.)

ANNIE: Where the hell is everybody?

JOSEPH: They took Aunt Katherine home. I told them to take their time, that we had to have a chance to talk. I thought you and I should discuss the arrangements alone.

ANNIE: Arrangements! What arrangements? The only thing left to do is go home and arrange to never come back and that's exactly what I intend to do. The sooner the better.

JOSEPH: His ashes Annie.

ANNIE: His what?

JOSEPH: His ashes. We have to decide what to do with his ashes.

ANNIE: What do you mean, DO with them?

JOSEPH: How to dispose of his ashes.

ANNIE: I thought they did that.

JOSEPH: Who?

ANNIE: The people . . . at the Crematorium.

JOSEPH: They give the ashes to the family. One of us has to pick them up Wednesday morning.

ANNIE: Oh shit!

JOSEPH: We can't ask Barbara to do that. It's not right. They were only married for nine months.

ANNIE: Since when did this family ever care what's right or not right? He left every damn cent to her, didn't he? Not that I care. Not that he ever gave either of us anything but grief. Let her hire someone to pick up the ashes, as if I give a damn.

JOSEPH: Annie, I know you are capable of talking without swearing.

ANNIE: *(Under her breath.)* Shit. Shit. Shit.

JOSEPH: Listen, this is just as hard on me as it is on you. That's why I wanted a chance to talk to you alone. I'll pick them up . . . you want me to pick them up. I'll do it if that's what you want. Just say so.

ANNIE: I can't do it. That's all I know. If you want to, fine . . . then you do it.

JOSEPH: *(A little irritated.)* There is no WANT to. One of us has to do it. But you've got to help me decide how to dispose of them. It's our responsibility, both of ours.

ANNIE: Oh God, Joseph. What do they come in . . . the ashes . . . what are they going to hand you?

JOSEPH: A box I think.

ANNIE: Jesus' tits!

JOSEPH: We could have them put into an urn. I mean, if we want to keep them. What do you think?

ANNIE: Are you crazy? An urn for Chrissake! This is our father, Joseph, who came home drunk every night and beat the shit out of our mother. The father we used to hide from under the covers. Why don't we just build a god-damned altar to him and petition the Pope to make him a saint?

JOSEPH: I should have known better than to think you'd be any help on this.

ANNIE: Well, how do we know they're his ashes? They could be anybody's . . . they could be sweepings from somebody's fireplace.

JOSEPH: You're overreacting again. And you keep changing the subject. Are you going to help me with this or not? *(No answer.)* Listen, Annie, I know you don't want to deal with this. You think I want to? I know what you're doing. You think if you can just act out, just *(Frustrated.)* act like you can't handle it, then I'll have to do it. You always do that. Ever since you were a little kid you've done that.

ANNIE: Well maybe it's not acting. Maybe I can't handle it.

JOSEPH: Well maybe I can't either, but I just get stuck with it because I'm the man. Is this some kind of revenge because you think you're going through the change of life?

ANNIE: Don't be ridiculous. It has nothing to do with anything. You just seem to care and I don't. Isn't that fairly clear? You just seem to want everything to appear normal. Our father dies and we settle arrangements. Just like in a real family. Except we aren't a real family. How old were you before your nightmares stopped, Joseph? I was thirty-two years old and I still woke up screaming.

(No answer. Joseph is very tense.)

ANNIE: Oh God! You still have them, don't you? Oh this is really shit! Don't you see. This is not fair. I'll just tell Barbara to give me a million dollars and I'll carry his God-damned ashes around in my purse for the rest of my life.

JOSEPH: I thought you said you didn't care about the money.

ANNIE: Well, I've got three sons to raise, don't I? It's not like I'd buy a Mercedes with it. I'm a single mother and I'm a secretary. Not that I expected anything from him anyway. Listen, Joseph, don't bother with the ashes. You shouldn't have to do that. Just go home and let them keep them.

JOSEPH: We have to go there on Wednesday morning and pick them up. Barbara asked us to, to tend to the final arrangements.

ANNIE: Just don't show up.

JOSEPH: I can't do that. It isn't right.

ANNIE: Oh well, now for the first time in history the Timothy O'Malley family is interested in what's right. Now that he's dead, we can all just start pretending we're just like everyone else. And for starters we will sit rationally and discuss what to do with his burnt corpse.

(Joseph makes a visible effort to stay composed.)

JOSEPH: We should have them strewn at sea. That's what he wanted. We have a choice . . . the crematorium provides a boat or a plane. We can take either. They do a nice service and let the ashes out at sea.

ANNIE: I don't believe this.

JOSEPH: Well, what do you want? A plane or a boat? We can arrange for either on Wednesday. We should both go.

ANNIE: Go? What do you mean go? We're supposed to be there? We're supposed to dump the ashes? Forget it. I can't do it.

JOSEPH: You can. You just don't want to.

ANNIE: You got that right. And you're not fooling me. You don't want to either. He was a monster to you, Joseph. Anyway, I'm terrified of planes and you know that. That leaves the boat. That's disgusting, what with the wind blowing and everything and ashes flying all over, all over our faces and into our hair . . .

(Joseph is at the end of his rope.)

JOSEPH: They stop the God-damned boat, Annie. There is no God-damned wind. They say a little prayer and you simply pour the ashes into the fucking sea.

ANNIE: Sort of like garbage night at sea, huh?

(Joseph is very agitated. Goes to the cabinet. Pours himself a large whiskey.)

JOSEPH: What do you want from me, Annie. Just what the hell do you want?

ANNIE: I'll have a whiskey thanks.

(Joseph pours drinks. Brings one to Annie.)

JOSEPH: That's not what I meant, and you know it.

(Annie studies her drink.)

ANNIE: Daddy was drunk out of his mind every day of their lives almost until the day he died. He broke our mother's heart with his other women. She died an early death, unhappy and miserable. The only time I ever remember laughing as a kid, I remember laughing with you. And as an adult, when I see your face I remember the pain we suffered. That's the worse thing they did to us. I can't look into your eyes without remembering pain.

JOSEPH: We've got to start letting go of the pain, Annie. I think he loved us in his own way.

ANNIE: I want the ashes.

JOSEPH: What?

ANNIE: I'll pick them up Wednesday. I don't want you to have to deal with this.

JOSEPH: Why don't I believe you? I appreciate the gesture, Annie, but I know you better than that. You'd just dump them some place.

ANNIE: So what's the matter with that? When I die, Joseph, I want you to promise you will throw away my ashes.

JOSEPH: Annie, please, I'm exhausted. Please discuss this with me. Like an adult, if that's possible.

ANNIE: Will you promise me that?

JOSEPH: Where?

ANNIE: In the garbage.

JOSEPH: OK. If I'm still alive and that's what you want. I promise I will dump your ashes in the garbage.

ANNIE: In a bag.

JOSEPH: Fine.

ANNIE: Paper, not plastic.

JOSEPH: Fine.

ANNIE: There's no law against that, is there?

JOSEPH: Annie, if there is a law against it, I wouldn't care. If you want to go to your maker in a paper bag, then by the grace of God, that's the way you'll go. A promise is a promise.

ANNIE: Thanks, Joey. Now can I have Daddy's?

JOSEPH: I wouldn't trust you for a minute with them.

ANNIE: Fuck it then. Do it yourself, if that's the way you want it.

JOSEPH: Fine. I will.

ANNIE: Well, that's settled then. I knew you'd see it my way.

(Annie walks to the window, looks out.)

ANNIE: Where the hell is everybody? I'm starving. I made your favorite pork chop casserole because I knew today would be tough on you.

JOSEPH: *(Sarcastic.)* Gee, Annie, you're so thoughtful I just don't know what to say.

ANNIE: I love you too, Joey.

(Annie looks directly at him — serious.)

ANNIE: More than anything or anyone. Always have, always will.

END OF PLAY

THE ATOMIC PINEAPPLE
by David A. Sullivan

FIRST PERFORMANCE
January 1997

ORIGINAL CAST

Ludwig Wittgenstein . . . . .Scott Harrison
Werner Heisenberg . . . . .Malte Frid-Nielsen
Directed by . . . . .Evan Hunt
Sets by . . . . .Donna Teague

CHARACTERS

LUDWIG WITTGENSTEIN: A sixty-year-old philosopher with piercing eyes and wavy dark hair laced with gray who is dressed in a rumpled, brown, herring-bone patterned jacket with a white button-down shirt —open at the collar, matching brown pants, socks and shoes.

WERNER HEISENBERG: A forty-seven-year-old balding physicist whose remaining fringe of hair is a salt-and-pepper halo around his ears. He is dressed in a crisp blue sports jacket with brown patches on the elbows, blue slacks, socks, shoes and a stiff white shirt with a blue tie.

SET

Upstage center, a five foot tall wooden bookcase. The top is half full of neatly stacked books, the bottom is a two-door cupboard. Downstage center are two wooden folding chairs.

THE ATOMIC PINEAPPLE

As the play opens, Wittgenstein is seated cross-legged between the two chairs attempting to finish a bridge of books he has been constructing from one to the other. Heisenberg is standing behind him, upstage left, looking on bemusedly. Wittgenstein holds a brown notebook in one hand, in the other a blue one. He makes a tepee shape from them and places it onto the cantilevered bridge, which collapses, leaving him holding the two books, which he lowers onto his own head as a dunce cap, then slowly turns towards Heisenberg.

WITTGENSTEIN: Scheiße!

HEISENBERG: I could've told you it wouldn't work. There wasn't enough counterweight.

WITTGENSTEIN: Ah, counter weight. *(He places the tepee of journals on the floor between the two chairs. Then he picks up the fallen books and begins to arrange the stacks so they cantilever over the gap again.)* But were you certain it wouldn't work?

HEISENBERG: *(Advancing.)* Natürlich.

WITTGENSTEIN: Yet you watched me without assisting?

HEISENBERG: *(Picks up black journal with a piece of paper protruding. Hands it to Wittgenstein.)* Yes.

WITTGENSTEIN: *(Takes the journal and adds it to one of the stacks.)* As you watched the Nazis deplete the Universities in Germany and said nothing? Did atomic bomb research and said nothing about the implications? My grandfather was a Jew you know — before he converted to improve his business opportunities. He used to squinch corks into his eyes and chase me around the dining table when I was a boy shouting: "The Golum's going to gobble your tender flesh!" Funny man, but two-faced.

HEISENBERG: *(He grips the back of the chair.)* Two-faced? Is that what you asked me down to Oxford for? To lecture me about my uranium fission research for the Reich? It's 1950, Herr Wittgenstein, and I've heard all this rot before.

WITTGENSTEIN: *(Stands with black journal in hand.)* No no.

HEISENBERG: *(Advancing.)* I had to do some fancy footwork to get my Leipzig chair, I wasn't going to throw it away because of a fanatic's crackpot policy concerning Jews.

WITTGENSTEIN: *(Retreating behind the other chair.)* No lecture.

HEISENBERG: *(Stalking.)* The Copenhagen Spirit was finally being accepted! Verstehen Sie das?

WITTGENSTEIN: *(Circles the chairs, followed by Heisenberg, until he arrives at his original spot. He spies the paper that sticks out of the black journal he's holding.)* I just thought you might want to see . . .

HEISENBERG: *(Interested.)* You have something for me?

WITTGENSTEIN: *(Placing the black journal on the left stack.)* . . . your mistake. Only in hindsight do we find certainty. You weren't certain the books would fall until they fell.

HEISENBERG: I don't see what this has to do with the Heisenberg uncertainty principle, since the scale is so vastly different. You did interrupt my trip back from the International Congress of Mathematicians to talk about my principle didn't you?

WITTGENSTEIN: *(Gesturing to the chair, stage left.)* Here, stand on this chair, Werner.

HEISENBERG: *(Stepping back.)* What?

WITTGENSTEIN: *(Taking his hand and leading him back to the chair.)* You'll be my counter weight. *(Reluctantly Heisenberg steps onto the chair and sits on its back, his feet on the books.)*

HEISENBERG: This isn't child's play I'm talking about.

WITTGENSTEIN: *(He rearranges the stack beneath Heisenberg's feet, picks up the two journals from the floor, then moves to the other chair, which he mounts.)* Oh but it is, it is. They're the ones who play language games best because they don't think about them — Marco?

HEISENBERG: *(Involuntarily.)* Polo.

WITTGENSTEIN: See? You can still play; you just don't take the time.

HEISENBERG: You seem to do nothing but play games.

WITTGENSTEIN: They aren't all idle. I'm working on some notes on certainty now — or maybe they should be on uncertainty? — anyway they're about the basic propositions we think we know. *(He holds up his left hand.)* Such as: "Here is my hand," *(Placing his hand on his chest.)* or: "I know that I am a human being." Think of how unclear that proposition is by looking at its negation. What would it mean to say "I know I'm not a human being" or "I know I'm a chimpanzee"? — which wouldn't make you any less human.

HEISENBERG: *(He dismounts from his perch and straightens his tie.)* This is mindless!

WITTGENSTEIN: No, mind full, and that's the point. Since the proposition depends on others, such as *(He taps his head with his finger.)* "I know I have a mind." But do you? It might be sawdust for all you know. You've never seen it. You've only inferred it's not sawdust.

HEISENBERG: Yours seems to be.

WITTGENSTEIN: I have a five-year-old niece in Germany. Before I left we were playing house — my spread legs were her door — when she stopped suddenly, and asked, "Uncle Ludwig, how do you think?" It's a very good question. *(Pauses. Lost in thought. Returns.)* Ready?

HEISENBERG: *(Exasperated.)* For what?

WITTGENSTEIN: To test your counter weight theory.

HEISENBERG: Wahnsinnig! *(He pulls up his hairs. Then flattens them back down.)* When we were developing quantum physics we had to create our own vocabulary — so we called an illogical but necessary mathematical invention an "Unsinn" — a nonsense, and then we made a word from the Yiddish for "swindle" and the Greek for "schema," which we christened "Schimmel." If you added two nonsenses successfully you'd get a "Schimmel." *(Wittgenstein gestures to the chair, he remounts.)* This foolery reminds me of those times, but without the content.

WITTGENSTEIN: Perhaps the content is in the doing — as your new language game created quantum physics so our game may produce something surprising.

HEISENBERG: I hope so. *(They stare at each other. Long pause. Heisenberg waves.)* Ludwig?

WITTGENSTEIN: *(Startled.)* Problem. How to place the notebooks over the gap while remaining seated.

HEISENBERG: Here. Throw me one and we'll lean out together.

WITTGENSTEIN: *(Tossing Heisenberg one of the journals.)* Right. Well Schimmeled!

HEISENBERG: *(Both stand unsteadily on their chairs, leaning towards each other until they're forced to grab hands or fall.)* Ich habe dich! *(With their downstage hands locked together they attempt to lower the notebooks into place, but again the bridge collapses, they lose their balance and — kicking the chairs free — fall onto the pile of books.)* Scheiße!

WITTGENSTEIN: Again.

HEISENBERG: No. Different this time. It's what I said at the end of my uncertainty paper. *(He holds the black journal up.)* Causal law states that if we know the present we can calculate the future — so if we knew precisely how much counterweight to exert and the span of each book, plus the friction of the covers, the density of the air . . . und so weiter, we could be certain of the outcome. But we can only increase the probability of any event, not its occurrence. It's not the conclusion that's wrong but the premise.

WITTGENSTEIN: *(Taking the journal.)* We can't know the present?

HEISENBERG: *(He stands, picks up a chair and moves it in closer, checking that he's not seen by Wittgenstein.) Because each time we attempt to measure two variables at the subatomic level our own measuring causes one of the variables to shift. As a mathematical consequence the standard deviation — the imprecisions in the values of p and q, say of space and time — are inversely related to each other. We batten down p and q slips away.

WITTGENSTEIN: *(He stacks the books vertically in two towers between the chairs.)* My p and your q cannot be known at one and the same time. So the game's up?

HEISENBERG: *(He picks up the other chair and moves it in closer.)* That game — yes.

WITTGENSTEIN: When I was a child the bathroom was a terrible place for me, you see some plaster had fallen down from the ceiling, and it was shaped like an open-beaked duck. *(He makes a duck shadow puppet with his fingers.)* Or, I always thought, it could be a rabbit. *(Both turn their heads sideways to see the rabbit.)* And as it changed from one to the other it reminded me of those monsters Bosch found while painting the Temptations of St. Anthony. *(He uses his free hand to make another duck which attacks the rabbit.)* I was never certain which would eat the other — or whether they'd turn on me. *(He attacks himself with the hand animals.)* That uncertainty was terrifying.

HEISENBERG: You want to extrapolate from quantum mechanics in a way I find ludicrous.

WITTGENSTEIN: Because you've lost control of the application?

HEISENBERG: *(Sitting down, he pulls in his chair even closer.)* Because it's a false application. It's Unsinn.

WITTGENSTEIN: Let's refresh ourselves before we attempt the bridge again. Here. *(He takes a metal tray from out of the cupboard at the base of the bookcase and places it on the pile of books to form a table. On it is a plate with a pineapple, two forks, and two smaller plates.)* I picked this up at the open market this morning — you wouldn't believe how I had to haggle for a decent price.

HEISENBERG: *(Standing up suddenly, so his chair falls over.)* A pineapple.

WITTGENSTEIN: Good!

HEISENBERG: *(Righting his chair.)* A pineapple?

WITTGENSTEIN: Identification complete. We can move on now.

HEISENBERG: *(Gripping the chair.)* A PINEAPPLE? What do you want me to do, confess my sins?

WITTGENSTEIN: If you'd like, but I simply wanted you to eat. *(Both sit. He takes apart the pineapple, which has already been sectioned, and pierces a pineapple chunk.)* I see three stages in life: the aesthetic, where you try to squeeze the maximum amount of enjoyment from life. *(He eats a chunk of pineapple and closes his eyes, chewing.)* The ethical, where you surrender to a duty which demands renunciation of those enjoyments. *(He pierces another slice and proffers it to Heisenberg, who leans — open-mouthed — to take it, but Wittgenstein pulls it away.)* And the religious, where renunciation itself becomes a source of joy. *(He steps off the stage and offers a piece of pineapple on the end of his fork to an audience member.)* Here, would you like some? *(He flicks the fork so the pineapple chunk flies off over the heads of the audience.)* Can't have any — and neither can I. *(Pause.)* Didn't enjoy that? I did.

HEISENBERG: *(Exasperated.)* You can't do that. You're changing the rules of the game.

WITTGENSTEIN: *(Returning to the stage.)* Nonsense — I'm just Schimmeling — as you once did.

HEISENBERG: *(Turning away.)* I don't have the stomach for this.

WITTGENSTEIN: *(Piercing another piece of pineapple, he holds it out.)* Come, just a sliver.

HEISENBERG: All right. *(He leans forward to bite the chunk of pineapple, then hesitates and grabs Wittgenstein's hand to assure he won't pull it back. Chews.)* What tender flesh!

WITTGENSTEIN: Now then. *(Spearing another chunk of pineapple.)* I've been reading about World War II a bit, and I was hoping you'd tell me your story of the final days before you were captured — what was it like creating an atomic bomb? *(Eats pineapple.)*

HEISENBERG: February, 1945. *(He stands, swallowing.)* We were in Heigerlock in Tübingen, working in a cave at the base of a mountain crowned by a monastery. In our atom cellar — it'd been an old wine cellar for the local innkeeper — we tried to create a critical reactor. It was so stupid of us to go ahead, the war already lost, without even making adequate preparations to save ourselves if it worked. *(He hoists the silver tray with the pineapple and slowly lowers it down, as if it were very heavy, onto the books.)* As we winched the uranium blocks into place over the cylindrical reactor vessel and began filling it with heavy water, the neutron multiplication rate increased. *(Lifts the pineapple.)* But then it died out. *(Lets the pineapple fall.)* We didn't have enough heavy water to go nuclear. *(Pause.)* Of course we really didn't want to be successful.

WITTGENSTEIN: Pity.

HEISENBERG: Yes. *(Pause. Wittgenstein reaches to spear another pineapple chunk, Heisenberg hoists the tray and stands on his chair.)* Wait. Was it a pity it didn't go nuclear, which would have revealed German scientists' superiority? Or was it a pity it didn't go nuclear, because then those scientists would have been incinerated?

WITTGENSTEIN: Now see here, Werner, you're a guest in the Anscombe's house — oh, right, so am I. *(He stands on his chair, arms crossed, back turned. Long pause.)*

HEISENBERG: *(Descending from his perch.)* Oh, all right, have your bloody piece of pineapple.

WITTGENSTEIN: *(Petulant, he waves it off, eyes closed.)* Not interested.

HEISENBERG: Come now, you wanted it a second ago. *(He holds the tray aloft towards Wittgenstein.)*

WITTGENSTEIN: No. I've found religion. *(Pause. Speaks while turned away.)* During the war the Germans made a steel, bomb-proof container to convey the consecrated host to the troops on the front line. *(Heisenberg steps out into the audience and distributes the pineapple, plates, and forks to those in the front row, gesturing for them to eat.)* What a disgusting invention! The host should have no protection from humans at all, but be transferred from hand to hand, to hand to mouth — as in a relay. *(Heisenberg comes back on stage, places the tray on the stack of books and claps his hands. Wittgenstein turns around and looks for the pineapple. He steps off his chair and looks behind the cupboard, throws the cupboard doors open, looks inside, feels around as if there could be a false bottom. He advances to the front of the stage and glares at the audience.)* Gone. *(Gesturing.)* Poof?

HEISENBERG: Right. Now about your bridge. *(He stands up, holding a book in each hand.)* Got it!

WITTGENSTEIN: *(Looks up, then resumes his search.)* Yes, but it's not a human bridge we're attempting.

HEISENBERG: No, not me. *(He moves to the bookcase and places the books in it.)* Stack the books in here.

WITTGENSTEIN: *(Putting one hand on his head, one on his heart.)* Here?

HEISENBERG: Help. *(He tips the bookcase towards Wittgenstein, who catches it. Together they lift it and place it onto the chairs.)* So! Your bridge of books.

WITTGENSTEIN: No, that's simply a bridge of boards with books stacked on them.

HEISENBERG: You disapprove of my move in your game. But it's sound as this bridge. *(He thumps the bookcase with his hand and it crashes to the floor. Apologetic, he shrugs. Together they right the bookcase and begin to place the books in it again. Righting one chair, he edges it in closer, checking Wittgenstein doesn't see.)* Ludwig.

WITTGENSTEIN: *(Staring, distracted.)* I know my own name only because I use it over and over again.

HEISENBERG: *(Righting the other chair, he again moves it in closer.)* Ludwig, I'm using it over and over again to get your attention. *(Pause.)* LUDWIG!

WITTGENSTEIN: *(Startled.)* Hello?

HEISENBERG: You said earlier you had something for me.

WITTGENSTEIN: Right. As you know I've been researching the activities of the Copenhagen group in Stockholm in 1939. *(He extracts the black journal from the pile and pulls out the loose piece of paper.)* Mixed in with some transcripts I found a page torn from Albert Speer's notebook — same blue-ruled stationary with a watermark of a peacock. I'm sure it's his.

HEISENBERG: Speer's notebook?

WITTGENSTEIN: Yes, Speer's. Here's what it says: *(Unfolds the piece of paper and reads.)* "The uranium club consisted of Otto Hahn, Carl Friedrich von Weizsacker, and Werner Heisenberg. W.H. lectured at the Harnack House on atom smashing, the development of the cyclotron, and the possibilities for an atomic bomb."

HEISENBERG: Here. *(Advancing, he attempts to snatch the letter. Wittgenstein mounts one of the chairs and keeps him away with his foot.)* Let me see that.

WITTGENSTEIN: "Field Marshal Milch asked how large it would have to be to destroy a city the size of London, and W.H. said about the size of a pineapple." Curious choice of fruit! — were you thinking of a spiky exterior or the slightly acidic taste?

HEISENBERG: *(He relents and sits in the other chair.)* You don't understand what it was like for me. We'd come so far, built something . . . lasting in physics. I thought — I thought it would be for the best if we won the war. I don't condone my actions, but I love my country. And afterwards they tore Germany apart. Cleaved it in two as if it were a rotten piece of fruit. The money for research was spent, the spirit dried up, the Geist gone.

WITTGENSTEIN: *(Sitting down in his chair.)* You stopped believing?

HEISENBERG: I'm not a bad man. I only wanted to do my work — ok, to be famous for my work — I wanted to be a name.

WITTGENSTEIN: Werner Heisenberg? *(Heisenberg nods. Wittgenstein stands, turns towards the audience.)* Imagine if you will, that I am not L.W. — Ludwig Wittgenstein — but an actor playing Ludwig Wittgenstein. And in my part I say the words, "I, Ludwig Wittgenstein, dot dot dot." That actor is no more right than I am, when I say I am Ludwig Wittgenstein. For names carry us, we don't carry them.

HEISENBERG: *(Stands.)* As I've been embodied in an idea of uncertainty only vaguely like my own.

WITTGENSTEIN: We're called to our names from before our births — if we're lucky enough to have parents who consider us worthy of such a gift.

HEISENBERG: *(Staring off at the audience.)* The Nazi authorities traced my family back five generations looking to see if I was tainted by Jewish blood. They found the Heisenberg clan in the town of Heidenoldendorf — Heisenberg brandy burners, Heisenberg master coopers, Heisenberg locksmiths — some dropped an S, some added it back in — but still, no Jews. So I was exonerated. *(Shrugs.)* Yippee.

WITTGENSTEIN: And now live split in two, like one of your atoms. *(Heisenberg nods. Long pause. Wittgenstein begins to stack the books on one of the chairs.)* I have an idea. Once more onto the bridge!

HEISENBERG: *(Reluctantly he stacks books on the other chair.)* Must we?

WITTGENSTEIN: Yes. And perhaps it was a mistake to think of the books as solid objects.

HEISENBERG: What else are they?

WITTGENSTEIN: *(Shaking the journal page.)* Mobile, changeable atoms arrested in the form of paper.

HEISENBERG: Paper?

WITTGENSTEIN: Which burns. *(He places the metal tray beneath the bridge, tears the journal page in two and places one on each side of the gap.)* Do you smoke? Do you have a lighter?

HEISENBERG: A pipe, yes. *(Fishes out a lighter from his pocket. Wittgenstein grabs it, unscrews the top and douses the books and the journal page on both sides of the bridge with the fluid.)* Now see here Ludwig, that was a gift from my wife, Elisabeth. *(Pause.)* Is that the only copy of Speer's journal page in existence?

WITTGENSTEIN: At present, yes. *(He pulls a pack of matches from his pocket and hands a match to Heisenberg and takes one himself.)* Lights! *(The lights are lowered. At the same time, they light their matches.)* Two Unsinns equal one Schimmel.

HEISENBERG: Eins, Zwei, Pineapple! *(They each light their half of books. The flame crawls up the stack and leaps across the gap igniting the paper which falls, burning, onto the tray. Wittgenstein bends and keeps it burning.)* I don't know how I can repay you for this.

WITTGENSTEIN: You've talked out your sins, now go and sin no more. When I was in my forties I confessed two crimes to my friends, that of being Jewish and denying it, and of having used a ruler on a female student in one of my classes, and then denying I'd done any such thing when the headmaster confronted me. Denial atrophies the flesh. I had to chop off a limb or two, but those that remain are the healthier for it. So with you.

HEISENBERG: What is it with you, do you want us all to be perfect?

WITTGENSTEIN: Of course I want us to be perfect.

HEISENBERG: Even if armless and legless?

WITTGENSTEIN: As long as we're not headless or heartless. *(He bends to the smoldering embers. Pinches some between his fingers and lets them sift between his fingers.)* Care for some ashes?

HEISENBERG: *(Tapping his head, then heart.)* No thanks, my head's full already. And my heart's overfull.

WITTGENSTEIN: *(He lifts the tray, steps to the front of the stage, and blows the ashes off.)* Poof!

(Blackout.)

END OF PLAY

DINNER
by Richard Markgraf

FIRST PERFORMANCE
January 2001

ORIGINAL CAST
- Sally . . . . .Lisa Hadley
- Bill . . . . .Scott Harrison
- Brenda . . . . .Manirose Brendsel Raley
- Directed by . . . . .Stuart Serman and Rita Wadsworth
- Set Design by .William "Skip" Epperson

CHARACTERS
SALLY: the wife, thirty-four.
BILL: the husband, thirty-five.
BRENDA: the daughter, fifteen.

DINNER

Sally, Bill and Brenda are at their dining room table eating dinner. The characters eat throughout the play.

SALLY: *(After a very long pause.)* Would you repeat that?
BILL: *(A long pause. Between mouthfuls.)* I said I'm leaving you for Wendy McDonald.
BRENDA: *(A long pause. Between mouthfuls.)* Pass the spinach.
SALLY: *(A pause. Between mouthfuls.)* She the one always late for choir?
BILL: That's Wendy Chang. McDonald, Chang — how can you confuse McDonald with Chang?
SALLY: *(To Brenda.)* Go easy on the spinach.
BRENDA: Mom, Wendy Chang is *sexy*.
SALLY: *(A pause.)* For my money, Wendy Chang is a lot sexier than Wendy McDonald.
BILL: You think so? You *really* think so? To tell you the truth, Sally, I've never thought to compare the two. *(Reflecting.)* I'd say they're both sexy.
SALLY: They're both married.
BILL: *I'm* married.
BRENDA: Thank goodness. That makes me legitimate. Doesn't it?
BILL: How come Brenda eats spinach but won't eat ice cream?
SALLY: *(A pause.)* You know, Bill, out of the blue like this, this is a monumental shock. This is an extraordinary event. A not an everyday occurrence. And bringing it up at dinner — just blurting it out. And with Brenda here. This could really stunt her emotional growth. She might have to go into advanced counseling.
BRENDA: It's not *my* marriage.
BILL: Don't sass your mother.
SALLY: How's your liver?
BILL: I don't drink excessively.
SALLY: On your plate.
BILL: I never have liked liver. And you never fix it with onions like they do in restaurants. Liver and spinach — what kind of a dinner is that?
SALLY: I suppose Wendy serves stir-fried veggies and rice and monosodium glutamate.
BILL: That's Wendy Chang. I'm seeing Wendy McDonald.
SALLY: How do I know you're not seeing both of them?
BILL: You're the one who brought up Wendy Chang.

SALLY: I always thought, if you ever left me, Bill, it would be for some fox. Some kind of Madonna. Wendy McDonald is plain, and that's being charitable.

BILL: Plain?

SALLY: Brenda, wouldn't you say Wendy McDonald is plain?

BILL: Plain?

BRENDA: Is she the one who walks that funny dog — the one that's lopsided?

BILL: It's Wendy who's lopsided.

SALLY: You'd think she'd fix that.

BILL: Pass the butter.

BRENDA: It's margarine.

BILL: *(To Sally.)* I make enough money, I work hard, why are we always cutting corners? At my own table, I can't eat butter?

BRENDA: Ruins your arteries.

BILL: That's hearsay.

SALLY: That what you see in Wendy? She serves butter?

BILL: We've been eating out.

SALLY: When's the last time you took me out?

BILL: Last night, where did we eat last night? Remember? Out.

BRENDA: McDonalds.

SALLY: She's the one you're leaving me for — not Chang.

BILL: Right.

SALLY: *(A pause.)* You think you know a person. I have to tell you, I'm in a state of shock. We see each other every day, a fifteen-year marriage, and I could have sworn you still loved me.

BILL: Can't I love both you and Wendy? It's possible.

BRENDA: *(Startled.) Fifteen* years? Hey, that's how old I am — fifteen.

BILL: Doesn't matter.

BRENDA: Not to you it doesn't matter, but if this ever leaks out I'm trashed.

SALLY: Brenda, please, one family crisis at a time. Right now, I'm the one being devastated.

BILL: You don't think this is affecting *me* any?

BRENDA: I'm absolutely flabbergasted. You know, I was just turning the corner in my therapy, getting my act together. Dr. Spitz was saying I could maybe start seeing him just twice a week, and now this. You could knock me over with a whisper. I'm a love child. Or weren't you two in love?

BILL: Count on it.

SALLY: It could be Wendell.

BILL: You always told me it wasn't Wendell.

SALLY: But it could have been.
BRENDA: Wendell?
BILL: Eat your spinach.
SALLY: His thing broke too, you know.
BILL: But you've said all along he and I ravished you a week apart.
SALLY: I could be wrong. My memory's fuzzy.
BRENDA: Wendell?
SALLY: A week, a day — who was keeping track?
BILL: I think you should make a real effort to remember, Sally. Anyway, Brenda doesn't look at all like Wendell.
SALLY: Clifford. She looks a lot like Clifford.
BRENDA: Clifford?
BILL: Clifford Parkington? That guy in the band who played trombone. The big brown-noser?
BRENDA: Clifford?
SALLY: It couldn't have been Clifford. His never broke.
BILL: *His!*
SALLY: *(Patting Brenda on the head.)* So never you worry, it wasn't Clifford.
BRENDA: Wendell?
BILL: Wendell?
SALLY: *(To Bill.)* What's the difference now you're leaving?
BRENDA: *I'm* not leaving.
BILL: Well, it certainly does make a difference. I might not have to pay for Brenda's braces.
SALLY: It wasn't Wendell.
BILL: You can't be sure of that.
SALLY: It's coming back to me. You two *were* a week apart.
BILL: But was I first or was he first?
SALLY: I've told you a million times, he was first.
BILL: No, you always said I was first.
SALLY: Well, she certainly doesn't look like Wendell.
BRENDA: Who do I look like?
BILL: You look like Sally.
SALLY: *(To Brenda.)* I don't think we look alike at all. I've always been uneasy about that.
BRENDA: I never knew you've been married *just* fifteen years. I'm fifteen.
BILL: You'll be sixteen soon. Then it won't matter.
SALLY: *(To Bill.)* See what you've done? You've upset both of us. I bet if I told

that Wendy Chang or McDonald how callous you are, she wouldn't up and get a divorce and marry you. What do you bet?

BILL: If she ever asks I'm going to tell her things went as smooth as silk. Piece of cake. *(A pause.)* You've never mentioned Clifford before.

SALLY: He never came up.

BRENDA: Then it couldn't have been him.

BILL: My attorney will probably want Brenda's DNA sample. I don't think I should be buying braces for a perfect stranger.

BRENDA: Dr. Spitz is going to make me come in daily, for sure. And double sessions.

SALLY: It's the uncertainty that's bewildering her, Bill. Haven't you noticed she's not eaten a bite since Wendell came up?

BILL: She probably doesn't like liver.

BRENDA: *(Rising.)* May I be excused? I'm going to be sick.

SALLY: If you hold your nose you won't taste anything.

BRENDA: *(Holding her nose.)* I'm *already* tasting it. Ahhhhhh! *(Runs offstage.)*

SALLY: You should be ashamed.

BILL: Me?

SALLY: Bringing up the Wendys.

BILL: I brought up just one.

SALLY: Don't you think one was enough?

BILL: Look, if I'd known it was going to snowball into something totally out of control, that you were going to get so unhinged, both of you, I would have kept it all a secret. Don't I get points for being honest? I mean, you're not being very modern about this.

SALLY: I'm going to be sick myself.

BILL: It *must* be the liver.

SALLY: *(Feeling ill, rising.)* You'll never know, will you, if she's Wendell's or yours. *(Holds her nose, calling offstage to Brenda.)* Step aside, I'm coming. Ahhhhhh! *(Runs offstage.)*

BILL: *(A long pause. To Sally offstage.)* Will I be getting any ice cream?

END OF PLAY

ETAINE AND ETAIRE
by Karen Villeneuve

FIRST PERFORMANCE
January 1998

ORIGINAL CAST

    Etaine . . . . .Olivia Goldsmith
    Etaire . . . . .Alisa Peck
    Directed by . . . . .Maria Crush
    Sets by . . . . .Mark Hopkins

CHARACTERS

ETAINE: Etaire's siamese twin sister.
ETAIRE: Etaine's siamese twin sister.
    The twins are attached at their backs. They share three lungs and the main arteries of their hearts are intertwined. They are in their early twenties.

ETAINE AND ETAIRE

In a dark chamber-like room. Bright spot on the twins; they are sitting on a special backless chair with two seats. Two video cameras with monitors are set up so that each can see the other. Monitors are visible to the audience. Etaine and Etaire perform elaborate hand gestures in unison.

ETAINE: How is the fish?
ETAIRE: The fish in the dish?
ETAINE: No, how is the fish?
ETAIRE: In the dish, OK? How is the fish?
ETAINE: The fish in the dish?
ETAIRE: No. How is the fish?
ETAINE: In the dish, OK? How is the fish?
ETAIRE: *(Stumbles.)* The dish in the fish?
   (They giggle.)
ETAINE: The dish in the fish! I mean the fish . . . the fish!
ETAIRE: In the dish, OK? I mean . . .
ETAINE: Fish! How is the fish! You were right!
   (They giggle painfully until laughter tapers off, then silence.)
ETAINE: The dog in the fog . . .
ETAIRE: Climbed an old log . . .
ETAINE: To fetch him a frog . . .
ETAIRE: *(Stumbles.)* A fog in the frog. *(Starts to laugh.)*
ETAINE: *(Interrupting.)* It's frog in the fog. Frog . . . say it again!
ETAIRE: The frog in the fog. Climbed the old log.
ETAINE: To flee . . . *(Pause, anxiously.)* Have you ever thought what it would do?
ETAIRE: I'm tired.
ETAINE: Of us?
ETAIRE: Of the Game. Etaine, Etaine . . . who falls down the drain.
ETAINE: Etaire, Etaire . . . who combs mother's . . . *(They clasp hands, squeezing three times, letting go.)* We're scared.
ETAIRE: Don't think of that. *(Beat.)* Look. *(Looking into the monitor.)* You look sad. Don't look sad.
ETAINE: We were like two rose bushes grafted to the same stock. Now we know about our hearts. 'Twined together like roots.
ETAIRE: And one lung between us, and one lung of our own.
ETAINE: So how can they possibly separate us?
ETAIRE: They'll put some stranger's in us.

ETAINE: No. We won't let them!
ETAIRE: Don't think of it! *(Silence.)* You're my twin sister, always. Here . . . catch a memory!
ETAINE: The fire?
ETAIRE: In the hills. We found that mouse . . .
ETAINE: Its feet were burned off. We saved it. We brought it home where he could die in peace. They loved us there, in our town. Remember how much they loved us? We were famous.
ETAIRE: *(Inhaling.)* Smells.
TOGETHER: Eucalyptus.
ETAINE: That was when it rained. Mom took us to the beach. We rode a huge tortoise. We wore a dress.
ETAIRE: The Red Dress.
ETAINE: With zig zag trim.
ETAIRE: Wasn't the trim black?
(They fall silent. Simultaneously, they panic.)
ETAIRE: I've got the Scaries! Breathe — breathe!
(They breathe deeply, Etaine becomes calm first.)
ETAIRE: You win.
(Lights dim to black. Lights up.)
ETAINE: *(With alacrity.)* Cheek?
(They press their cheeks together, shutting their eyes.)
ETAINE: They said we have a 90 percent chance. What if one of us dies?
ETAIRE: If you died, I promise to die too.
ETAINE: Like two rose bushes planted together, from cradle to grave . . . from one root came two, and their roses did merge so that no one knew where the roots had begun. *(Pause.)* I would too. If you die, then I will die too.
ETAIRE: Hush. Don't think of it.
ETAINE: *(Suddenly.)* Red Car! *(They blow three times looking at opposite walls as if seeing the same vision.)* Hands!
(Performing the same hand gestures as in the beginning, this time with more speed and intensity.)
ETAIRE: *(Looks at her monitor.)* You've been looking thin.
ETAINE: I haven't felt well.
ETAIRE: You are like I was when we were ten. I was weaker then. Now I'm the stronger one. Maybe you need some time alone. How would you feel about taking down the cameras?
ETAINE: *(Terror stricken.)* I can't find my hands! *(Etaire grasps her hands.)*
TOGETHER: HANDS! DANCE!

(They lock elbows and start rocking back and forth, pressing the backs of their heads together and moaning. They long to be held and loved. This is the closest they are able to get.)

ETAINE: *(Abruptly stops, looks at her monitor.)* We can't see it — how they'll do it. How will we choose? They'll put us to sleep. *(Beat.)* We can tell them not to wake us up if one of us dies.

ETAIRE: They won't. That would be "murder."

ETAINE: We can't do it then.

ETAIRE: We can promise . . . promise to kill ourself, the one who lives.

ETAINE: Oh God.

ETAIRE: You're being weak. We will live — both of us. I wish you weren't so weak right now when what we need is strength. We're fighting the Disease. In the lung — it's there, waiting for whoever is weakest. I can't tell it what to do! *(With disgust.)* You want to be in love.

ETAINE: Yes! I want to be in love! I want you to go away! I want you to go away! GO AWAY!

(Etaine starts to struggle to get away from Etaire. She stops suddenly, shocked at what she sees in her monitor. Etaire's head hangs limp, she is wheezing. Etaine gets up, standing Etaire up with her.)

ETAINE: ETAIRE! ETAIRE! Who combs Mother's hair! *(She takes deep breaths, Etaire doesn't respond.)* Etaire — do this!

(She grasps Etaire's hands, squeezes them rhythmically, counting. Etaires comes to.)

ETAIRE: *(Catching her breath.)* Juniper willow. Lawns are still . . .

ETAINE: Still. And pepper?

ETAIRE: Pepper mint.

ETAINE: No! No! You did it wrong! It's pepper tree . . . don't you remember? Now we have to do Hands. DO HANDS!

ETAIRE: *(Turns off her video monitor.)* I'm tired of this!

(Etaine goes into a fit; she claws at Etaire, they try and get at each other. They fall to the floor and fight, squirming to get at each other. Etaine grabs one of Etaire's hands and bites her fingers, Etaire cries out, then they both cry as Etaine continues to gnaw Etaire's fingers, gradually sucking them until both are calm.)

ETAINE: Don't cry, Etaire. We're going to make it. Don't cry. Hands . . . *(They languidly clasp hands.)* Up! *(They roll together until they are sitting up.)* Now, let's dance perfectly. *(They clasp elbows and rock back and forth until they are standing.)* Cheeks! *(They press their cheeks together.)* Oh, Etaire. You have such lovely eyes!

ETAIRE: Oh, thank you, Monsieur.

ETAINE: Would you like this dance?
ETAIRE: Indeed, that certainly would be most lovely.
(They begin to dance a tango only back-to-back.)
ETAIRE: I must say, Monsieur, you lead ever so nicely.
ETAINE: Oh, thank you, Madame. You follow quite nicely yourself. Like a field of wheat bending gently in the wind. Your complexion is a rose warmed by the tender light of dusk . . . your eyes are pools, and I'm a mere fish . . . shall we go to the balcony?
ETAIRE: Oh, Monsieur, look at the stars!
ETAINE: They are lovely tonight, I agree.
ETAIRE: But not as lovely as your eyes!
ETAINE: *(Drops her head back in a mock swoon, sighs.)* Oh, Monsieur!
ETAIRE: Wait, you are playing the man!
(Etaine has a laughing fit, Etaire joins her.)
ETAIRE: *(Mockingly.)* Mon-sieur! To-night!
ETAINE: *(Stops laughing, wearily.)* I'm tired.
ETAIRE: Now it's your turn. Are you sick?
ETAINE: I'm feeling all right.
ETAIRE: Maybe we need a nap.
ETAINE: Maybe. Yes. *(Inviting Etaire to dance again.)* Shall we?
ETAIRE: I don't mind if I do.
(They fox trot with extreme care and precision. They stop abruptly as if it were ritual.)
ETAINE: Red Car! Toot! *(They blow into the corners.)* HANDS!
(They clasp hands. Etaire screams and lets go.)
ETAIRE: Those hands! They're going cold!
(Etaine collapses, gasping for air, pulling Etaire down with her.)
ETAIRE: From the self-same womb we came, wounded, wombed-in . . . Lunatics! Your hands are gone. Oh, Etaine! Your heart squeezes me! It bleeds in me! Don't leave me! Don't leave me alone! I love you! Don't die! *(Angrily.)* That lung! It was the statue in that dream — our dream — then the rain came — washed it down. Then the red clouds, falling — like mother's hair — like the fire — it was the lung. Collapsed. Oh, Etaine — I am Etaire! I love you! I'm scared! Breathe! Breathe! Breathe!
(Etaine starts to breathe, but with effort.)
ETAIRE: *(Desperately.)* Come back! Etaine! Etaine! Who falls down the drain! HANDS!
(They lock elbows with military precision.)
ETAIRE: Now! DANCE PERFECTLY!
(Lights fade to black except for one video monitor.)

END OF PLAY

FRIED CHICKEN, HOT OR COLD
by Ann MacGregor Gibb

FIRST PERFORMANCE
January 1998

ORIGINAL CAST
    Charlene . . . . .Mara Luthy
    Harlan . . . . .Aaron Woods
    Bert . . . . .Ian Kleinfeld
    Directed by . . . . .Colette Searls
    Sets by . . . . .Mark Hopkins

FRIED CHICKEN, HOT OR COLD

A small town diner anywhere in the South today. There's a pay phone beside the kitchen door. Harlan (forties), the only customer, is seated at a table with the kitchen door behind him. He's wearing a suit and has a briefcase, but it's clear he's a local as he chows down on the fried chicken special. He's so engrossed he doesn't notice Charlene (thirties) enter quietly from the street. She's dressed young for her age and upholding the tradition of big hair.

CHARLENE: *(Her accent dripping with honey.)* Why hey — Harlan?! I don't believe it!

HARLAN: Well, hey — Charlene?!? What are you doing here?

CHARLENE: I just stopped in for a bite. Aren't you going to ask me to join you?

HARLAN: Charlene, you can't just — I can't ask you — you're wanted by the police!

CHARLENE: You never used to be the type to let a little warrant get in the way of love.

HARLAN: Would you keep your voice down? You better start thinking about what you're saying and what you're doing. There's something you need to know.

(Bert, the waiter, enters from the kitchen.)

BERT: Hello, Miss. Are you joining Harlan here?

CHARLENE: Yes.   HARLAN: No

(Charlene sits.)

BERT: Uhh . . . all right then. What can I get you?

CHARLENE: I'll have what he's having.

BERT: One fried chicken special. Anything to drink?

CHARLENE: Iced tea, please.

BERT: Coming right up.

(Bert exits.)

CHARLENE: Harlan, just sit on down and tell me what I need to know.

HARLAN: It's my wife.

CHARLENE: I know you're married now, don't worry, I won't turn up on your doorstep.

HARLAN: That's right, you better not, because my wife, she thinks, well, it's like this. My wife thinks you're dead.

(Bert enters with iced tea.)

BERT: Here you are. Chicken will be right up.

(He exits.)

CHARLENE: Why in the world would she think I'm dead?
HARLAN: Well — because, she trusts me and she believes me and I told her you're dead.
CHARLENE: What?!?
HARLAN: I had to, to make things easier.
CHARLENE: For you, maybe, but not for me!
HARLAN: Take it easy now, it's not like you opened up the Times-Picayune and saw your own obituary.
CHARLENE: It would be easier for you if I was dead.
HARLAN: Now don't talk like that. I don't want you dead, I just wanted my wife to think you're dead.
CHARLENE: Oh, I get it! Harlan, you are so clever. You . . .
(Bert enters with the special.)
CHARLENE: *(Continuing.)* . . . can't romance a dead woman, so who's going to suspect anything?
BERT: Here you go, Miss. *(To Harlan.)* How's the chicken?
HARLAN: Just fine, Bert, just really fine.
BERT: That's what I like to hear. And Miss, you let me know if there's anything else I can get you.
HARLAN: Isn't there something you need to check on in the kitchen?
BERT: Ahh . . . I do have pie in the oven. Guess I could take a look.
(Bert exits.)
CHARLENE: Where were we? Oh yes that's right, we were discussing my being dead so you and I could have some fun.
HARLAN: Now hold on there, I didn't say anything about having any fun.
CHARLENE: Harlan . . . Honey . . . don't be like that. Why just the other night I was thinking about that summer when we had a picnic down by where the railroad goes over the river, remember?
HARLAN: We had a lot of picnics down there.
CHARLENE: I was thinking about the time you bet me I wouldn't dive naked off the trestle. Guess you didn't mind when I made you pay up.
HARLAN: Only time I've been happy to lose a bet.
CHARLENE: As I recall, we had some very good times.
HARLAN: We sure did.
CHARLENE: And there's no reason we can't have some more.
HARLAN: There sure is. And it's called "failure to appear."
CHARLENE: Don't you worry none about that police thang, it's going to blow right over, you'll see.
(Bert enters.)

BERT: The pie's fine. Say . . . what's the matter, Harlan?

HARLAN: What do you mean?

BERT: You're not finishing your chicken. You always finish your chicken. You feeling all right? Want me to call Rose and have her take you over to the doctor?

HARLAN: No I do not want you to call Rose! I'm fine.

BERT: All right then. Let me know if there's anything I can get ya'll.

(Bert exits.)

CHARLENE: I can't believe you married Dozie Rosie.

HARLAN: It's Rose, and we've been married for two years now.

CHARLENE: My goodness, two whole years — congratulations. Did ya'll have a big wedding?

HARLAN: Enough folks to fill the VA Hall.

CHARLENE: And what did Dozie Rosie, I mean, what was Rose's dress like?

HARLAN: What do you think, it was white.

CHARLENE: I'm sure it was white, but was it floor length or more like tea length, you know, to about here —

(She stands to demonstrate.)

CHARLENE: *(Continuing.)* — and was it sort of formfitting around the bust —

(She illustrates "formfitting" on her own bust.)

HARLAN: Just sit on down and I'll tell you what it looked like. It was big, and kinda poofed out . . .

(He stands and uses his body as a mannequin while he describes the wedding dress. At this moment Bert, unknown to Harlan, enters.)

HARLAN: *(Continuing.)* . . . and long, all the way to the floor, and it stuck out all around, and up here, *("Up here" being the bodice.)* . . . were these flowers, not real ones, and there was this thing, I think you call it a bustle, that stuck out like this —

(Harlan sees Bert.)

BERT: Hey Harlan.

HARLAN: Hey Bert.

BERT: Thought ya'll could use some more water.

HARLAN: Thanks.

BERT: Sure, no problem

(Bert exits.)

HARLAN: Oh shoot, I've got a picture here in my wallet.

CHARLENE: Ah . . . how sweet . . . her hair's a little flat, don't you think?

HARLAN: The veil kind of squashed it down.

CHARLENE: But you, now *you* look so handsome. This must be ya'll's first dance, right?

HARLAN: That's right.

CHARLENE: I thought so. Now let me guess, don't tell me . . . okay, I've got it.

(She stands.)

CHARLENE: *(Continuing.)* Come on now, stand up.

HARLAN: I don't think so —

CHARLENE: I ain't gonna bite you, come on, what are you so afraid of? It's the middle of the day!

HARLAN: That's exactly what I'm afraid of.

(But he gets up.)

CHARLENE: *(Embracing him as if to touch dance.)* I bet ya'll's first dance together was a waltz.

HARLAN: No, Charlene —

CHARLENE: I'm wrong? Was it a foxtrot?

HARLAN: Charlene, wait —

CHARLENE: Oh, Harlan, don't tell me it was a tango — you racy devil, you.

HARLAN: Charlene, I don't tango.

CHARLENE: We did some pretty good mambos in our day.

HARLAN: I gave up dancing when you left town.

CHARLENE: Didn't you ever miss me? Or even just think about me?

HARLAN: I thought about you a whole hell of a lot after I saw this.

(He rummages through his briefcase and throws a clipping onto the table.)

CHARLENE: *(Snatching up the clipping.)* Oh my god! I don't believe it! Is this from the Times-Picayune?

HARLAN: Yep.

CHARLENE: I hate this picture, it makes my eyes look all little and piggy! And besides, none of this is true. You know how those reporters lie, just to sell newspapers. You wait and see, I will never go to prison.

HARLAN: Maybe not, if you stay on the run.

CHARLENE: Oh, you don't care about me, you go around telling people I'm dead.

HARLAN: Now just because I said you're dead doesn't mean I don't have fond memories.

CHARLENE: Really? How fond?

HARLAN: Not *that* fond.

CHARLENE: Wait a minute — I could turn myself in.

HARLAN: But you just said you'd never go to prison.

CHARLENE: I won't. But I'm entitled to my day in court. And then, after the case is over and all, I can stop running and pretending.

HARLAN: Ah, I don't know, Charlene, I don't know — those prosecutors can be pretty tricky. Things might not work out the way you reckon.

CHARLENE: Would you mind handing me my purse? What's the number for the sheriff? With my looks I can get any public defender I want. Maybe even a real lawyer. Hey, wait a minute, I could surrender right here, to you! Are you still a judge?

HARLAN: Ah, yes, yes, I am still a judge but . . . I'm not sure surrendering here is a good idea. You see how the legal system works is, the trial can't be here because the crime — I mean the alleged crime — wasn't committed in this state. So we'd have to extradite you. But until all the paperwork went through, you'd sit in jail for, oh I don't know how long, could be months.

CHARLENE: Exactly, that would give us time to get reacquainted, what with your office being right next to the jail and all.

HARLAN: But I don't want to get reacquainted.

CHARLENE: Harlan, you are breaking my heart! It's this being married, it's changed you!

HARLAN: Yeah that's right, it's made me a better person.

CHARLENE: Sounds thrillin'. Makes me wanna run right out and get hitched.

HARLAN: Now you stop being mean. I'll tell you why marriage is good. When you're married you've got somebody who's always ready to help you out.

CHARLENE: You mean like an accomplice?

HARLAN: That's the idea, but I prefer the term partner.

CHARLENE: Not the kind of partner you might turn in to make a better deal with the DA?

HARLAN: Nope, the kind you'd never betray.

CHARLENE: I wish I had a partner like that. Maybe I can find myself one in another town.

HARLAN: Now that is an excellent idea, an *excellent* idea. And no hard feelings, okay?

CHARLENE: Oh all right. Only . . . Harlan . . . things might have been different, if you'd stayed the same.

HARLAN: I know it. I just got to where I didn't want to be that guy who got you to dive naked into the river. I have to go back to court, so . . . good luck, Charlene.

(He exits.)

CHARLENE: Oh, shit!

(She pulls her wig off and throws it to the floor. Bert enters.)

BERT: Can I get you — where'd he go?

CHARLENE: Back to the courthouse. You and your big ideas! "Harlan takes one look at you and he'll fall for you all over again, Harlan can fix it so you never go to jail, blah blah blah blah blah!" And I believed you!

BERT: But Sweetheart, when I saw your picture on that TV show it was just . . . love at first sight, Baby. The happiest day of my life was the day your momma told me where you was hiding out. I'd do anything for you.

CHARLENE: I know you would, Sugar Pie, it's just all so — disappointing. I'm tired, I don't want to go back on the road.

BERT: I don't want you to, Baby. Maybe there's something else we could try.

CHARLENE: Hey, hold on — is Harry Bailey still the police chief?

BERT: Oh yeah, he's got that job for life.

CHARLENE: And does he like your fried chicken?

BERT: Never misses it.

CHARLENE: Well now, Sweetheart, why don't you call old Harry up and let him know what's on the menu for this afternoon?

BERT: All right, Sugar, you got it!

END OF PLAY

HABITS
by Steve "Spike" Wong

FIRST PERFORMANCE
January 2000

ORIGINAL CAST
- Kim .... Sara Bickford
- William .... Ryan Thomas Murphy
- Directed by .... Marjorie Young
- Sets by .... Dohn Grube

HABITS

A small table at a stereotypical ten-year high school reunion. Drinks, plates and pulled out chairs. A drink table is near. Festive signs.

KIM: So, apartment, condo, or house?
WILLIAM: Small house. You?
KIM: Townhouse. Own or rent?
WILLIAM: Own, of course.
KIM: Bedrooms?
WILLIAM: Two. One bath. You?
KIM: Two and two. Backyard?
WILLIAM: Small. Mostly lawn.
KIM: Gardening?
WILLIAM: Difficult. Allergies.
KIM: Gas stove?
WILLIAM: Electric.
KIM: Wash dishes?
WILLIAM: By hand.
KIM: Towel or air dry?
WILLIAM: Air.
KIM: Not enough time?
WILLIAM: Lazy.
KIM: Move the furniture when you vacuum?
WILLIAM: No.
KIM: Hmmm.
WILLIAM: Paper towels?
KIM: Love 'em. Smoke?
WILLIAM: Quit.
KIM: Take-out food?
WILLIAM: Chinese, of course, or pizza.
KIM: Often?
WILLIAM: No.
KIM: Drink from the milk carton?
WILLIAM: Yeah, but I don't let my lips touch it.
KIM: Drink from the faucet?
WILLIAM: When I'm in a hurry.
KIM: Coffee?
WILLIAM: Fresh ground. Every day.

KIM: Wow. Every day. Beer or wine?
WILLIAM: Both. More wine.
KIM: Me, too.
WILLIAM: White or red?
KIM: Merlot.
WILLIAM: Pets?
KIM: A dog.
WILLIAM: Lab?
KIM: Too big.
WILLIAM: A wiener dog.
KIM: Too small.
WILLIAM: Spaniel?
KIM: Almost. Heinz 57; he's a mix.
WILLIAM: Birthday?
KIM: November 10. With friends.
WILLIAM: July 8. With friends. Holidays?
KIM: My folks. You?
WILLIAM: They're gone. No problem.
KIM: Cable TV?
WILLIAM: Sure. ESPN?
KIM: Only for tennis. Old movies?
WILLIAM: Yes. Here's looking at you kid. Public TV?
KIM: Masterpiece Theater. Cartoons?
WILLIAM: No. Well, a little "Batman." Soaps?
KIM: God no. "Melrose Place"?
WILLIAM: Only for fashion advice.
KIM: Right. You like the women.
WILLIAM: O.K. CDs or tapes?
KIM: CDs. Rock and roll, classical, New Age. You?
WILLIAM: Tapes and CDs. Country, rock and roll, one Mozart.
KIM: Token classical.
WILLIAM: A gift.
KIM: Run?
WILLIAM: Usually.
KIM: Weight lift?
WILLIAM: Of course. Work out?
KIM: Aerobics, bicycle, throw sticks for the dog. Well . . . shower or bath?
WILLIAM: Bath. You?
KIM: Mostly shower.

WILLIAM: Shower cap?

KIM: Sometimes.

WILLIAM: Ugly things. Scrub brush or wash cloth?

KIM: Loofah. Brush your teeth in the morning?

WILLIAM: Seldom. Mouthwash. You?

KIM: Brush, first thing. Sleep in on weekends?

WILLIAM: Can't stand to.

KIM: Never?

WILLIAM: Unless there's something worth keeping me in bed.

KIM: Ha.

WILLIAM: Pajamas?

KIM: Silk. You?

WILLIAM: Cotton. Underwear. Always.

KIM: Shave?

WILLIAM: Electric. Twice a day. You?

KIM: Armpits every other day. Legs daily.

WILLIAM: Every day. Wow. Love your perfume. Chanel.

KIM: Yes. Good nose.

WILLIAM: Gave some to my mom every Christmas.

KIM: Cologne?

WILLIAM: Brut.

KIM: Figures. Republican?

WILLIAM: Democrat.

KIM: Reagan.

WILLIAM: Mondale.

KIM: Bush.

WILLIAM: Clinton.

KIM: Taxpayer Relief Act.

WILLIAM: Social Security reform.

KIM: NRA.

WILLIAM: ACLU.

KIM: Dow Jones.

WILLIAM: Goodwill Industries.

KIM: Plastic?

WILLIAM: Visa.

KIM: American Express Platinum.

WILLIAM: Figures.

KIM: Anne Klein.

WILLIAM: Tommy Pull-My-Finger.

KIM: So, sports car?
WILLIAM: No, Honda Civic. You?
KIM: BMW.
WILLIAM: Ooooh, fancy.
KIM: It's my baby. Um . . . Toilet paper rolls off the top or off the bottom?
WILLIAM: Oh . . . off the bottom. Um . . . B.O.?
KIM: Never. My perspiration doesn't stink. So I've been told.
WILLIAM: So you've been told?
KIM: By one of my . . .
WILLIAM: lovers.
KIM: Old boyfriends. You?
WILLIAM: Smell like old shoes, after working out.
KIM: Burp after meals?
WILLIAM: Never in restaurants. Pick your nose?
KIM: Hah. Yes.
WILLIAM: Which finger?
KIM: Little. You?
WILLIAM: Thumb and forefinger, like so.
KIM: Fart in bed?
WILLIAM: Only when I'm alone. Snore?
KIM: Don't think so. Fred said no.
WILLIAM: Fred?
KIM: Last lover.
WILLIAM: Boyfriend.
KIM: Right.
WILLIAM: Very many of those?
KIM: Three.
WILLIAM: Serious?
KIM: Once. Girlfriends?
WILLIAM: Oh . . . six or seven.
KIM: No wonder you flunked math.
WILLIAM: Don't want to look promiscuous. So, birth control?
KIM: What?
WILLIAM: On the pill?
KIM: Yes.
WILLIAM: Whew.
KIM: Condoms?
WILLIAM: Sometimes. It depends.
KIM: On?

WILLIAM: Trusting the woman.
KIM: Do they trust you?
WILLIAM: Oh yes. I was a boy scout. French kiss?
KIM: Love to.
WILLIAM: All the time?
KIM: Yes.
WILLIAM: Ticklish?
KIM: Very.
WILLIAM: Good. Slow to get passionate?
KIM: Not after wine. Are you fast in bed?
WILLIAM: Depends.
KIM: On?
WILLIAM: How long it's been since the last time.
KIM: And . . . ?
WILLIAM: Two or three months.
KIM: Long time?
WILLIAM: Yes. You?
KIM: Long time.
WILLIAM: When you get up in the morning and look in the mirror, what do you see?
KIM: Busy. Tired. Hopeful. And you?
WILLIAM: Same old same old. Sometimes satisfied. Wondering.
KIM: Alarm clock?
WILLIAM: Clock radio. 6 A.M. I can change it, though.
KIM: I don't think you need to. Want to share it?
WILLIAM: Absolutely.

(They rise and entwine their arms. As they start to leave, William reaches back and steals a flower or perhaps a wine bottle from the table. They exit with delicious expectation.)

END OF PLAY

THE HARD CEL
by Philip Pearce

FIRST PERFORMANCE
January 2001

ORIGINAL CAST

    Apollodora . . . . Daria Elise Troxell
    Flint Brady . . . . Ryan Murphy
    Steep Mitchell . . . . Daniel D. Hughes
    Directed by . . . . Dohn Grube
    Sets by . . . . William "Skip" Epperson

CHARACTERS
APOLLODORA: a Nordically blonde food service technician.
FLINT GRADY: an intense photographer.
STEEP MITCHELL: a model.

SCENE
The Bistro Akropolis in Beverly Hills.

TIME
A weekday afternoon.

THE HARD CEL

The Bistro Akropolis on a street somewhere off Rodeo Drive, Beverly Hills. A couple of wrought-iron lunch table settings under a striped awning. Door leading to the bar and grill inside.
Apollodora is by the door, holding a local free newspaper and talking on her cel phone.

APOLLODORA: *(Phone.)* So, it's either Iranian One-Act Folk Comedies at the Hudson — or the new Kubrick at the Westwood Cineplex. Life is choice, Gary. Work on it. I've got orders to pick up. *(To someone inside, as she goes off.)* The Moussaka and the grape and feta omelet are mine, Demetrius!
(Flint Grady enters, pauses under the awning and continues talking on his cel phone.)

FLINT: *(Phone.)* Because the woman has just phoned through to say she took an earlier plane, that's why . . . A United flight arriving one-forty-three instead of an American Eagle at four something . . . How's that for screwing up a whole afternoon's schedule in one fell swoop?
(Apollodora returns.)

APOLLODORA: Well, hi. Outdoors today?
(Flint grunts, still absorbed in his phone call. She shows him to a table.)

APOLLODORA: Are we on our own this lunchtime?

FLINT: *(Phone.)* Hell, no. I want you to drop whatever you're doing and meet her flight at LAX . . .

APOLLODORA: I'm not off till half-past five . . .

FLINT: *(To Apollodora.)* I wasn't talking to you — ! . . . Alone? No, no. I'm being joined by a friend . . . *(Phone.)* Be reasonable. Andrea — you don't cancel *the* Steep Mitchell at zero minutes' notice . . . Have Shirley call your two o'clock and explain while you get yourself out to meet United Flight — *(Referring to notes.)* Four-eight-two into LAX . . . What? From Seattle . . . or Portland. Vancouver. One of those places. Use your initiative, girl, and don't bug me with a lot of goddamned details. Meet the flight, have the lady paged, make my apologies and keep her happy till I can meet you both at the Bev Wilsh. Say about six-fifteen . . . *(To Apollodora.)* If my friend asks for me, my name is Flint Grady —

APOLLODORA: Well, sure, but if he's your friend he'll recognize you for himself, right?

FLINT: Wrong. I used the term "friend" loosely — I hope he'll be a friend by the time we've had lunch. I need the kind of good food and ambience that will persuade him to be my friend and let me do a shoot with him.

APOLLODORA: *(Phone.)* The one who just walked in is Mafia.

FLINT: Photography.

APOLLODORA: *(To Flint.)* Whatever . . . *(Phone.)* So what did you decide?

FLINT: You'll have seen him thousands of times. Billboards . . . TV commercials. If you thumb through that newspaper, you'll probably spot him modeling shirts or cologne. His name is —

APOLLODORA: *(Phone.)* Tom Cruise? Well, of course I'd prefer him to some Iranian standup comic . . . .

FLINT: He's not that famous.

APOLLODORA: *(Phone.)* . . . but don't let that influence you — I'm just a poor female media addict, aren't I?

FLINT: I'm sure you're being too hard on yourself . . . *(Phone.)* Borrow Eddie's car! Steal a UPS van! Just get your butt out to the arrivals lounge now — now. Call me when you're on your way and I'll update you on the lady . . . *(He hangs up.)* I think I'll hit the men's room before my friend shows . . .

APOLLODORA: Right the other side of the bar. Have a look at our specials on the board as you're passing through. May I bring you something to drink while you're waiting for —

FLINT: Steep Mitchell.

APOLLODORA: Steve Mitchell.

FLINT: Not Steve. Steep. Like a cliff. Trust me, the minute he walks in, bells of recognition will ring . . . Drink? Let's see: what do I want to drink . . .?

APOLLODORA: *(Phone, shouting.)* It's a simple, straight-forward choice, boy-san! All I'm asking is that you make it sometime between now and five thirty, if that's not too big an effort!

FLINT: Well, all right! Evian with a twist.

(He goes.)

APOLLODORA: *(Noting it on her computer.)* Good choice! . . . *(Phone.)* Because I've got orders to deal with and that is what "hold" is for, Gary . . . What do you mean you can't hold any longer? Either you hold or you raise your hand and get permission to leave the room the way you did in middle school . . . O.K., O.K., I'll call you back! . . . Give me an Evian with a twist, Demetrius!

(She goes. Steep enters talking on his cel phone.)

STEEP: *(Phone.)* No, that suite that looks out on the slopes and has a big white bear skin rug in front of the fireplace . . . My client won't accept any accommodation that doesn't include a bear skin rug . . . Yes, I'll hold while you check.

(Apollodora rushes out with mineral water.)

APOLLODORA: One Evian with — oh, hi!

STEEP: *(Taking the glass from her.)* Thanks. I'm supposed to be meeting a photographer named — *(Fumbling in his pockets.)*

APOLLODORA: Grady. He's in to the rest room. He said I'd recognize you and I do.

STEEP: Tight. My name is —

APOLLODORA: Steep. Like a precipice . . . I'll be your food service technician for lunch today, Steep. If you have any questions, I'm Apollodora . . .

STEEP: Cool name.

APOLLODORA: Thanks.

STEEP: Spelled —?

APOLLODORA: I don't know. It was Manny's idea. The manager. He made all of us change when we did a total make-over of this place last month . . . When we were still the Scandia Grill, I was Erika — with a K. And believe me, it was a lot easier endorsing my paycheck.

STEEP: You've never been in Greece, then?

APOLLODORA: No, but I sold souvenir programs at a benefit performance once . . . Just a joke. Steep . . . Here's Flint —

(Flint returns from the rest room. He is talking on his cel phone.)

FLINT: *(Phone.)* A university demonstration on Santa Monica Boulevard? . . . Oh. A diversity demonstration. Well, I'd suggest you check a left immediately. Maybe, like, La Cienega or Beverly Boulevard. Call me back . . . *(To Steep.)* Mister Mitchell — Steep! Flint Grady. We've never actually met —

STEEP: No, but I love your work . . .

FLINT: Well, I do too. I mean yours.

STEEP: Hold on just one tick, er —

FLINT: *(Prompting.)* Flint.

STEEP: Right. *(Phone.)* Shit! . . . Couldn't he move? If he's had four days in that same suite, he'd probably welcome a change of scene . . . It's vital. My client is coming all the way from London and if she doesn't have a bear skin rug in front of her fireplace, she won't put out — er — put out tenders for a construction project we're considering . . . Well, you can at least ask him — and phone me back A.S.A.P. My number is Area Code three-one-zero, slash six-three-nine dash nine-nine-nine-zero. *(He hangs up.)* Aspen . . .

FLINT: You ski?

STEEP: God, no. I'm terrified of heights. I just go on location and wear the gear. You know. For pix . . . *(He punches numbers on his cel phone.)*

APOLLODORA: Our specials are on the board. I'll just slip in and get you another twisted Evian while you're deciding . . . *(She goes in.)*

FLINT: Pix. Right . . . I'm really excited about the possibility we might work together on this children's book project, er —

STEEP: Steep.

FLINT: Thanks. I'm Flint . . . I believe Maurey Hersch at Vantage Books has briefed you on the concept? I suggested lunch instead of the office, Steep, because I feel it's terribly important to establish some kind of interpersonal relationship before launching a project like this one . . .

STEEP: Love it. Love it. *(Phone.)* Come on, Rudolpho. Pick up. I know you're there, man!

FLINT: Without some preliminary bonding, I say, what's the point, you know, Steep?

STEEP: *(Phone.)* Will you pick bloody *up,* you lard-assed wop?

FLINT: Now here, for instance, is the other lead character in the story —

STEEP: *(Phone.)* Rudolpho, Sweetheart. I thought you'd fallen in and flushed yourself down. Now listen carefully . . .

FLINT: He's called Stanley. As you can see, he's a squirrel.

STEEP: Cute. Oh, very cute . . . ! *(Phone.)* I'm expecting a call from London. A Brit chick called Felicity . . . Felicity Haynes-Waltham. Don't bother to write it down. She calls herself Flick and she sounds just like that horse-faced girl on "Good Neighbors." The point is, I'm in this Greek place with that photographer guy named Clint —

FLINT: Flint. Flint Grady.

STEEP: *(Phone.)* Grady . . . . *(Sotto voce.)* Because he's Brock Wilson's brother-in-law, Rudolpho. Brock — you know, my new agent — and I owe Brock a favor. It's for some kind of kiddie commercial or public affairs spot or something . . .

FLINT: Stanley's girlfriend is called Marilyn. Here she is. She's a muskrat . . .

STEEP: *(Phone.)* Point is, Rudolpho, when Flick phones I want you to tell her to phone me here — but *not* on this number. N-O-T *not*. Got it? Tell her to call me on — *(With a "May I?" smile, he takes Flint's phone.)* Area Code three-one-zero — six-six-two . . . nine-zero-zero-eight . . .

(Flint's phone rings. He grabs it back from Steep.)

STEEP: *(Phone.)* Hullo? . . . Andrea! Where the hell are you?

STEEP: *(Phone.)* Because I have got to keep this line open for Aspen to call back about the bear skin. Rudy . . . No — B-E-A-R. But don't bother writing that down either.

FLINT: *(Phone.)* I don't care if they're about to stage the Battle of Armageddon, Andrea, stay on La Cienega.

STEEP: *(Phone.)* It's the least you can do for me. Don't forget that long, dismal night I spent solo at the Ramada just so you could have the whole apartment all to yourself and that tall blonde from Utah . . .

FLINT: *(Phone.)* No, no — straight onto 10. Then exit 10 onto 405. Call me when you've hit the first freeway . . . *(He hangs up.)* Wonderful to rap with you this way, Steep!

STEEP: *(Phone.)* So? Was it my fault she turned out to be a Mormon?

FLINT: *(Handing him a menu.)* The overall concept is that we combine these fantasy cartoon figures with an established, real-life role-model. That's you, of course.

STEEP: Right.

FLINT: *(Nervous laugh.)* We hope! . . . As you'll see from the sketches, this book aims at something like what M.C.I. did with Michael Jordan and Tweety-Bird . . .

STEEP: That sounds tight.

(Flint's phone bleeps.)

FLINT: *(Phone.)* Andrea! Listen carefully — . . . What? cut the cockney hi-jinks and get serious, girl. Where are you now? . . . Hammersmith? Never heard of it . . . Sorry. I think you have . . . Steep Mitchell? Oh, yeah. Sure. He's right here.

STEEP: *(Phone.)* Flick!

FLINT: I'll need that phone back, Steep. I've got a colleague who needs to check in for a briefing before she gets to LAX . . . But, meanwhile, just to brief you. We're hot to trot with Ben's characters, but having a recognized personality like yourself is obviously going to make or break the whole project. Are you reading me?

STEEP: *(Phone.)* Clear as crystal, you sexy creature . . . !

FLINT: Well, er — that's great . . .

STEEP: *(Phone.)* You could be sitting at the next table. What time is it over there?

FLINT: Pop-ups, of course.

STEEP: *(To Flint, taking up a menu.)* No, just a salad.

FLINT: We'll do half the pages three-D, with pop-up pictures . . .

STEEP: Love it. Love it. *(Phone.)* Are you packed?

FLINT: You talking fitness and sports to Stanley Squirrel . . . you doing hair, grooming and deodorants with Marilyn Muskrat . . .

STEEP: Well, get cracking, as you Limeys say. How's Hampstead Common looking?

FLINT: Possibility of a film, of course — if the book takes off. Big possibility of action-figure tie-ins with McDonalds or Burger King. All kinds of possibilities floating around out there. Right?
(Steep's phone rings. Flint picks it up.)
Andrea?

STEEP: *(Snatching his phone from Flint.)* That's Aspen! Hullo? . . . *(Phone: to Flick.)* Hold a tick, Flick. *(Phone: to Aspen.)* No, a Navajo rough weave lap robe will not do!

FLINT: Ben and Maurey are flex, of course — wide open to any additional character or story ideas you might want to throw in . . . I'll need my phone back pretty quick, if you don't mind . . .

STEEP: Very cute. Love it. Love the concept . . .*(Phone: Aspen.)* No. I'll hold . . . *(Phone: Flick.)* What's your flight number?
(Apollodora comes in.)

APOLLODORA: *(Phone.)* Five-forty at the Cineplex. You're on, Gary. Got to go.
(She hangs up.) Flint? A message from your office.

FLINT: Yeah?

APOLLODORA: They say don't forget your shoot at Malibu.

FLINT: Christ! I'm half an hour late already. Bit of an emergency, Steep old man. I wonder if you —
(Steep shrugs helplessly toward both phones. Flint shrugs and turns to Apollodora.)
Could I borrow your phone for a second?
(He checks numbers across Steep's shoulder, punches them in.)

APOLLODORA: Be my guest!

STEEP: *(Phone: to Aspen.)* Because she was born and raised in the Yukon and is deeply concerned about the endangered polar bear population —!

FLINT: *(Phone.)* Steep — it's Flint Grady . . . So good to meet and share with you at the Bistro Akropolis today . . .
(Steep continues to talk on Flint's phone to Flick in London and to the hotel in Colorado. Flint, while talking on Apollodora's phone at the same time pays the check, shakes hands with Steep arranges the sketch book on the table and finally departs.)

STEEP: *(Phone.)* Sweetheart, of course I'll drive in to Denver and meet your plane . . . Woops! Looks like I've got Call Waiting on my Aspen line, but time, tide and British Telecom wait on no man — or woman either, am I right? Hold a tick . . .

FLINT: What I'm going to do, Steep, is FAX you the Stanley Squirrel book contract.

STEEP: *(Phone: Aspen.)* Then you'll have to sneak in and move it to the fireplace in Ms Miss Haynes-Waltham's room . . . Pinned to the floor? Well un-pin it! . . . Colorado pine pegs? Shit!

FLINT: *(Phone.)* I'd suggest you check it over and if you feel favorable, FAX me your initials, care of Vantage Books, on the places I mark with a single check — and a full signature on the ones marked with a double check. I'll then be in touch with you by e-mail to talk details like set-ups for the pix and computer graphics work with Ben and his staff . . .

STEEP: And of course it's all arranged about that big, white, fuzzy, you-know-what, dolly girl — !

APOLLODORA: *(Shouting after Flint.)* Hey — ! Hey, come back here —

FLINT: *(Shouting from offstage.)* You can keep the change — !

APOLLODORA: That doesn't mean you can keep my cel phone!

(She rushes off after him as Steep continues to crack trans-Atlantic jokes and set up meeting times in Colorado.)

END OF PLAY

ID
by Kyle Wood

FIRST PERFORMANCE
January 2001

ORIGINAL CAST

Morality	Zane Basler
Paranoia	Kai Lillie
Superficiality	Christopher Sugarman
Ego	Misti Boettiger
Confidence	Jim Eckhart
Sex Drive	Andrea Chappell
Inner Child	Ryan Murphy
Robin	Lauren Goldring
Daniel	David Rudesill
Directed by	Bill Peters
Sets by	William "Skip" Epperson

CHARACTERS

EGO: Male or female. Any age. He/she organizes thought process rationally and governs action.

CONFIDENCE: Male or female. Any age. He/she firmly believes in Daniel's own abilities. Confidence believes he/she will prevail in all disputes and is willing to prove it with violence.

SUPERFICIALITY: Male or female. Any age. He/she lacks depth of character and enjoys using others to benefit his/her shallow attempts at happiness. A true kiss ass.

MORALITY: Male or female. Any age. He/she understands the difference between right and wrong. Morality's main goal is to teach others moral quality and guide them in the direction of good.

PARANOIA: Male or female. Any age. He/she is constantly aware of Dan's faults and imperfections. He/she has delusions of persecution. Paranoia believes the whole world is out to sabotage him/her and Dan.

INNER CHILD: A full grown adult male. He wears blindingly bright yellow lederhosen and a matching yellow bonnet. He has extra big brown shoes with silver buckles and yellow socks pulled up to his knees. His face is rough and covered with stubble. He carries a large lollipop around with him.

SEX DRIVE: A stocky man. He has very long mangled hair with streaks of gray in it. He has a beard to match with bits of grime and food in it. He is wearing nothing but a tattered loincloth. He has poor hygiene and a vulgar personality. This part may also be played by a woman.

DANIEL: A thirty-two-year-old single man. He works as a budget advisor for the city of Denver, Colorado. He lives alone in a studio apartment in the suburbs. All of the characters, except for Robin, live in Dan's ID and influence his life. Dan has trouble communicating with others.

ROBIN: A twenty-nine-year-old woman. She lives across the street from Dan. Robin and Dan have been dating for two months now. Robin is very free spirited and outgoing.

ID

A day in the life of Daniel's ID. Sex Drive is completely wrapped up in his sleeping bag, asleep. Ego is clicking her pen as she studies a report. Paranoia is on perimeter patrol. Morality is immersed in deep meditation. Confidence is on three-hundred-eighty-sixth push up. Superficiality is listening to his Walkman.

MORALITY: Are we happy? *(Pause.)* I mean . . . what is happiness? The pursuit of happiness is, at its core, the very meaning of life itself. Paranoia, are you happy?

PARANOIA: That's a trick question. No matter what I say it's a trap. Just leave me alone.

MORALITY: Superficiality, what about you?

SUPERFICIALITY: When you have an ass sculpted by the gods that can hypnotize the entire population of France, that is happiness.

MORALITY: Is Daniel happy?

EGO: I received another memo from Lord Soul this morning. He is *not* happy with current circumstances here within Daniel. Lord Soul believes Daniel is drifting aimlessly. Our Daniel is not happy, because of all this constant bickering. We need to come together.

CONFIDENCE: Excuse me, Ego. Sorry, "Chief Ego."

EGO: Yes, Confidence, what is it?

CONFIDENCE: My main man Dan is great. In fact, he's better than great. If it weren't for Morality and his mind numbing babble, we wouldn't have to see Dr. Fritz twice a month.

MORALITY: You can lead a horse to water, but you —

ALL: *(Finishing Morality's line.)* can't make him drink.

MORALITY: I suggest yoga and a daily mantra.

(Telephone rings.)

PARANOIA: Telephone! Put a trace on that.

(No one notices Sex Drive waking up.)

EGO: Places everyone. *(Everyone listens.)*

PARANOIA: It's Robin!

SUPERFICIALITY: Robin?

CONFIDENCE: Dan has been going out with her for three months now and you still don't remember her?

SUPERFICIALITY: Petty details in Dan's life are beneath me.

PARANOIA: Hang up. *(Everyone argues for and against hanging up.)*

MORALITY: She's coming over! . . . and she says she's staying for breakfast.

PARANOIA: Oh no, what could that possibly mean?

SEX DRIVE: *(Wakes up.)* AAAARRRRGGGGHHH! Sex. Now. Me. Want. *(Sex Drive goes berserk, pushing the others and trashing the room.)*

EGO: Code red!

(Confidence grabs Sex Drive's favorite toy and lures him back inside the sleeping bag. Sex Drive with a toy begins to satisfy himself.)

EGO: These outbursts have become too frequent of late. Sex Drive wants for only two things in his primitive life: Sex and then Sleep. *(Sex Drive stops moving and begins to snore.)* His vulgar displays of power have increased with each passing day. I fear he will soon be strong enough to destroy all of us if he does not get what he wants.

MORALITY: Then Sex Drive will be the only one steering Daniel through the pitfalls of life.

PARANOIA: We're doomed. There's no hope for us.

MORALITY: His aggressive behavior will only scare Robin away.

EGO: Precisely, it is our responsibility to satisfy Sex Drive. With Robin. Tonight.

CONFIDENCE: I'm all for getting Danny laid, but it will only work for so long. In this handbag I have the means to put him down permanently! Now, who's with me?

EGO: No! That can never happen. He has a contract with Lord Soul. *(Ego produces contract and reads from it.)* "Sex Drive must have an influence in everything Daniel does." The contract further states —

PARANOIA: Contract? Wait a minute. How come none of us have ever met him? Or . . . seen him? Or anything?

EGO: Who?

PARANOIA: Lord Soul. He doesn't exist! We're alone, all of us! Vulnerable to the evil intentions of a cruel world! Tortured by a life of agony! Every day we are faced with life altering decisions: paper or plastic.

SUPERFICIALITY: *(To Paranoia.)* Boxers of briefs.

PARANOIA: The pressure is too much for me!

SUPERFICIALITY: Please, you're getting too deep for me. *(Looking up as if speaking to Lord Soul.)* I don't doubt the Soul's existence for one minute. Lord Soul, my master, I stand before you oiled and manicured. Gaze into my incredibly gorgeous eyes and you will see me for who I am. Your delicious servant.

CONFIDENCE: *I've* never seen him. *I've* never even heard him. Just these damn contracts.

MORALITY: The soul expresses itself through us. Like listening to Beethoven on the radio. Beethoven is not actually inside the radio. We are the radio, trapping the soul's essence. For Lord Soul has no location in time or space. The radio is on: birth. The radio is off: death. But Beethoven's symphony is always there.

SUPERFICIALITY: *(To Morality.)* Kiss ass.

INNER CHILD: *(Loud booming voice through house speakers.)* I AM LORD SOUL! WHAT BUSINESS HAVE YOU?

EGO: Ah, yes. That reminds me —

SUPERFICIALITY: *(Kneels before Lord Soul.)* Yes, your most Handsomeness. Command me. Tease me. Whip me! I will drag my tongue across shards of glass if you so desire.

INNER CHILD: WHAT FUTILE PERSON DARES DISTURB MY SLEEP!?

SUPERFICIALITY: Oh, Master of Loud Words of Intimidation. Spit on them for they need to be punished, not me. But if you feel I'm not worthy, spit on me a thousand times so that I may bathe in a shower of all your bodily fluids.

CONFIDENCE: That's a pretty neat trick, Morality. You had ole kiss ass here shakin' in his boots, but if you don't zip your lip Dan is going to take us all back to Dr. Fritz for some more "therapy."

MORALITY: Trust what you know, not what you assume. Sometimes a voice is just a voice.

EGO: I think it's time I let you in on some new developments. As you know, last Monday we had a two-hour visit with Dr. Fritz. And while Daniel was regressing, something happened.

INNER CHILD: *(Loud bellowing laugh.)* COWARDS! ALL OF YOU!

EGO: Or should I say *someone* happened.

(Lighting changes to reveal Inner Child's silhouette cast upon the up stage paper wall.)

CONFIDENCE: I don't friggin' believe it. You mean —

EGO: That's correct. It is Daniel's: Inner Child.

(Inner Child breaks through the paper wall and swaggers out to center stage.)

INNER CHILD: Well fuck me runnin'. Look at what a bunch of losers you all turned out to be. Ya thought you got rid of me, huh? Wrong! Thanks to a little piss ant psychologist, I'm back baby!

PARANOIA: He—He's a psychiatrist.

INNER CHILD: What did you say, ya little shit?

PARANOIA: . . . uh . . . I—uh . . . well, um . . .

INNER CHILD: That's what I thought. You're scared of me, huh? Ooooh I'm the boogieman. Well are ya going to cry or piss your pants?

PARANOIA: Do I have to choose one?

INNER CHILD: *(Looks down at Paranoia's crotch. Paranoia has soiled himself.)* Looks like you already did. Now get the fuck out of my sight! And as for you, Ego, you can kiss my fat ass until you turn blue in the face. *(To everyone.)* I am, now, master and you are all my little bitches.

SUPERFICIALITY: *(Rushing to Inner Child's side.)* Hey, that thing you did with the shadow and the scary voice and all . . . pure genius. You and I, we have a lot in common. You hate Ego. I hate Ego. We're a team. By the way, I love this outfit, it's so —

INNER CHILD: SHUT YOUR PIEHOLE!

EGO: NO, YOU SHUT YOURS! Your contract expired when Daniel hit puberty. So unless Lord Soul decides to extend your contract, consider yourself banished.

INNER CHILD: Soul? Fuck Lord Soul. What has he ever done for me? Nuthin'. Except tuck me away deep within the bowels of Dan's subconscious with nuthin' but Lincoln Logs and Tinker Toys to pass the years away. Oh and don't forget the Slinky. "It's Slinky, It's Slinky . . ." — the Slinky sucks!!

MORALITY: Everyone loves the Slinky.

(Paranoia notices Sex Drive mumbling: "Bubbles, Bubbles . . .")

INNER CHILD: My ass. That piece of crap was fun for about two minutes. Ooh, it rolled down the stairs . . . and that's all it fuckin' did. I'm thirty-two years old! I'm not going back and you can't make me so "Na, na, n-na, na."

(Sex Drive awakens from his slumber in a wild rage.)

SEX DRIVE: Sex. Me. Want. Now.

(Paranoia rushes downstage to listen in and find out what happened.)

INNER CHILD: *(Curls up in a fetal position and begins to cry.)* Mommy. Help. It's a monster.

(Everyone attempts to restrain Sex Drive.)

PARANOIA: *(Panics.)* Uhhh, Ego? Ego, I think you should hear this!

EGO: Not now, Paranoia, as you can see we are a little aroused at the moment.

SEX DRIVE: *(Howls out like a wolf at the moon.)* aaaaWWoooooo!

PARANOIA: I know. I'm taking a ride on Danny's train of thought and —

EGO: Superficiality, grab a leg!

SUPERFICIALITY: And risk premature wrinkles? Never. You "grab a leg."

EGO: What pray tell is Daniel doing?

SEX DRIVE: *(Pants.)* Lust . . . *(Pants.)* Crave . . . *(Pants.)* Hot . . .

PARANOIA: He's talking to a girl named Bubbles on his cellular. I think he's having phone sex!

SEX DRIVE: ssseeEXXXXXXxxx!

EGO: Robin will be here any moment. We can't see her with Sex Drive like this. Confidence, go get one of his toys.

CONFIDENCE: No! It's time for the Handbag of Horror. *(Produces a bag of photos. Superficiality decides to help and grabs some photos for himself.)* I've been stock piling powerful memories for just this kind of horny predicament.

SEX DRIVE: *(Slobber, slobber.)* Mmmm. Yummy. MORE!

CONFIDENCE: Image number one: Bucky, the neighbor's cute little doggy . . .

ALL: Awww.

CONFIDENCE: Licks his genitals!

SEX DRIVE: Eee. Rrr . . . Bubbles . . .

CONFIDENCE: Then he —

SEX DRIVE: Nooooo!

CONFIDENCE: Licks your face!

ALL: Ooooh.

SUPERFICIALITY: Great Grandma Blanche *(Picture: a.)* has just stepped out of the shower *(Picture: b.)*. Her towel drops to the floor *(Picture: c.)*.

SEX DRIVE: Ack! Nooo!

CONFIDENCE: And a gust of wind makes a flapping noise against her skin.

SEX DRIVE: Ugh . . . *(Choke.)*

(Sex Drive falls to the ground, unconscious. Inner Child sits up and sucks his thumb.)

SUPERFICIALITY: All this excitement has given me the vapors, *(Feels his hair.)* but my hair is *(Looks in mirror.)* still perfect.

PARANOIA: I hope he's dead. I hope that vicious slobbering beast roasts in the fires of Hell!

MORALITY: Needs must as the devil drives. We had to do what we had to do.

(Doorbell rings.)

ALL: ROBIN!

(Robin and Daniel enter.)

DANIEL: Come on in. So, how's it going?

ROBIN: *(Drops her purse and takes off her jacket.)* Oh, *(Relaxing sigh.)* it was a little hectic at work today, I'm all right now. How about you?

PARANOIA: I'm doing good.

DANIEL: I'm doing good.

PARANOIA: Except for this enormous urine stain on my pants.

EGO: Stop that!

INNER CHILD: Wanna play with my slinky?

(Confidence pushes Inner Child away.)

DANIEL: Wanna play with my slinky?

68 Kyle Wood

ROBIN: What!? Did you just say slinky?
(There is an uncomfortable silence.)
EGO: Someone say something? Anything? Anyone? Morality?
MORALITY: You cannot draw blood from a rock. I have nothing.
CONFIDENCE: Conversation is overrated. The silence demonstrates Dan's ability to think deep thoughts. She thinks he's smart. She thinks it's cool.
PARANOIA: *(The pressure consumes Paranoia and he lashes out.)* Stand up straight, you're slouching. Close your mouth, you've got crooked teeth. You're sweating like a fat disgusting pig! Take off that scarf, you look like Mr. Furley. You missed a zit on your forehead —
INNER CHILD: *(Overlapping. Laughing.)* What a dumbass.
PARANOIA: Stop staring, that's too much eye contact. No! Not her chest. Don't look at her chest! You can look at a girl's butt, because they can't see you, but never ever stare at her TITS!
SUPERFICIALITY: Please. You're going to give the poor boy a complex. This is my area of expertise, so back up and let me operate. Dan, my boy, get a hold of yourself. Take a deep breath, relax and repeat after me: Robin?
DANIEL: Robin?
ROBIN: Yes.
MORALITY: Beauty is in the eye of the beholder. And I behold you.
SUPERFICIALITY: *(Scoff, at Morality.)* I apologize for my actions. I'm just in awe of you and your beauty.
DANIEL: *(Nervously fighting to speak.)* I-I-I'm sorry. I'm in awe of you.
ROBIN: Oh wow, really? Well, what do you think of my new dress?
(Sex Drive wakes up.)
SUPERFICIALITY: That's a very nice dress.
DANIEL: That's a very nice dress.
SEX DRIVE: It would look good crumpled on my floor!
DANIEL: It would look good crumpled on my —
SUPERFICIALITY: Department store!
DANIEL: *(Confused.)* in the department store — window . . . On the mannequin.
ROBIN: Oh. Thanks . . . I guess. Hey, I thought we might go out and sing some karaoke tonight?
SUPERFICIALITY: Mmmm, to hear you sing. Snook'ems, your voice is so sweet and rich it makes —
DANIEL: Billie Holiday sound like a test tone for the emergency broadcast system.
ROBIN: Oh Daniel. I don't know what to say. I'm blushing.
SUPERFICIALITY: The melody is so alluring. It invites me. Controls me —
SEX DRIVE: COMMAND ME!!!

DANIEL: Command me.
SEX DRIVE: FONDLE ME!
DANIEL: Fondle me.
SEX DRIVE: HURT ME!
DANIEL: HURT ME!!
DANIEL AND SEX DRIVE: *(Together in unison.)* WHIP ME!
DANIEL: Strip me naked and force me to wrestle savage ferrets —
SEX DRIVE: While you snap my ass with a wet towel!
ROBIN: *(Angrily surprised.)* What!?
EGO: No! What have we done!
PARANOIA: That's it. We're doomed. Finished.
ROBIN: *(Gathers her things and heads for the door.)* I don't know what's gotten into you, but I think I should leave.
(Chaos ensues as Robin begins to leave. Ego begins to sing Beethoven's "Ode to Joy" to Sex Drive. Sex Drive hears the music and joins in with Ego. Everyone else sees this and begins to join in as well. Simultaneously, Robin stops at the door and turns to Dan. Dan rises from the ashes of despair and moves toward Robin. Dan serenades Robin. They embrace and kiss.)
ROBIN: Oh Dan, you're so unpredictable. *(Laughs.)* I like it.
ALL: Thank you.
DANIEL: Thank you.
ROBIN: Now, I know we've only been going out a few months, but . . . well . . . I love you.
SUPERFICIALITY: It's been real. I'm so out of here.
(Stunned and dazed, the members of Dan's ID run off. Dan and Robin are the only ones left on stage. Dan is like a deer caught in the headlights. A beat.)
(Lights fade to black.)

END OF PLAY

LOVE AND DEATH
by Kathyrn Chetkovich

FIRST PERFORMANCE
January 2000

ORIGINAL CAST
    Celia . . . . .Patti Fitchen
    James . . . . .Philip Slater
    Directed by . . . . .Bonnie Ronzio
    Sets by . . . . .Dohn Grube

LOVE AND DEATH

Motel room. Celia is pacing, waiting. A moment later, James enters.

CELIA: There you are! I was starting to worry.
JAMES: I told you not to expect me any earlier. I had a meeting.
CELIA: I know. I just . . . worry.
JAMES: What about?
CELIA: Oh, you know, everything. Don't you?
JAMES: No, actually. I don't. Do you think I should?
CELIA: Of course not. That's part of what I love about you. Aren't you going to kiss me?
(They embrace.)
What's wrong?
JAMES: Nothing. What do you mean? Nothing's wrong.
CELIA: You seem tense. Something's the matter.
JAMES: Celia, I'm fine. Is something the matter with *you?*
CELIA: No, of course not. Sorry. How long do you have?
JAMES: I have to be home by eight-thirty. You?
CELIA: Tonight is Richard's men's group. Nine-thirty at the earliest. I know it's not the right thing to say, but I liked men better before they started talking so much.
JAMES: You're just an old-fashioned girl.
CELIA: That's what I love about you: You don't *say* everything. And everything between us is so . . .
JAMES: Temporary.
CELIA: Intense. How are you feeling?
JAMES: Fine.
CELIA: You always say that.
JAMES: Because it's true.
CELIA: You don't have to be brave for me, you know.
JAMES: I thought that's what you just said you liked about me.
CELIA: Loved.
JAMES: Loved, then. Look, Celia, I have to tell you something. Some news. I went to the doctor's today.
CELIA: I knew it. I knew there was something. It's worse, isn't it?
JAMES: No, it's not what you think. It's *good* news. I — I'm not sick, it turns out. I'm not dying!
CELIA: What are you talking about?

JAMES: The lab made a mistake, apparently. Some mixup with the slides or something. I'm fine! There's nothing wrong with me!
CELIA: What do you mean, a mistake? You mean you're not sick?
JAMES: No!
CELIA: You're not going to die?
JAMES: No! Well, not right now. Not that I know of, anyway.
CELIA: But how can that *be?*
JAMES: Just one of those freak confusions, I guess. But listen, it means I'm fine!
CELIA: James, that's — well, that's great. Obviously. What — what great, great news.
(They embrace, but awkwardly.)
Well. This kind of changes everything, doesn't it?
JAMES: Does it?
CELIA: I mean, in a *good* way, of course. But still.
JAMES: I don't see why it has to.
CELIA: Well, we can't very well go on having an affair if you're going to *live*, can we? Your wife is my best friend!
JAMES: What are you saying? You only loved me because you thought I was going to die?
CELIA: Of course not! I've loved you for years. But I only *slept* with you because I thought you were going to die.
JAMES: That's perverse.
CELIA: It is not! It's moral!
JAMES: What?! What is this, the "terminally ill" clause of the seventh commandment?
CELIA: You're a fine one to talk!
JAMES: I'm the one who was dying, remember?
CELIA: You only *thought* you were dying.
JAMES: Look, let's not argue, OK? Celia?
(Pause.)
CELIA: I'm sorry. This just — I'm surprised, is all.
JAMES: Imagine how I feel!
CELIA: How *do* you feel?
JAMES: What do you mean?
CELIA: Someone just gave you your life back. That doesn't happen to most people. What does it feel like?
JAMES: Well, great, you know. It feels great.
CELIA: "Great"? That's it?
JAMES: I'm not good at talking about things. You said so yourself, remember? You said that's what you love about me.

CELIA: Like.

JAMES: Oh, come on, Celia. This is good news. We can worry later. We're together now. Let's celebrate.
(Pause.)

CELIA: Do you remember how it started? Do you remember the day you told me?

JAMES: Of course.

CELIA: But do you remember what you said?

JAMES: I called you from a pay phone. I remember that.

JAMES: You said you were downtown with an hour to kill and was I free for lunch.

JAMES: I remember. I remember feeling like that was the one phone call you're allowed to make before they lock you up.

CELIA: Three glasses of wine, and then you told me.

JAMES: Yes.

CELIA: We were sitting there. You'd just been to the doctor. You said he'd asked you to get dressed and meet him in his office.

JAMES: God, yes, I remember.

CELIA: Six months, you said he said.

JAMES: You remember.

CELIA: Everything. Six months. Remember that?

JAMES: I couldn't very well forget *that*, could I?

CELIA: You bastard.

JAMES: What? Because I thought I was going to die and now I'm not?

CELIA: Because you lied.

JAMES: About what?

CELIA: He didn't say six months! He said a year, maybe two!

JAMES: So, I forgot exactly what he said! It was a stressful conversation! Besides, what difference does it make, if it turns out I'm actually fine?

CELIA: You would *not* have forgotten a thing like that, unless . . .

JAMES: Unless what?

CELIA: Unless you made it up in the first place.

JAMES: What are you saying, that I made the whole thing up? That I was never going to die?

CELIA: James, how could you *do* that? How could you lie to me about a thing like that?

JAMES: It wasn't a lie. I honestly thought I *would* die without you. I *had* to have you.

CELIA: That's sick, you know that? For a well man, you're incredibly sick.

JAMES: Listen to me. I *did* go to the doctor's that day. We talked about my heart, how sometimes it throws in this extra beat, which was probably nothing to worry about, although sometimes perfectly healthy people do drop dead on the golf course, you never know. We'd had dinner with you and Richard the night before, do you remember? I do. I remember everything about that dinner. I remember sitting next to you and thinking if I couldn't touch you I was going to die. I literally thought that. And then I had this conversation with the doctor the next day. And when I left his office the sun was just incredibly bright. It was bouncing off the cars in the parking lot so, so *intensely* that I could hardly keep my eyes open. And I thought, if there's a phone here, and if I've got change, and if she's listed, I'm going to call her. And if she answers, it's a sign.

CELIA: Why didn't you tell me that? Why didn't you just tell me the truth?

JAMES: Because the truth wasn't enough!

CELIA: The truth is always enough!

JAMES: Since when?

CELIA: Since *always*.

JAMES: Well, I'm telling you the truth *now*.

CELIA: But *now* everything is different. Now I can't trust you.

JAMES: Now is exactly when you *can* trust me. It was *before*, when you thought you could, that you couldn't.

CELIA: Is that supposed to make me feel better? Because it doesn't.

JAMES: Well, what about *you*? You're the one who wanted a deathbed romance! How do you think that made *me* feel, knowing that you were only with me because you thought I wouldn't be around in another year?

CELIA: Maybe two.

JAMES: You're cruel.

CELIA: You would know

(Pause.)

Does Meredith know?

JAMES: About us?

CELIA: That you're not *dying*.

JAMES: She never thought I was!

CELIA: You didn't tell her?

JAMES: Why should I tell her? It wasn't true! Good god, *you* didn't tell her, did you?

CELIA: How could *I* tell her? "Oh, by the way, you'll never guess what James mentioned while we were at lunch the other day"?

JAMES: I thought she was your best friend.

CELIA: Now who's being cruel?

JAMES: I'm sorry. I am. For everything.

CELIA: So you're really fine?

JAMES: You sound disappointed.

CELIA: I'm just adjusting to the news.

JAMES: Did you really *want* me to die?

CELIA: Of course not! It just . . . it made everything . . .

JAMES: Easier?

CELIA: More *alive,* somehow. More real. But of course, this is better. I mean, obviously! It just takes a little getting used to.

JAMES: Well, the doctor *did* seem a little concerned about one thing . . .

CELIA: Really? What was that?

JAMES: Well, my cholesterol. It's a bit high.

CELIA: *(Disappointed.)* Oh.

JAMES: But my heart. It *does* throw in that extra beat now and again.

CELIA: But you said that was nothing to worry about, right?

JAMES: Well, ordinarily not. But, you know, with elevated cholesterol — and I *do* have high blood pressure.

CELIA: So in your case it *might* be a bit more serious?

JAMES: Well, you never know. My uncle died young.

CELIA: Heart attack?

JAMES: Farming accident. But still! I could, you know.

CELIA: What?

JAMES: Die. It could happen.

CELIA: Oh, James!

(They embrace, passionately this time.)

END OF PLAY

MATCHING COLORS
by Edith Cooper

FIRST PERFORMANCE
January 1997

ORIGINAL CAST

    Joan ....Birte Frid-Nielsen
    Eve ....Billie Harris
    Jake ....Simon Kelly
    Directed by ....Marjorie Young
    Sets by ....Donna Teague

SET
Joan's living room. Sofa or two chairs with loose cushions. Portrait of a woman in her thirties.

TIME
The present. Late afternoon.

MATCHING COLORS

Joan and Eve are sitting with their shoes off . . .

JOAN: It went well, didn't it . . .
EVE: More a party than a funeral. Nobody talked about her.
JOAN: It was a lot of work . . .
EVE: Sorry I couldn't come sooner. My case just dragged on.
JOAN: *(Undertone.)* Yeah, your big important case.
EVE: Important to the client, a nurse with a back injury. The hospital claimed it was her own fault, but we got her a nice settlement . . .
JOAN: Mom would have loved it: her family, her friends. Her portrait where everyone could see it. Nice touch, don't you think?
EVE: Who was that man who stared at it so long?
JOAN: I don't know. There must have been a hundred people. You might have talked to him, acted more like a hostess.
EVE: I didn't feel like talking. I had the funniest feeling, as though we were all waiting for her; as though she'd walk in at any moment and light up the room the way she always did — and I missed her terribly . . .
JOAN: I can only remember her as she was at the end.
EVE: Poor you. — Try to think of the good thing. We had the best birthday parties. Remember the time it rained, and we had an indoor picnic, with egg sandwiches. And you and she put on a puppet show?
JOAN: Those old puppets! She let me paint their faces, and put a new dress on the princess. Pink georgette! . . .
EVE: And when the crocodile swallowed her, we kids were all terrified. — I wonder if she kept them.
JOAN: The attic's a mess. We have our work cut out. And I'm so tired.
EVE: Of course you are. *(Pause.)* Your house looks beautiful. So light and fresh.
JOAN: I had it painted. That's one thing they drilled into us at school: "Your home is your best advertisement."
EVE: Aren't those new pillows? Lovely colors . . . I really have to hand it to you. I wish you could do my apartment.
(Beat.)
Say, the pillows are exactly the colors of the picture! . . .
JOAN: You noticed! I used it for my focus . . . It pulls everything together, don't you see?
EVE: *(Beat.)* Did you have it hanging here, or how —
JOAN: I borrowed it so I could work with it. *(Getting carried away.)* I couldn't

find matching pillows, so I bought silk and dyed it . . . It took quite a few tries. Don't you think the match is perfect?

EVE: Yes, that underwater green, and the purple of her dress —

JOAN: Plum — I think the room color's good too: Cream with a touch of Sienna. Sets it off nicely, doesn't it?

(Small pause.)

EVE: How did you manage, with so little time?

JOAN: I started a month ago.

EVE: You went to all that trouble just for today? *(Pause.)* You weren't planning to *keep* the portrait?

JOAN: *(Beat.)* Well, yes of course I am.

EVE: Without even talking to me? Because it happens to be the one thing *I* want.

JOAN: I'm entitled to it. I took care of her.

EVE: I've always loved that picture.

JOAN: It's perfect here.

EVE: It would look perfect in my place.

JOAN: In your small rooms? With your modern furniture? It would look awful. What you want is things to scale, like those delicate Japanese brush paintings Dad had in his den. Group them together, it'll make a stunning statement.

EVE: I don't want to make a statement. I want the portrait, because it's her. And don't do the decorator bit on me.

JOAN: It's what I am. Trust me, the portrait would loom; it would make your room look small and cluttered.

EVE: I'll love having her loom. — You have no right to it, no legal right.

JOAN: And why is that? Because you wouldn't talk her into making a detailed will.

EVE: I tried.

JOAN: You couldn't have tried very hard; you can argue anyone into a paper bag.

EVE: She said: "Oh you two get along so well, you'll split everything up between you."

JOAN: I know: you didn't try because you knew she'd leave it to me.

EVE: That's how *your* twisted mind works. And you accuse me of lying! I DON'T LIE. Or steal our mother's property.

JOAN: I borrowed it, for God's sake! I did not steal! And do you think it was easy, taking care of her all these years? Oh she was unreasonable! I'd hire help and she fired them. Phone calls, at all hours! Said I never came to visit, when I'd just been . . .

EVE: You rushed in and out, she told me. That's not visiting. — I came as often as I could . . .
JOAN: Yeah, you took her out. Wore her out.
EVE: It's what she wanted. We shopped; you know how she liked giving little gifts. And then we'd have tea in that little sidewalk cafe. She had a good time.
JOAN: She stayed in bed for days, after . . .
(Pause.)
EVE: Joan, did you grudge her a good time? Are you that mean-spirited?
JOAN: (Overlap.) Rubbish. She was frail, I —
EVE: I won't let you keep the portrait.
JOAN: Try and take it from me.
EVE: I'll take you to *court* if necessary . . .
JOAN: You'd do that? You . . . bitch! Cold-blooded lawyer-bitch! That would fix me all right. I can see the papers: "Bennett sisters fighting over mother's portrait." My reputation in shreds, my career over before it got started. But you don't care.
Well, I have friends, they know how hard I worked all these years, taking care of her.
(Long pause.)
Eve, don't do this. Have a heart. I'm good at decorating, you said it yourself. Let me have my chance. I've got my brochures made: "Timeless elegance for gracious living." A photo of my living room on the front, with the portrait.
I want it, Eve. I need it. (Pause.) Say something!
EVE: Your commercialism leaves me speechless. You'd use the portrait for an advertisement!
JOAN: Commercialism! Shit! Just trying to get my life together! But you don't care. You don't care about me or anybody, you just care about winning. You always wanted to have the last word. Debating champion. "Queen of Words" we used to call you . . . (Small pause.)
But *I* was queen of the ball.
EVE: Because you'd go to bed with anybody . . .
JOAN: You never went to bed at all . . .
EVE: Of course I did . . .
JOAN: With who?
EVE: Whom. — Nobody you know.
JOAN: Probably spent the night discussing points of law with some dried-up old fart.

EVE: I won't stoop to discuss my sex life with you. — You can't have the picture, because you only want it as part of your pretentious decor. And you didn't really like Mother . . .
JOAN: Liar! I loved her . . . And what's pretentious about my decor?
EVE: Just ignorance, I guess, judging by your atrocious mixture of Hepplewhite and Biedermeyer.
You'll never make it anyway, with or without the portrait. Let that be your consolation.
JOAN: Oh, you — you fiend from hell!
(She grabs Eve by the shoulders and shakes her. Eve kicks her in the shins. Joan pushes her down on the floor where they wrestle, sit on top of each other, pull each others' hair, etc.)
(Enter Jake.)
JAKE: Excuse me —
(The women stand up, smooth down their hair and dresses.)
JAKE: *(Charming smile.)* Very sensible of you, doing a little wrestling . . . been under a lot of strain . . .
EVE: Did you forget something?
JAKE: You fought like that even as children.
EVE: I don't remember you. You were a friend of Mother's?
JAKE: Since before you were born, Eve . . . You were an ugly little baby, and fussy. I used to rock you on my knee. That made you laugh.
(Sings.)
The Camptown ladies sing this song:
  doo dah, doo dah.
At the Camptown racetrack five miles long,
  all the doodah day.

Gwine to run all night,
Gwine to run all day,
I put my money on the bobtail nag
Somebody bet on the Bay.
JOAN: Uncle Jake!
EVE: We don't have an uncle Jake.
JOAN: Mother made me call him that.
JAKE: *(To Joan.)* You flirted charmingly with me at age five . . . Even then you had style, sometimes just a ribbon or a necklace. And now you're striking, like a model. Tres chic.
EVE: And I was an ugly baby.

JAKE: But you turned out well — I see your mother in you: that look, that probing gaze.

JOAN: That attorney-for-the-prosecution-look.

EVE: Just how well did you know my mother?

JAKE: *(Beat.)* Intimately. *(Beat.)* We clicked, right from the beginning . . . We liked the same food, the same music — all kinds, from classical to jazz to gospel; jokes, the more corny or vulgar the better. What a lovely laugh she had! And she was sensuous, a toucher, like me. Oh, she was fun to be with. And, bless her, she laughed at my imitations. I was a good mimic. Hell, I still am!

(In a George Bush voice.)

No, I don't mind being retired. In fact . . . I'll let you in on a little secret — you don't mind, Barbara, do you? — When we get out on the yacht, all by ourselves, we do it — you know, the sex thing? — right out there, on the deck, floating along . . . Of course we're gettin' a little creaky. Can't do everything they show on those videos —

(Joan titters, Eve laughs.)

JOAN: This is our mother you're talking about? . . .

EVE: What about Dad?

JAKE: He never knew.

(Long pause.)

When it was over, I lived in France for a while . . .

(Pause.)

JOAN: *(Slowly.)* So you and Mother met before Eve was born . . . *(Looks from him to Eve.)* . . . She has your coloring. *(Pause.)* Is she — could she be — your daughter?

EVE: Good Lord!

JAKE: It's possible.

EVE: What do you mean, possible. You must know!

JAKE: Your mother wasn't very good at keeping track of things.

JOAN: You can say that again.

(Pause.)

EVE: But there are ways: blood tests —

JAKE: Your father and I are the same blood type.

EVE: Were. He's been dead for years . . .

(Pause.)

So why did you come? To see how I turned out?

JAKE: That was one reason.

EVE: The other?

JAKE: To get the portrait. She left it to me . . .
JOAN: To you! She couldn't have . . .
EVE: She left a will in which we inherit everything.
JOAN: And I get the portrait because I took care of her.
JAKE: I have a letter from her. *(He takes it out of his pocket.)*
EVE: Let me see.
(He gives it to her, she reads it, with Joan looking over her shoulder.)
EVE: *To whom it may concern: After my death, Jacob ("Jake") Feldstein is to have the portrait of me, painted November 1943 . . . Laura Bennett, Springfield, June 1944.*
(Long pause.)
JOAN: It's her writing all right.
EVE: Notarized.
JOAN: Is that really . . . legal?
EVE: I'm afraid so. *(To Jake.)* But why should you want it? You were only a brief episode in her life.
JAKE: Because I painted it, and because it's the best thing I ever did.
(He takes down the portrait.)
JOAN: Don't! Stop him, Eve!
EVE: What about me? How can I live not knowing who I am?
JAKE: It'll give you that air of mystery which men find so appealing.
(Close to her, looks at her searchingly.)
I'd be proud to call you my daughter, Eve. — Meet me again?
(She nods. He kisses her on the lips. She remains standing very still. Jake approaches Joan who backs away. He turns, picks up the portrait, starts to walk out.)
JAKE: Au revoir.
(Joan, sobbing, tosses a pillow at him.)
JAKE: *(Picks it up.)* Thanks! I can use that. — Ciao!
(Carrying pillow and portrait, he walks out . . .)
(Curtain.)

END OF PLAY

MRS. SCHEINBAUM
by Frank Hilmes

FIRST PERFORMANCE
January 2000

ORIGINAL CAST
    Esther Scheinbaum ....Audrey Filippini
    Maury Goldman ....Brian Rosen/Richard Lockie
    Directed by ....Maria Crush
    Sets by ....Dohn Grube

MRS. SCHEINBAUM

Setting: An Insurance Adjusters office.
At rise: Esther Scheinbaum, in her mid-eighties but still fighting, is seated in the institutional "customer's" chair. She wears a nondescript, gray striped dress with sleeves that are obviously too long. A small foil-wrapped package sits on the desk. A mid-level Insurance Adjuster, in his late forties, Maury Goldman, enters and drips into his too soft, too old, leather chair. His clothes match the grungy feeling of the office and its furniture.

GOLDMAN: Mrs. Scheinbaum.
ESTHER: Esther, please. I brought you some cake; your grandmother's recipe. *(Pause.)* I think hers was better. *(Long pause.)* You decide.
(Goldman regards the package, then sets it to the side. Esther's demeanor deflates.)
GOLDMAN: Mrs. Scheinbaum. Your request for this procedure has already been rejected six times by this office. Why have you come again?
ESTHER: To get approval.
GOLDMAN: Your approval has been denied.
ESTHER: I need the approval. You will give it to me.
GOLDMAN: Why did you think I would grant —
ESTHER: I knew your grandmother, Shoshana Goldman. I know you are Jewish, Mr. Goldman.
GOLDMAN: My heritage . . . or my grandmother has nothing to do with this claim.
ESTHER: It has *everything* to do with it!
GOLDMAN: No —
ESTHER: Yes! It has everything to do with it! I was a best friend to your grandmother. She raised you to be a good boy. To be fair. This I know.
GOLDMAN: I cannot approve this request. This is for *cosmetic* surgery.
ESTHER: Cosmetic! This is my life here!
GOLDMAN: Mrs. Scheinbaum. This company's policy is that this removal is a cosmetic procedure, not a medical one.
ESTHER: Again with the cosmetic! My husband and I paid premiums to this insurance company, the insurance company you work for, Maury Goldman, for over forty-five years and you refuse to help an old woman who was best friend to your grandmother?
GOLDMAN: Mrs. Scheinbaum. This company, my company, has paid all of your legitimate medical bills for over forty-five years. True?

ESTHER: True.

GOLDMAN: During that time we have paid for: the birth of three children, with complications on the third; two miscarriages; a gall-bladder removal; an appendix removal; a radical mastectomy; a total hysterectomy; removal of cataracts; two broken legs; a broken hip, and a hip replacement. Then we have your husband's three heart attacks, one triple bypass, removal of his prostate, two strokes and six years of recuperative physical therapy. I will not even go into your children's medical histories. *(Long pause.)* I think you have done well by this company. My company, Mrs. Scheinbaum.

ESTHER: Like we had a choice for you to spend this money?

GOLDMAN: Mrs. Scheinbaum. Please understand —

ESTHER: No. I do *not* understand! And *you* do not understand!

GOLDMAN: I think I understand perfectly well, Mrs. Scheinbaum.

ESTHER: Do you know where I met your grandmother, Mrs. Shoshana Goldman?

GOLDMAN: No.

ESTHER: Where we met, you should never have to go. People dying all around us. People killed all around us. And those damned —

GOLDMAN: Wait!

ESTHER: For what?

GOLDMAN: I know where this is going.

ESTHER: And? Where is it going?

GOLDMAN: You met my grandmother in Auschwitz.

ESTHER: Buchenwald

GOLDMAN: A camp is a camp.

ESTHER: Oy! Would your grandmother's heart ache.

GOLDMAN: I've seen the stories a thousand times, Mrs. Scheinbaum, and I don't want to see them again. That happened to *them.* Not to me.

ESTHER: But it did happen to your grandmother! That is your *heritage!* You must honor it! It will not go away, no matter how much you want it to!

GOLDMAN: Mrs. Scheinbaum. My grandmother never said a word about the camps, I had to learn about them from *Schindler's List* and the History Channel! If she wanted me to have a heritage, she should have told me!

ESTHER: Your grandmother saved many children —

GOLDMAN: *(Shouting.)* I do not care how many children she saved! I do not care how cruel the Nazi bastards were! I *do not care* how noble all of you were! It is *over!*

ESTHER: For *you* it is over! For me it will never be over! For your grandmother it was *never* over!

GOLDMAN: She died peacefully.
ESTHER: I know. *(Long pause.)* Now I want to die peacefully.
GOLDMAN: That is your business.
ESTHER: No, Mr. Goldman. It is your business. Only you can help me die in peace.
GOLDMAN: I think you should leave.
ESTHER: I think you should approve this removal!
GOLDMAN: No.
ESTHER: No?! You cannot say no!
GOLDMAN: I just did!
ESTHER: You did not mean it!
GOLDMAN: The hell I didn't!
ESTHER: Do not curse at me!
GOLDMAN: Leave now or I will have you arrested!
ESTHER: Arrested! Me! Just because I ask for what is fair?
GOLDMAN: *(Cooler.)* Mrs. Scheinbaum. You are dying of lymphatic cancer, you know that. I cannot approve a procedure such as this for someone of your age and medical condition. It is not —
ESTHER: Not what?
GOLDMAN: *(Pause.)* Prudent.
ESTHER: Prudent?
GOLDMAN: Prudent.
ESTHER: Could we say it is not . . . cost effective?
GOLDMAN: Your words, not mine!
ESTHER: The Nazis were cost effective.
GOLDMAN: *(Coldly.)* Stop. Now. *(Very long pause.)* Mrs. Scheinbaum, at your age, the skin is thin and fragile. It would cause scarring.
ESTHER: Scarring! You think I should care about scarring! I have scars from the camps, I have scars from the operations your company paid for! What do I care about scarring?
GOLDMAN: I'm sorry.
ESTHER: That is your final word?
GOLDMAN: It is.
ESTHER: Then can I ask a question.
(Goldman sits, silent.)
ESTHER: If this tattoo, this thin skin, should be burnt, say in a small fire, or by an acid burn . . . would the insurance company pay for that treatment . . .
(Goldman still sits, still silent.)
. . . and how much would that be?

GOLDMAN: I don't know.

ESTHER: Would it be more or less than the removal by a laser?

GOLDMAN: *(Realizes he's fallen into a trap.)* I will deny that claim as fraudulent!

ESTHER: Not fraud. It is what I deserve!

(Esther slowly raises her sleeve to reveal her death-camp tattoo.)

ESTHER: Mr. Goldman. I do not want to be marked like this in my death as I was in my life. *(Long pause.)* Did your grandmother die with the mark?

GOLDMAN: *(Long pause.)* That's not fair, Mrs. Scheinbaum.

ESTHER: Did your grandmother die with the mark?

GOLDMAN: That's not fair, Mrs. Scheinbaum.

ESTHER: Did your grandmother die with the mark!

GOLDMAN: No!

ESTHER: And why not!

GOLDMAN: She burned it off!

ESTHER: How!?

GOLDMAN: Lye. *(Pause.)* She burned it off with lye.

ESTHER: Did she hurt?

GOLDMAN: Painfully.

ESTHER: Did she scar?

GOLDMAN: Horribly.

ESTHER: Did you turn down her request?

GOLDMAN: *(Long pause.)* That is *not* fair, Mrs. Scheinbaum.

ESTHER: Denying *my* removal is not fair, Mr. Goldman.

(Very long pause before she rises to exit; just before she reaches the door, guilt and tears overwhelm him.)

GOLDMAN: Approved.

ESTHER: *(Startled.)* What?

GOLDMAN: I'll approve your request.

ESTHER: Thank you, Mr. Goldman.

GOLDMAN: Under *one* condition . . .

ESTHER: *One* I can live with.

GOLDMAN: *Never* file another claim with this company, Mrs. Scheinbaum. For anything.

ESTHER: I have no plans to do so, Mr. Goldman. *(Long pause.)* Your company has already paid for my prescriptions . . . Like your grandmother, I, too, can keep a secret.

(Esther exits.)
(Lights down.)

END OF PLAY

MY HIGHER POWER
by Melissa Klein

FIRST PERFORMANCE
January 2001

ORIGINAL CAST
  Naomi .... Daria Elise Troxell
  Directed by .... Ian McRae
  Sets by .... William "Skip" Epperson

MY HIGHER POWER

Naomi, a young homeless woman, white, about eighteen to nineteen, holding a Burger King soda and wearing a backpack with a sleeping bag attached, is standing at a San Francisco bus stop. It is drizzling intermittently. Naomi is addressing people getting off the bus.

Hey man, you got a extra transfer? . . . 'Scuse me ma'am, do you have an extra transfer by any chance? . . . 'Scuse me, you got a transfer you don't need? . .. Do you — *(A passerby hands her a transfer.)* Hey, thanks, man. Thanks a lot. Hey, do you want a soda? I haven't drank out of it yet. No? Okay. Well, thanks for the transfer.

(Rubbing her arms, shivering a little.)

Damn, I'm cold. All my clothes are getting wet and my sleeping bag's soaked. It sucked sleeping outside without Marla last night, especially when it started drizzling. I don't wanna drink this soda, it'll just make me colder. I should have gotten coffee but I just couldn't think when I got to the counter. They know me by now at that Burger King and they don't let me use the bathroom anymore without buying something cuz they know I go in there to shoot up. I wasn't even trying to get high, I don't wanna go all the way out there to visit Marla and then have them not let me in to visit her because they think I'm high. I just needed to get well.

When I came out of the bathroom the manager behind the counter was giving me that look that says, "You fucking junkie," and I walked out as quick as I could. I was wishing Marla was there cuz she's not afraid to talk shit to anyone. One time me and Marla were in the supermarket, we had sparechanged a couple bucks, we'd gone through one forty and we were about to drink another. It was when we were trying to just drink instead of do dope. We were kinda drunk and we were walking through the fruit section, and Marla grabbed a cantaloupe, set it down on the floor and kicked it like a soccer ball. I kicked it back and we were laughing and yelling, "Goal! Goal!" until this big beefy security guard came over and said, "No horseplaying in here," and Marla said, "We're not playing, we're in serious training." That shit was funny even though they made us pay for the cantaloupe and then we didn't have enough change left for another forty. But we kept the cantaloupe and when we got outside we threw it at the glass door. It splattered orange goop all over and we ran away laughing. They don't let us in that supermarket no more though.

(To passerby.)

Hey, you got a extra cigarette?

(Taking cigarette.)
Thanks a lot. Can I get a light off you?
(Naomi lights cigarette and begins smoking.)
I wish this bus would hurry up. I guess the rain makes everything go slower. I hope I remember where I have to get off to transfer to the hospital where she's at. It's not General, it's one of those other ones, out towards the ocean, they just took her there cuz it was closest. I hope I can find my way back from yesterday. She's the one with the best sense of direction and I usually don't pay that good attention. I gotta take this bus and then get off somewhere and catch another one, take that one till near the end of the line. They have morning visiting hours and I wanna be there for as much of it as I can, I wanna sit there and hold her hand cuz even though they say she doesn't realize I'm there, I know how Marla is, and she always knows more than she lets on.
(In response to a passerby asking her for a cigarette.)
Sorry man. I just bummed this one off someone. Hey, do you want this soda though? Sure, no problem.
Some kids don't like coming down here cuz they say there's too many crackheads, but that shit's stupid. The junkies all got junkie pride — "At least I ain't a crackhead," and the crackheads saying, "At least I don't stick no needle in my arm." Marla used to shrug her shoulders and say, "What, you're hot shit cuz you got track marks down your arms instead of smoking rock? So you're a track star, they're rock stars, don't begrudge anyone their talent." But it's funny how everyone's gotta look down on someone else, you always gotta find someone you think is lower than you. It's like when I was little we were poor as shit and making sandwiches out of the same big old white government tubs of peanut butter as everyone else, on welfare like everyone else but my mom letting it be known "at least we're not black." And that whole thing's a trip too cuz after all that look at me and Marla. I can think of about five things right off the bat that my mom would find wrong with that picture.
My mom was pretty good at that, finding things wrong. And I guess I've been pretty good at making things wrong too . . . and maybe that's where heroin comes in. Cuz it's part of making things that are wrong feel all right for a little while but in the end it's just another thing gone wrong. Heroin, it's like debt consolidation, you know what I mean? I mean it gets rid of all your little problems but then you got one big problem, one big debt to pay and pay.
And this thing with Marla is freaking me out and I'd like to kick, but I think the only way you can really kick is to leave this city and where the hell am I gonna go? I can't go back home. And even if you try to leave, this city

will drag you back every time, suck all the money from your pocket, all the pride from your guts.

I've gone to those meetings a coupla times and I guess it's cool for some people but that shit doesn't work for me. They say admit that you're powerless, you're powerless over your addiction. But I mean that's the whole thing, isn't it? Being powerless. I mean I feel like there's enough people in my life telling me I'm powerless, enough people who've told me I'll never be shit. Maybe if someone for once had told me I could be something I wouldn't be in this situation. And they're all talking too much about God in there, and I don't believe in God. I mean I grew up with God telling my mom not to spare the rod but that just beat God out of me with every stroke. And Marla's the same way. She says she can't walk into a church and look at all those people praying in the pews without thinking, "All these people would act all scandalized about shit I do for money but look at them all kneeling here, giving God a blowjob." At those meetings they say you don't have to think about God in the traditional sense. They say it doesn't have to be a dude with no beard and sandals. You can just think about your higher power, the force that's by your side. But where was God when I got kicked out of the house and all the shit that's happened to me since? I'm not saying I'm perfect, I'm not saying I never hurt anybody but I always hurt myself worse. The only one who's ever been by my side for any of it is Marla.

After that night that things gotta outta hand with Ace, Marla's the one who cleaned the blood off my face and then a month later she's the one that went to General with me for the abortion, held my hand fierce while all the machines sucked out the little thing that would have been half me and half that fucking asshole. Marla's the one who was in the recovery room while I was lying there still dizzy and the nurse was trying to tell me to get those sticks in my arm, she kept trying to convince me. I was shaking my head no and she was saying, "We just don't want to see you here again in a couple of months honey," and hot dizzy tears were coming to my eyes and Marla's the one who looked straight at the nurse and said, "Look she don't need that shit. a) It don't protect you from HIV or any STDs. b) That shit's bad as fuck for you and you ain't even telling her none of the side effects. c) She was raped, okay? I'm her girlfriend and she doesn't need birth control cuz I'm not gonna get her pregnant.

The funny thing is I always wanted to have a baby. I know it's not realistic — I mean look at my fucking life, it would just be one more baby that got taken by CPS. But in this other world, this fantasy world, I could imagine me and Marla with a kid. This one time me and Marla hitchhiked to Santa

Cruz, just for the day, just to get away for a little while, and they've got these computer things at the boardwalk that morph your face with someone else's to see what your baby would look like. So just for kicks me and Marla did ours and it came out this beautiful little girl with fat cheeks, lighter skinned than her, with eyes kinda like mine and a big smiley mouth like hers. I said, "Too bad biology's not on our side with this" and Marla leaned over and kissed me and she said, "I guess we can't have her but you'll always be my baby."

So, what if your higher power's a smart-ass chick with cinnamon skin and a big wide grin she can stick three sticks of gum in at once and still crack jokes out of? What if your higher power's another junkie just like you and the inside of her arms is bruised a twilight blue where the needle missed its mark, but sleeping inside those arms is the only safety you've ever known, even if it's in a park or in some nasty-ass hotel?

And what if last night for the first time in a long time you slept alone cuz your higher power's lying on a bed in a sterile room in a powder blue hospital gown, and they've taken off all her bracelets made of beer tabs and safety pins and replaced them with a plastic band with her name on it, last name first.

I mean, I know it's gonna be okay, I know she's gonna get better cuz she's a tough ass bitch and nothing so stupid as an OD is gonna take her out. I know she's gonna get better cuz she's got too much to say to the world to lie there with her mouth shut for too long. I know she's gonna get better — but what if she doesn't? Well your higher power supposed to always be there with you, right? But what if one day she isn't? Well then what?

Shit, this bus is taking forever. Can't believe I still have to take the other one after this. I wish I could remember for sure where to get off. I know I gotta take it almost till the end of the line. I just wish Marla was here to help me figure out where I need to go.

END OF PLAY

NOCTURNE, WITH APPLES
by Scott Munson

FIRST PERFORMANCE
January 2000

ORIGINAL CAST

    Nora . . . . Kristen Vaughn
    Rudy, the cat . . . . Steve "Spike" Wong
    Scott . . . . Kiet Tran
    Directed by . . . . Marcia Taylor
    Sets by . . . . Dohn Grube

For F.D.
Black cat with a mouse,
How proud, the mighty hunter.
Yellow lanterns shine!

CHARACTERS

NORA: The Literary Manager at a small but well-thought-of theater. Early-to-mid thirties. Slight, disheveled, perplexed.

RUDY: A cat. Male. Supple. Pretty black coat. White belly and a milk mustache.

SCOTT: A playwright at the beginning of his career. Open and candid.

SETTING/TIME

A bare stage, except for two stools, one at left, the other at center. Beneath the second stool there is a blanket on the floor.

There are three time frames operating in the play. They freely move back and forth like the themes in a nocturne. They are:

- Yesterday morning when Scott and Nora speak about the production of his play.
- Yesterday evening when Scott eats the pie and tries to sleep.
- The present where Scott addresses the audience directly and tells his story.

NOCTURNE, WITH APPLES

At rise: Lights up on stool at stage left. Nora enters and sits down. She directs her remarks at the audience.

NORA: Scott, I just want you to know that nothing has changed. We're still positively committed to doing your work.
(Lights up on the rest of stage. We see Rudy, curled up in a ball, sleeping on the top of the blanket. Scott enters and sits on the other stool. For the moment, he ignores Nora. Each of them speaks to the audience as though oblivious of the other.)
SCOTT: My wife made a pie today. Actually, a tarte tatin. From France. So the whole house smelled of apples. Wonderful!
NORA: There is something different about your writing. A quality we very much like.
SCOTT: Apples. Burnt sugar. Cinnamon. Nutmeg. And butter. Lots of butter.
(Gesturing.)
And she flips it over so the crust is on the bottom and there's this beautiful golden-brown glaze on top . . . so it's a little like an upside down cake . . . only with apples . . .
(Beat.)
We ended up eating pie all day. With a little dessert wine from Alsace. Delicious!
NORA: There's a *sweetness* to it . . . Yes . . . a sweetness . . .
SCOTT: Maybe it was the smell that ended up attracting . . . our unexpected . . . intruder . . .
(Rudy wakes up with a start, looks around, and then closes his eyes, and sleeps again.)
SCOTT: *(Continues.)* Anyway, my wife always makes pies . . . or something sweet . . . when I get bad . . . No . . . *awful* . . . news. I guess she thinks it cheers me up . . . or something . . . so when everything with the theater just started . . . *falling apart* . . . she thought, "Now would be a good time for some really good pie . . ."
(With a sigh.)
Because I really felt . . . *crushed* . . .
(Scott turns to Nora and the two of them talk directly.)
NORA: Unfortunately, a lot of things have changed. Money, for starters. A lot of grants we've been counting on just haven't come through.
SCOTT: What about the money from that bakery?

NORA: Well, Sara Lee is hardly a *bakery* . . . They're a very big national corporation . . .
SCOTT: But I thought you said that money was *guaranteed* . . .
NORA: Well, only half of it came in . . .
SCOTT: *Half?*
NORA: And that half had to go to . . . Well . . .defray . . .
SCOTT: *Defray?*
NORA: . . . our ongoing expenses . . . Salaries . . . Upkeep . . . Admin . . . Unfortunately, it was the other half . . .
SCOTT: The half you *didn't* get . . .
NORA: . . . that we were going to use to do your play . . .
SCOTT: Oh . . .
NORA: But that's not the only problem . . .
SCOTT: There's more?
NORA: We're having . . . and please don't tell anybody this . . .
SCOTT: Believe me . . . My lips are . . . absolutely . . .
NORA: . . . *Internal* difficulties . . . *Serious* ones . . .
SCOTT: Serious?

(Nora nods. The lights fade on her. Scott turns and is now back in the present and speaks to the audience.)

Normally, I maybe eat one or two pieces of pie . . . depending on the nature and severity of the crisis . . . But this time . . . Well, I pretty much ate the whole thing . . .

(Gesturing.)

. . . except for this one little piece for my wife . . .

(Beat.)

So, when it was time to go to bed, I had a terrible bellyache . . . from all that pie . . .

(After a beat.)

So, for the longest time I couldn't sleep . . . Finally, I got up and took a Lexomil. That's a French valium. My wife gets them from her folks back home. It helps calm you down . . . Just sort of turns your head right off . . . And I needed that . . . Because as I was lying there . . . with all that pie churning around inside me . . . my mind just racing . . . with nothing but depressing thoughts . . . I was just overwhelmed with *waves* of those good old existential flop sweats. You know the ones I mean . . . ?

(Taking a breath.)

They started with me staring at the ceiling and saying, "Yes, I'm going to die. Yes, this is going to happen to me. Yes, there's nothing anyone can

do to stop it." And that scared me so bad that . . . to cheer myself up . . . I started thinking about the whole fiasco with the theater again. Things like, "It's a good thing my career is going nowhere. I'm glad that they aren't going to do my play . . . because, if they did, no one would care . . . no one would like it . . . and the reviews would be *brutal* . . . because, in reality, I have no talent . . . and who am I trying to kid anyway?"
(Beat.)
But that started to cut a little too close to the bone . . . so . . . just to change the subject . . . I got to thinking, "My house is going to be invaded by some crazed killer . . . Godzilla and his brother. Yeah, the one who's the *real* badass in the family . . . they're going to take turns torturing me . . . before they get around to killing me . . ."
(Beat.)
So all this stuff was *tumbling* inside my head . . . and I got up and took a Lexomil . . . and washed it down with a jolt of brandy . . . to make sure I got the job done . . . and I finally got off to a very troubled . . . sleep . . . because it was just so hard . . . to let go . . .
(The lights come back on. Then Nora resumes her conversation with Scott.)
NORA: First off, I think the Artistic Director is having a nervous breakdown . . .
SCOTT: He is?
NORA: . . . because his wife . . .
SCOTT: They're *married?* I thought she was . . .
NORA: Well . . . she's not . . . She's the . . .
SCOTT: Really? I had no . . .
NORA: Anyway, she's leaving him and going to L.A.
SCOTT: What? To make it in movies? Not a chance! She'll be lucky to get commercials . . . *Industrials* . . .
NORA: She says he's abusing her . . . *Hitting* her . . .
SCOTT: What?
NORA: But it's only when he drinks too much . . .
SCOTT: That's horrible!
NORA: So we can hardly count on her for the lead.
SCOTT: Oh . . .
NORA: And he says, without her in the play, he wouldn't . . . feel *right* . . . playing "Chris" . . . I mean even if he wasn't having . . .
SCOTT: . . . a nervous . . .
NORA: Exactly.
(Beat.)
And then there's me . . .

SCOTT: You? What's wrong with you?
(Scott turns away from Nora as the lights fade on her.)
(Scott then addresses the audience directly.)
SCOTT: Okay, I got to sleep. But almost *immediately*, I started having very bad dreams. Very bad. Dreams about all this bullshit with the theater... We went over all this dead ground about not doing my play. Over and over again. But this time, in my dream, their theater...
(Louder — to Nora — who just shrugs in the dark.)
... their sorry-candy-assed-stinks-like-an-ashtray-in-the-lobby-of-a-Motel 6-in-Fresno-99-seat-my-red-ass-you couldn't get-*50*-if-50-people-were-ever-crazy-enough-to-pay-good-money-to-come-to-this-*decrepit*-saggy-butt-why-can't-you-paint-this-place-and-at-least-put-in-some-good-*seats*-while-you're-at-it-so-people-won't-have-to-have-a-Novocain-shot-in-their-ass-before-coming-to-this-so-called-"showcase"-for-the-performing-arts...
(Beat, taking a breath.)
Well, anyway, in my dream, their theater smelled... of *apples*...
(Beat.)
And then... as I was somewhere between asleep and awake... I heard this... *scratching*...
(The lights come back up on Nora.)
NORA: I'm getting married.
SCOTT: You are? Why that's... You are?
NORA: To my high school sweetheart.
(Beat.)
Tom.
SCOTT: Tom?
NORA: Tom.
SCOTT: But you're...
NORA: I never said I *was*... anything... *People* said that.
SCOTT: *People?* You've been the drama critic for a gay newspaper ever since I met you... Every other word out of your mouth is "queer theory" this or "lesbian flaneur" that.
NORA: So?
SCOTT: You're always wearing *buttons* and *ribbons* and... I don't know... *something*. I think *people* might be forgiven if... if... *people*... *leaped*... to the conclusion that maybe you're...
NORA: Okay, maybe I gave an *impression*... but if *people* ever *paid attention*... they'd know I've always thought of myself more as being...
SCOTT: Bi?

NORA: Flexible . . .
> (Beat.)
> Anyway, we're very much in love . . . *Tom* and me . . . and we're going back to his Dad's place . . . in the Midwest . . . to farm . . .

SCOTT: Farm?

NORA: So, you see, I won't be around to direct your play either.

SCOTT: Okay. Good. Let me see if I've got this straight. The company is going broke. The A.D. is a wife-beating drunk who is having a crack-up. The leading lady has skipped town and will next be seen, if she's very, very lucky, doing pantyhose commercials and pitching Mars bars. And you've discovered your latent heterosexuality and are going back to Iowa to grow tater-tots with Ma and Pa Kettle. Did I leave anything out?

NORA: It's Wisconsin. And it's a dairy farm. Although we'll have a garden . . . a very *big* garden . . . at least by California standards . . .

SCOTT: But you're still positively committed to doing my work.
> (Beat.)

NORA: I've got an idea.

SCOTT: What?

NORA: Why don't you write a play about *us?*
> *(The lights fade on Nora. Rudy goes over to Scott, sticks out one paw, and scratches one of the legs of the stool.)*

SCOTT: Okay . . . like I said . . . I was sleeping . . . tossing and turning . . . dreaming about a theater filled with apples . . . when I heard this very familiar *scratching* at the door . . .
> (Beat.)
> It was my cat . . . Rudy . . . letting me know about his own little agenda . . . what did he care if my heart was filled with dread and my career was going over a cliff? Not when it was time for his nightly . . . *patrol* . . .
> *(Scott and Rudy are now in the past, reliving their conversation last night.)*

RUDY: I want to go outside.

SCOTT: Stay in. It's late.

RUDY: But I want to . . .

SCOTT: Why? What's out there? Nothing but disappointment . . . and danger . . .

RUDY: It's fun.

SCOTT: Fun? There's "Slash" and "Gypsy" . . .

RUDY: You let me worry about Slash . . .

SCOTT: *(Making like a boxer.)* Yeah? How many times do I have to tell you? Keep that left up!

RUDY: Can I go outside?

SCOTT: And then there's that chocolate brown Siamese . . . he's *huge* . . . he's like a *goat* . . . And you're so little.

RUDY: I'll take my chances.

SCOTT: Look . . .

RUDY: Look . . .

(After a beat.)

Only one of us can have his way here . . .

(Rubbing up against him.)

Just open the door and then you can go back to sleep.

SCOTT: It's scary out there. Don't go. It's late.

RUDY: You said that before.

(Beat.)

Please. I'll be good all day tomorrow. I promise.

SCOTT: I don't want you to get hurt. I love you.

RUDY: If you love me, let me out.

(Beat. Now both Scott and Rudy return to the present.)

SCOTT: *(To the audience.)* So I let him out.

RUDY: *(To the audience.)* I knew I'd win.

SCOTT: But I was afraid. He's such a brave little boy. Always standing up for his territory. But he's so little . . . He only weighs about eight pounds . . . That Siamese . . . He's as big as a *tree* . . . But does my guy back away? No. Never.

(Petting him — as Rudy licks his paws.)

. . . and he comes home with scars and wounds . . .

(Showing Rudy's ear to the audience.)

Did you see his ear? The Vet just managed to stick it back on last time . . .

RUDY: *(Pulling away.)* It looks fine to me.

(Cleaning ear with paw.)

So tell them the scary part.

SCOTT: So I let Rudy out and go back to sleep . . . An *uneasy* sleep . . . and about four . . . four-fifteen . . . I woke up . . . Just like that . . . No drowsiness . . . No transition . . . I'm just awake . . . and I heard this *sound* . . .

(Scott and Rudy now both re-enter the past. Rudy should start that weird, repressed "whine-howl" that cats make just before a fight. He should do this on and off for the next few lines.)

SCOTT: It was just outside the sliding glass door. We live in an apartment complex . . . right beside this little creek . . . and we have a small . . . a very small . . . redwood deck . . . You know, just enough space for a couple of chairs . . . and a potted plant or two . . . and a little grill . . .

RUDY: *("Breaking" character.)* Get to the scary part, okay? . . . Geez . . . How long do you think I can keep this up?

(Rudy goes back to making the noise.)

SCOTT: So I heard this sound. And I was naked . . . because it was such a hot night . . . and I thought, "Oh, shit . . . another cat fight . . . I better break it up" . . .

(Scott should get up and pantomime the rest of the action as it describes what's going on. Rudy too should match his actions with the narrative.)

So I opened the sliding glass door and stepped outside. And as soon as my naked foot touched the redwood deck, I noticed a couple of things *immediately* . . .

(Beat.)

. . . how wonderful it feels to have the night air against your naked skin . . .

(Beat.)

. . . how wonderful it feels to have your naked foot on a redwood deck . . .

(Beat.)

And, third, I smell the most powerful, gamy, *wildlife* smell in my whole life . . . and I noticed that Rudy is also on the deck, right next to me . . . just *rigid* . . . and he is moving . . . very slowly . . . just a paw at a time . . . *towards* the edge of the deck . . . but his body is as stiff and elaborate as an actor in a Noh drama . . . And then I realize a couple of more things . . .

(Beat.)

I should have put on my glasses before going outside . . . because I am absolutely blind as a bat . . .

(Beat.)

. . . and there's *something* at the end of the deck . . . hiding in the shadows and the potted plants . . . just a few feet away . . . in the darkness . . . I can't see it . . . but that *smell* . . . and I can hear . . . *breathing* . . .

SCOTT: *(Continues. Breathing a little — then resuming.)* So I take a few steps . . . in the same direction . . . and I realize that *I'm* walking as stiff and elaborate as an actor in a Noh drama . . . and Rudy's right beside me . . .

(Beat.)

and we get closer . . . and closer . . .

(Beat — whisper.)

. . . and I'm thinking I really should've gotten a broom or something . . .

(Beat — whisper.)

. . . and I'm thinking, "What am I doing? Defending *my* territory? I thought that was something only cats . . ."

(Leaping aside.)

When boom! *Something* races out of the darkness and runs right across my feet and disappears into the creek below.

(Beat.)

It was so fast. I could barely see it.

RUDY: It was a raccoon.

SCOTT: And I look at my feet. And there are claw marks all over them . . . and they're starting to bleed . . . just a little . . . no big deal . . . from where his claws raked my skin when he made his escape . . .

RUDY: *(Flexing his paw.)* They're not retractable. His claws. Not like mine.

SCOTT: So I called the Vet . . . to see if I needed shots . . . for *rabies* . . . and he told me a raccoon can *eviscerate* . . . that's the word he used . . . a house cat . . . just like that . . .

(Making a clawing gesture)

Eviscerate . . .

(Petting Rudy.)

You're a brave soul.

RUDY: Vets? What do they know?

SCOTT: *(Taking Rudy in his arms.)* From now on, it's you and me, brother. We're staying home and eating pie.

RUDY: I don't like apples.

SCOTT: Because the world's a very dangerous place. And bad. And that badness is never, never, very far away.

(Beat.)

You know . . . right now? . . . I'd just love a piece of pie.

RUDY: *(Rubbing up against Scott.)* I'd like to go outside.

(Blackness.)

END OF PLAY

PARCHEESIED
by John Howie Patterson

FIRST PERFORMANCE
January 1996

ORIGINAL CAST

    Dad Perkins . . . . .Herb Rossman
    Darryl Perkins . . . . .Jeff Young
    Sylvia Davis . . . . .Lori Robertson
    Directed by . . . . .Marcus Cato
    Sets by . . . . .William "Skip" Epperson

CHARACTERS

DAD PERKINS: A man in his sixties.
DARRYL PERKINS: His son, late twenties.
SYLVIA DAVIS: Darryl's girlfriend, late twenties.

SETTING

The dining area of Dad Perkin's small apartment.

PARCHEESIED

At rise: Dad, Darryl, and Sylvia sit around a table, playing Parcheesi. Dad taunts Darryl by shaking his dice cup at him.

DARRYL: Just roll, Dad. Roll.

DAD: *(Whispering to his dice.)* I need a one. C'mon give me a one.

DARRYL: Dad.

DAD: Hey, can't a guy talk to his dice?

DARRYL: Like they're listening, Dad. Roll.

DAD: Okay, okay, okay, pipe down. This is an important roll — all right? The game's on the line here. Right, Sylvia?

SYLVIA: Right Mr. Perkins. Whatever you say.

DAD: *(To Darryl.)* Don't rush me. Gotta build a little heat up in these babies before I can —

DARRYL: You see me taking five minutes to roll? Jesus Christ —

DAD: There's nothing in the rules that says I can't take as much time as I want. Nothing. No time limit. If you'd just relax and shut up maybe we could get on with this thing.

DARRYL: Fine.

(Dad breathes on his dice and whispers a secret message to them.)

DARRYL: *(Crossing his fingers.)* No one. No one. No one —

DAD: *(Stopping, glaring at Darryl.)* Now how am I supposed to roll with you putting a hex on me, huh? How am I supposed —

DARRYL: You put a spell on your dice don't you? Aren't I entitled to —

SYLVIA: C'mon you guys, it's just a game. We were having a perfectly wonderful evening. Let's just get on with the game okay? It's supposed to be fun, right?

DAD: What's not fun about it? I enjoy seeing your boyfriend here get all flustered. Takes things too seriously, doesn't he?

DARRYL: You're one to talk, Dad. If you would just roll —

DAD: All right, all right, I'll roll. You want me to roll, I'll roll. I'll roll so fast you won't have time to cast a counter spell.

(Dad dumps his dice onto the board.)

DAD: A one and a five. It worked. It worked, it worked, it worked.

DARRYL: Shit.

DAD: *(To Darryl.)* Now let's see, as much as I hate to, I'll use the one to send you home. And this five —

(Darryl hits the table with his hand.)

DAD: Oh now, you're not going to flip over the board are you?
   (To Sylvia.) He's got that tendency you know. All through childhood. Monopoly, chess, checkers, you name it. And this baseball game they used to play with dice. Yes, my Darryl was always a board flipper —
DARRYL: Okay, all right, gloat away. Just gloat your heart out. I don't care. But remember this, I'm right behind you, Dad, right behind. And what goes around, comes around.
DAD: Oh, c'mon Darryl. It's just a game. Isn't that right Sylvia, that's what you said?
SYLVIA: Yes that's what I said.
DARRYL: Finish your move, Dad, it's Sylvia's turn.
DAD: Yes sir.
   (Dad finishes his turn.)
DARRYL: *(To Sylvia.)* Get him. You need a four or a five. Both would be even better.
SYLVIA: Shall I pray?
DAD: Nah, don't bother. If you don't have that relationship with your dice, like I have with mine, it won't do a thing. You gotta live with the dice, be close to the dice. Like me, I keep 'em right by the bed when I —
DARRYL: Just roll, Sylvia.
   (She rolls.)
DAD: Damn — a four and a three.
DARRYL: Yes, honey. Yes. Oooooh it feels so good. Victory.
   (He gives her a kiss on the cheek.)
   Thank you, Sylvia. You have done a great service to humanity.
DAD: She was lucky, that's all. I don't hold it against her.
SYLVIA: *(To Darryl.)* So what do I do now?
DARRYL: What do you mean what do you do now? You send him back. Move your guy four and send him back. Here, I'll do —
   (Sylvia slaps his hand away.)
SYLVIA: I'll move my own pieces thank you.
DAD: I believe that is within her right.
DARRYL: She's just learning, Dad. Remember? This is her first game. She's never played before. I'm just trying to speed things up.
   (To Sylvia.) Move the piece four, honey.
SYLVIA: Which one?
DARRYL: *(Pointing.)* That one.
SYLVIA: But I don't have to, do I? I could move the other four right? And move the other three —

DARRYL: Yeah but, you don't want to do that.

DAD: How do you know? Maybe she does.

DARRYL: You want to send him back. Move that one four, that one three. You want to win, don't you?

SYLVIA: I don't really care actually. I'm so far behind at this point.

DARRYL: Honey, what are you saying? You're not gonna —

DAD: Let her do what she wants, Darryl.

DARRYL: You're not going to send him back? You're not going to —

SYLVIA: What if I don't?

DARRYL: Sylvia, what is wrong with you? Send him back for crying out loud. You're supposed to. That's the whole point of —

DAD: Don't you tell her what to do. Let her make up her own —

DARRYL: Sylvia — you want to help him? Is that what you're saying? You're going to let him win?

(Darryl points to his father.)

This monster? This monster who —

SYLVIA: I didn't say I was going to. I just wanted to know what would happen if I did. And I think I have my answer.

(She moves her pieces.)

DARRYL: *(Smiling incredulously.)* You're not going to send him home. My own girlfriend betrays me, the woman I've spent the last two years with, getting to know, caring for —

SYLVIA: With the way you've been acting, Darryl, I think I'm doing you a favor.

DAD: You're talking sense, Sylvie, you're talking sense.

SYLVIA: *(To Darryl.)* Maybe you need to learn a thing or two about sportsmanship.

DAD: You tell him, Sylvie —

SYLVIA: *(To Dad.)* It's Sylvia, Mr. Perkins.

DAD: Sylvia.

SYLVIA: Right. Your turn, Darryl.

DARRYL: I'm not going to forget this. *Sylvie.*

SYLVIA: Darryl. Give it a rest okay? It's just a game.

(Darryl taunts them with his dice cup, then rolls.)

DARRYL: Yes. Yes. Yes. Double-fives. That'll bring me out.

(He moves a piece.)

And with doubles I can move another nine —

DAD: Hold it. Hold it right there.

(Dad picks up the box top.)

You can't do that.

DARRYL: Why the hell not? It's doubles. I used the five to get out and I've got nine left to use as I please. You count what's on the bottom of the dice too, remember?

(Dad studies the rules.)

DAD: Says here, and I quote, "after all of his four pawns have been entered, a player throwing doublets —"

DARRYL: I know the rule, Dad.

DAD: "— a player throwing doublets may count the numbers on both top and bottom of the dice —"

DARRYL: Which I did, so what's the problem?

DAD: All your pawns weren't entered. You can't use the doublet. You can use the five to get out. But you can't use the rest of it.

DARRYL: Oh, come on, Dad. We've been through this time and time again. Remember when we decided that was a vague rule?

SYLVIA: Oh my God, you two make me sick.

DAD: I don't recall that, Darryl.

SYLVIA: Can we finish this up please before midnight? Before you guys kill each other?

DARRYL: *(To Dad.)* Last Thanksgiving. The big blowup. Uncle Jerry? Remember?

DAD: Nope. Can't say I do.

DARRYL: We finally decided that when you roll double fives with just one player left on start and the rest on home, you can use the top and the bottom. So it is a legal move.

(Beat.)

And — I get to roll again.

(Dad fumes. Darryl rolls and moves his pieces in silence.)

DAD: *(Whispering to dice.)* Double-six baby, double-six —

(Darryl crosses his fingers.)

DARRYL: No sixes. No sixes. No sixes —

DAD: *(Whispering.)* Give me a fix, double-six.

(Dad rolls.)

DAD: Damn. A lousy one and a useless two.

DARRYL: Praise the lord. There is a God after all.

SYLVIA: Yeah and I wish he would hurry up and end this game.

DARRYL: What's the matter, Sylvie, aren't you having fun?

SYLVIA: It's Sylvia. Please. I don't call you Darrylie do I?

DAD: *(To himself.)* Now wait a minute here, Bill, things aren't so bad.

(He moves his pieces.)

I can keep the blockade.

DARRYL: You're keeping the blockade?

DAD: Why shouldn't I?

DARRYL: You are trying to win aren't you. You've had that blockade forever. Sylvia's no threat to you. Why don't you let her through?

DAD: Don't know. Just don't feel like it I guess.

(He looks at Sylvia.)

Or do I? Yes, I guess, maybe I do. She did do me a good turn once after all, didn't she? I think it's time to return the favor.

(Dad moves his pieces.)

SYLVIA: Thank you, Mr. Perkins. You're such a gentleman.

(Looks at Darryl.)

Unlike some people I know.

(Sylvia rolls.)

DAD: Well how about that. The double-sixes I ask for she gets.

(Dad shouts into his dice cup.)

DAD: *(To dice.)* What are ya deaf? I said double-sixes.

(To Sylvia.)

Your dice musta heard. Best hearing on a pair of dice I've ever seen. Better hold onto those.

SYLVIA: *(Studying the board.)* I plan to, Mr. Perkins.

(She looks up at Darryl.) That is, if Darryl will let me.

(Darryl studies the board nervously.)

DARRYL: Aren't you gonna move your pieces, honey?

SYLVIA: I thought I'd take my time. Or maybe I'm just waiting for you to tell me what to do.

DARRYL: You might want to concentrate on that piece you've got back near start. Move that fourteen —

DAD: Darryl, you think she can't see it? You think she doesn't know? Come on, Darryl, we're both sunk and you know it.

(Sylvia begins to move her pieces.)

SYLVIA: Let's see. Six here — *(To Dad.)* That puts one of yours back to start. Sorry, Mr. Perkins.

DAD: Quite all right, Sylvia, I'll just get started on the dishes.

(Dad starts to get up.)

DARRYL: It's not over yet, Dad. Sit down.

DAD: May as well be. May as well be. I'm tired anyway. Let her win.

(Dad exits to the kitchen.)

DARRYL: It's not over.

SYLVIA: Now let's see, where was I? That gives me another twenty to play with,

in addition to the other six and the two on the other side. Let's see, one, two, three, four, five, six, oh and that sends another of poor Mr. Perkin's back. Gives me another twenty. That's forty-two all together now.
(Beat.)
Yes, this is working out very well.
(Her hand hovers over the board.)
Now, I wonder, should I leave this little piece here, just to keep it interesting? You are dangerously close —

DARRYL: *(Fuming.)* You told me you didn't know how to play Parcheesi. Where'd you learn?

SYLVIA: No, I don't think so. Better move this one along.
(Sylvia makes her final move.)

DARRYL: Where'd you learn?

SYLVIA: Well isn't it obvious, I learned from watching you two.
(Darryl looks homicidal.)

DARRYL: Oh yeah?
(Beat.)
Well I quit.
(He flips the board onto the floor. Dad returns from the kitchen.)

SYLVIA: Mr. Perkins, why does Parcheesi always bring out the worst in people?

DAD: I don't have any idea, Sylvie. But if I did, I don't think I'd want to play anymore.

SYLVIA: Why's that?

DAD: It would take all the fun out of it.
(Blackout.)

END OF PLAY

PAY PHONE
by Wilma Marcus Chandler

FIRST PERFORMANCE
January 1998

ORIGINAL CAST
  Herb . . . . .Jay Kensinger
  Mahatma . . . . .Kassandra Liput/Wendy Betts
  Bookstore Patrons & Browsers . . . .Neil Coonerty, Paul Moriconi
  . . . . .Katryn Kinser, Lisa Squires, Jonathon Seagull
  Directed by . . . . .Evan Hunt
  Sets by . . . . .Mark Hopkins

CHARACTERS
HERB: a man in his early forties
THE WOMAN (MAHATMA): late thirties
PASSERSBY IN THE BOOKSTORE
BROWSERS WHO GLANCE

SETTING
A crowded bookstore on a rainy day. There is a pay phone on the wall next to a bulletin board filled with flyers and posters of upcoming cultural and spiritual events in the community. There are browsers in the store and people who cross in front of the phone on their way to the rest room, which is around the corner from the travel section. There is a sign for the rest room. People may cross in front of the action at any time during the play.

PAY PHONE

Action as lights come up: Herb is on the phone, in mid-conversation. He is wild-eyed and dressed in old tweeds with everything askew. His hair flies out from his balding head in curly waves and he has a handful of change which he shakes in his pocket, takes out from time to time, shakes again, and always places back in the same pocket as he talks.

HERB: So what am I supposed to do? Huh? I called. I called two, three times and it's not good enough! What am I supposed to do? She's driving me ba-zonkers . . . huh? Yeah, but what am I supposed to say??? She just goes off . . . Yeah!
So yesterday . . . huh? . . . yeah. Yesterday. Then I called my broker. I'm not doin' so great. He says he's finished with me. *(Laughs.)* Yeah! this is the worst year of my life! I tell ya Phil, I'm goin' down. I'm stuck.
An I told her, "Herb's here for you, Babe," but No, it's not good enough. I say, "It's all gonna work out" . . . I really believe that . . . huh? Yeah. Also, she's telling me she's wild for some adventure. Keeps tellin' me to get to the "edge" . . . live the "edge" . . . I don't know what the hell she's even talkin' about . . .
(Begins gesturing wildly and his voice gets louder.) I'm goin' down, I tell ya. Maybe south.
Miami, Phil, Miami . . . to check it out. It's gotta be better than here. At least warmer. I'm fuckn' freezing here . . . and then she says, "This isn't criticism." Like, right!!!! Like I don't have enough edge or whatever!!
I know!! She said that last week about the money.
Phil, Phil! You may be my brother . . . Phil! Don't even start with that. Oh, by the way . . . the car died on me right downtown here.
Yeah. A pay phone . . . downtown. I know it's long distance, but I'm stuck! The bookstore!!!
(The woman enters and stops about two feet behind Herb. She is waiting for the phone and leans against the bulletin board facing out. She will continue to just stand there patiently during the next section of Herb's tirade, reacting ever-so-slightly, with a bit of a nod or smile. She does not rush him in any way. The woman is dressed in a lovely tailored suit and carries a large black bag over her shoulder. She is neatly groomed and never gets disturbed at having to wait. Her voice is melodious. She is always straightforward and even joyful in her responses as the scene goes on.)

HERB: Absolutely stuck. And she was my ace in the hole, ya know?

So, I'm at a loss here, Phil . . . I'm goin' south . . .
Yeah . . .
Yeah . . .
(Notices the woman.)
Yeah . . .
I'm so over this!!!!!
I know!!
Phil, you got it!! You're my only friend! Like what did the rabbi say to the sweet potato?
(Laughs raucously.) Yeah! Yeah!
(To woman.) I'm gonna be a while, lady.
(She smiles.)
So I tell her to call her sister. She says, "no way, never, nada, forget it!" She means it. She always says what she means. No subtext, ya know?
I'm so over this. So how are you? I don't mean to go nuts here . . . but I'm stuck.
I'm a pushover, a nice guy, a soft touch . . . I think I think too much about other people, ya know? A shmatah, a rag, a damned dishrag, a doormat . . . I never, never put myself first . . .
(Other people are glancing at him. His voice has gotten very loud.)
Last! I'm last on the list and I got the weight of the world on my back right now.
(Looks back at the woman.)
This is a public phone, lady. I can talk as long as I want! There's a phone outside.

WOMAN: That's okay. I'm waiting for this one.

HERB: *(Looks around. Notices other people are watching him. He continues his phone conversation split between glaring at various browsers and the phone itself. He has an increasing awareness of the woman who is waiting and he is becoming more and more defensive.)* So I'll call her. Yeah. Right after this. Then I'll call my broker and . . . oh . . . you gotta come down here and give me a lift. Yeah. Now. My car . . . Now. NOW!
I asked her . . . She said no.
I gotta get things fixed up then I'm outta here. This is enough of an edge for me.
(Woman seems to be getting ready for her time on the phone.)
Anyway, bring the papers . . . all of them . . . in the third drawer on the left . . . and bring cash . . . in the first drawer in the middle.
(Woman seems to sag slightly at the renewed conversation.)

And hurry up, will ya?
"The edge" for chrissakes . . . You know what the edge really is . . . ?
This is what it is!!! . . . And oh, I forgot to tell you about the cat box. No . . . listen to this . . . This is how it all started . . . I say "the catbox is overflowing" and I say "it's your turn to clean it" and she just stands there . . . so I get mad and I feel like go over and dump the damn thing all over the new Balukistan throw rug that cost a fortune but, instead, because I'm so thoughtful . . . I clean it again!
I know! Too nice! I put everyone else first! . . so, anyway . . .
(The woman has moved closer and instead of sagging with impatience, she has begun rummaging in her purse.)
Would you give me some room, lady? You're invading my personal sphere of effect here . . . This is a public phone, lady . . . and . . .

WOMAN: *(Interrupting.)* Here. I want you to have this. *(She pulls a business card from her bag and hands it to Herb.)*

HERB: *(Taking the card.)* Whatever! Just get back!
(To the phone.) I know! Everyone else comes first in my book. But hey, that's the way I am and Phil, she tells me to get out!!!!! Can you believe it? Fine !!!!!
(Casually reads the card.)
I'll be happy to . . . You think I'm gonna feel guilty?
(Turns to the woman.)
Why do I want this?
What the hell is *this*? *(Woman smiles.)*
(To the phone.) Jesus . . . Hold on a minute . . . I gotta problem here . . . No! Don't hang up . . . Hold on. Go count how much cash you got and go look in the drawer . . . in the back . . . yeah . . . I'll hold on . . .
(To the woman while reading what's on the card.)
Mahatma Ginsberg, Waiter. You're a waiter?
(To the phone.) NO. I'm here. Yeah, but hold on . . .
(Reading.) "Counseling . . . individuals and couples?" You're a wait counselor?
(He's very annoyed, but mystified at the oddness of this and rather interested.)

WOMAN: Could you give me a sense of how long you expect this call to take?
(Takes off her shoes and opens purse again.)

HERB: Waiters?

WOMAN: *(Smiles . . . remains placid.)* Yes. Would you like some coffee? It's raining out and my feet are killing me and I do need to make a call, but I'm planning to wait here for you to complete your business and why not be comfortable? Take your time.

HERB: You carry coffee for people?
(*To the phone.*) Hold on! What? $84.50 . . . Great. That's enough for the car and . . .
(*She hands him the coffee from a thermos that she has pulled from her purse and poured into an attractive mug that has also come from the purse.*)
Don't forget the . . . (*Nods to her.*)
WOMAN: Cream? Soy milk?
HERB: (*To the phone.*) . . . stuff in the . . .
(*To her.*) You got cream in there?
WOMAN: Yes. (*She smiles and pours half and half into his mug.*)
HERB: (*To the phone.*) . . . it needs an oil change . . . yeah the red light came on . . .
WOMAN: Sugar? Nutmeg?
HERB: (*Dumfounded at her largesse. He stops and stares at her, then continues.*)
(*To the phone.*) . . . and call her for me, will ya? Tell her I DON'T KNOW WHAT SHE WANTS . . .
(*To the woman.*) Thanks again.
(*To the phone.*) AND I'M SICK OF THIS WHOLE BUSINESS AND . . . Hold on a minute. I gotta deal with this woman-waiter who needs the phone . . .
(*This is an excuse to drink the coffee and he does, with relish.*)
WOMAN: I'm not a waiter. I'm a wait-er; someone who waits. I do counseling and hypnotherapy. You seem on edge. I thought you could use my card, maybe make an appointment.
HERB: (*Drinking. When he hears her say, "You seem on edge," he becomes even more agitated. He takes the change out of his pocket and starts rattling it.*) Oh oh! What the hell is this? (*Hears the operator asking for more money for the call.*) Hold on a minute! (*Shifts cup to other hand while looking at his change, see it's all pennies, gets very frustrated.*) Oh Christ. I need a quarter here. (*Drops some of the pennies . . . Browsers look up at the sound of falling money.*)
WOMAN: Here. I know you need change. (*Offers him her change purse. While he fumbles through it and finds the correct change and puts it in the phone she continues speaking.*) Being open to waiting and the changes that occur therein. Being open. Waiting for the world to open to you. Passive waiting. Or, if you prefer, active waiting. I also do couples waiting, teen waiting, waiting as closure, waiting as non-waiting, the Zen of waiting, so to speak, the sexuality of waiting, the continuum of waiting . . .

HERB: *(He finishes the coffee in a final gulp and pounces on her last words.)* The sexuality of waiting?!

WOMAN: Yes. I'm . . .

HERB: *(To the phone.)* Wait a minute, will ya . . . and get the umbrellas in the closet on the right and the maps in the bottom drawer on the . . .
(He is looking at her card again now.) Who the hell named you Mahatma?

WOMAN: *(Taking a bottle of Evian water and a long stemmed glass out of her bag. She opens it and pours herself a drink while talking.)*
It's Sanskrit. I named myself. It means high minded soul, someone revered for wisdom and selflessness. I aspire to that. Anyway, go ahead with your call. I'm not in a hurry.

HERB: What was your old name?
(To the phone.) Hold on a minute, will ya!!!

WOMAN: It's not something I share. Although it shapes my persona in the deepest subtextual level of my being, it is beyond language and my external self reflects the philosophy of all sentient beings, those who suffer and those who are at one with the cosmos.
(Herb holds out his cup as if begging for more coffee. She obliges by pouring more from the coffee thermos.) Everyone's in a hurry. Enjoy.

HERB: *(He's very interested now.)* Thanks.
I bet I can guess your old name.
Lillian. *(She smiles.)*
Frieda?
Sarah?
Gertie? . . . Okay, okay. So those are *my* relatives' names . . . but come on, tell me . . . come on . . .

WOMAN: Do you have time for this?
(Indicates the phone.)

HERB: *(To the phone loudly.)* Phil! You there? Hold on, will ya please?
(Sotto voce.) I got somethin' goin' down here a second.
Yeah.
Yeah.
Yeah.
(Woman takes out her appointment book and a pen.)

HERB: Helen?
Judith?
Eva?
Evangeline?

WOMAN: No. No. Make an appointment.

HERB: *(Not daunted in his efforts.)* Okay . . . I'll start with the As.
Angela!
Amy!
Africa! *(To the phone.)* Hold on!
Alana! *(To the phone.)* Hold on!
Audrey!

WOMAN: I think we have a lot of work to do here.

HERB: *(Practically frothing at the mouth.)*
Betty!
Billie!
Bronwyn!!! *(To the phone.)* Hold on . . .
Carol!
Coral! . . . . Hold on!

(Lights begin to fade as he goes on with the list of names. Cs, Ds, Es until the lights are out. The browsers are all staring at him now, frozen with disbelief. The woman just smiles and holds her appointment book out to him and shakes her head "No" to each name.)

Cindy!
Cha Cha!
Doris!
Daisy!
Dahlia!
Debra!
Divina!
Divina!!!!
Elsie!
Elizabeth!

(Et cetera until stage is black.)

END OF PLAY

THE PERM
by Dale Elizabeth Attias

FIRST PERFORMANCE
January 1997

ORIGINAL CAST

Dinah . . . . .Patti Fitchen
Sandy . . . . .Irene Teagarden
Directed by . . . . .Jill Hofman
Sets by . . . . .Donna Teague

CHARACTERS
DINAH: A hairdresser.
SANDY: A customer.
    Friends since high school, both twenty-nine years old.

LOCATION
"The Cut 'N Curl" one-chair hair salon in Gunnison, Colorado.

TIME
The summer of 1982.

SETTING
The set need be only a hairdresser's chair, and a small caddy for curlers, combs, water bottle, etc.

THE PERM

Lights up to reveal Sandy seated in the chair, "draped" with a gaudy plastic hair salon cape. Sandy's hair is wet, and she's flipping through a magazine. Dinah calls from off stage.

DINAH: Found 'em!

SANDY: Great!

(Dinah enters carrying a box of permanent wave rods. Dinah wears a pink smock with "Cut 'N Curl" embroidered on the front. Her own hair is bleached, and tortured into curves, waves, and curls nature never intended. Dinah's eye makeup is exaggerated — she's certain that her customers will doubt her skill at hairdressing if she isn't "done" each day, from her blue eye shade to her frosty pink lip gloss. Dinah certainly was considered cute in high school, but now, twelve years later, her looks have begun to take on the patina of pathos.)

DINAH: I don't use the blue rods on nobody but you, honey. Every other one of my customers, these blue ones make 'em look like French poodles, you know?

SANDY: It's just my stupid hair. You can roll it tight as all get out, and next week it's straight as a string.

(Dinah begins the process of dividing Sandy's hair into small sections, wrapping each section with a paper, then rolling it onto one of the blue rods. She will continue to do this throughout the play.)

DINAH: You gonna love this new product I just got. Down to Denver at the Hair Show? They demo'd this stuff, and I couldn't believe it. It don't hardly smell bad at all.

SANDY: Can I wash my hair right away?

DINAH: Oh no! Gotta wait three days before you shampoo, but after that, you ain't gonna believe what you get. You gonna have volume, volume, volume. You gonna look like somebody straight outta Hollywood.

SANDY: *(Makes sour face.)* Yuck!

DINAH: Oh, that's right. You just come from there. How's your trip?

SANDY: You know, every single year we take the family car trip, and every year I tell myself never again.

DINAH: Until next year.

SANDY: Jason wasn't so bad this time. But I gotta tell you, Jennifer was . . . Well, I swear she just hates the sight of me.

DINAH: She doesn't hate her own momma.

SANDY: She does. I mean, we picked Hollywood, for the vacation, just to please Jenny. You know the way she loves the movies? So we drive all that way out to California. But don't you know every word out of my mouth was all wrong. And the way I dressed. The food I ordered in restaurants. Everything. It was the third . . . no it was the fourth day. We were at that "Walk of Fame" thing. You know, in front of that Chinese theater? Where they have the stars and the handprints and stuff.

Well, I was trying my hands in a couple of movie star's, and what do you know? My feet are loads bigger'n all of 'em. You should see it. I swear Ginger Rogers must have worn a size two shoe. But guess what? My hands fit Debbie Reynold's print exactly. It was uncanny. Just a perfect fit. Well I got all excited and I hollered for Mike to come see, and Jenny comes over and says, "Mother, do you always have to act like such a god damn hick?" She really said it. "God damn hick" she called me!

DINAH: It's a phase, honey. It'll pass. You oughtta hear the foul garbage coming out of my boys' mouths.

SANDY: There wasn't nobody there but Japanese tourists anyway. Nobody understood a durned thing I said.

DINAH: Sometimes I just lay in the bed and I wonder what the boys are gonna be like when they're teenaged. I mean, look at what a wild time Jack had when he was in high school.

SANDY: Boys will be boys.

DINAH: I suppose. Did you see anybody famous out there?

SANDY: No, I didn't. Mike and Jason saw Ernest Borgnine at a filling station, but I was in the ladies and missed the whole durned thing.

DINAH: Well, what would you say to a movie star anyway, if you met one face to face?

SANDY: Darned if I know. "Like your movies" I guess.

DINAH: Unless it was Harrison Ford. I'd sure know what to say to Harrison Ford.

SANDY: What?

DINAH: I seen in "People" magazine that they put down a big slab of cement for Harrison Ford. Did you see that one?

SANDY: Can't miss it. Right down front. It's a real big slab.

DINAH: Does he have big feet? Did you notice that?

SANDY: Bigger'n Mike's by about a size and a half. His foot print was tennis shoes. Nobody else had tennis shoes in there. I couldn't get over how tiny Ginger Rogers . . .

DINAH: But it was big? Harrison Ford's? Then that means his, you know, is . . .

SANDY: His what?

DINAH: His thing. Jesus H. Christ, Sandy, I got to draw you a picture or what? You know what they say. Big feet, big noses, big . . .

SANDY: *(Dawn breaks.)* They were huge!

DINAH: Is it a sin to think about Harrison Ford in a carnal way?

SANDY: Hell, yes. But honey, there's fifty ways to Sunday to commit sin with every stitch of clothes on your back. You can be fantasizing 'bout Harrison all you want. Cause you ain't never gonna hear complaint one from Jack, when your eyes are shut real tight and you pretend that slim waist and those big shoulders belong to Indiana Jones.

(Sandy and Dinah giggle and blush together.)

DINAH: Uh huh.

SANDY: Doesn't the Lord tell us to honor thy husband?

DINAH: Sure.

SANDY: Well, there you go. You pretend you're underneath Harrison Ford, and your old man is gonna have himself one fine time.

I forgot to ask. Did Jack ever get his truck?

DINAH: Finally. A couple of weeks ago.

SANDY: Well?

DINAH: God, I never thought he'd make up his mind what truck he was gonna get. I don't know how many trips to Durango and the dealers we made. Finally, he makes up his mind and he's gotta go on a Sunday. I have to explain to mother why it is that I can't teach Sunday school. Believe me, Sandy-darling, buying a truck is no excuse for missing church. Not in my family. She gives me that look of hers. Like I'm eight years old.

SANDY: My mother can do that too. You think we'll ever be able to give that look to our kids?

(Both practice the "evil mother look" in the mirror together.)

DINAH: He finally got his durned truck. Don't you love that new car smell?

SANDY: I do. When my dad was still alive he used to trade in his Chevy for a new one every model year. September. I just loved that. I'd go sit in the new car and breathe it in.

DINAH: I know it's just plastic. But it's really kinda intoxicating.

SANDY: Mmmm. Intoxicating.

DINAH: Well, we took the new truck out for a test drive the next day. Fiona had the boys. She just spoils them rotten every time they're over to her place. She got a pantry jammed with junk for 'em, Nestle's Quik and cookies, and cakes and stuff like that.

SANDY: Same with Mike's mom.

DINAH: Anyway, we drove on over Monarch Pass.

SANDY: Monarch?

DINAH: I know. I says, "We going all the way to Denver or what?" Jack says we're just testing it out and I should sit back and enjoy the ride. It was easy. Cause of that smell. Before I know it, we're just about to Buena Vista. Jack says, "I'll buy you a malt." You know that burger place along Highway Fifty? I forget the name.

SANDY: I know the one you mean.

DINAH: Jack, of course, won't let us eat in the truck, so we have our lunch at that place, with the trucks and the tourists blasting by us at seventy-five miles an hour.

Jack says, "There's a place up in them rocks with a great view. Wanna go to the Submarine Races?" You coulda knocked me over with a feather. My Jack. On a Monday afternoon. In broad daylight. Maybe it was the new car smell getting to him.

So I says sure, and we go driving along Highway Fifty looking for the cut-off to get you to that great view.

(Dinah steps away from the chair. She still has the comb in her hand, but isn't rolling any more rods.)

Then all of the sudden. Outta nowhere this girl jumps in front of the car.

SANDY: What girl?

DINAH: Jack must have layed seventy feet of brand new tire on the road trying to stop. She just come from outta no where. You know how it is along there . . . along there, you either got your sheer wall of rock on one side, or your two hundred foot cliff on the other. There was no way to avoid her. No way at all.

SANDY: *(Quiet.)* Oh my Lord!

DINAH: It was horrible. She flipped up and over the hood of the truck. Her head broke the windshield.

SANDY: Oh my Sweet Lord.

DINAH: Jack somehow, I don't know how, he didn't lose control of the truck. Soon as he stopped, why I ran back to where she was lying. She was just . . . in the road. She looked just like a sack of something thrown outta somebody's car.

SANDY: Was she dead?

DINAH: No. But she was awful broken up. Horrible. You could see that just at a glance. Her arm was all funny. And her leg had one of them, what do you call that when the bone pokes through?

SANDY: Compound fracture.

DINAH: That's right. It surprised me that she was awake. But she couldn't talk. I knelt down beside her.

(Dinah kneels on the floor beside the chair.)

She tried to make a sound but there was nothing but blood. A kind of bubbly noise. Her eyes was looking at me. She had real skinny eyebrows. You know, when you pluck 'em too much. They was all pinched together in the middle of her forehead. She was only about nineteen or twenty. That's all. I lifted her into my arms there on the dirt. I could feel her blood running into my clothes. Real quick, I'm feeling all warm and damp underneath her.

Her eyes looked so scared. I thought, I just gotta make this poor girl not afraid. Somehow I got to help her. I knew she was gonna die and it was me who was supposed to help her over to the other side. So I says, "Don't be afraid. Sweet Jesus Christ is coming for you now and I'll be here to pray with you and hold you until he comes. He'll fill you up with his love and he'll take away all your hurts. You won't have no more fear nor worry. I promise. Only the love of your sweet saviour."

She made that bubble noise again, but then that place between her eyebrows, it just kinda relaxed. Her eyes closed part of the way. Her skin was a terrible color. The color of wood when you leave it out in the winter with no paint on it. And I remember thinking I never seen any human skin this color before. Not ever. And I think, I gotta make this girl rest easy. She don't need to be afraid. And I started to sing. I couldn't remember the words to anything 'scept "Amazing Grace." So I sang it real soft like it was a lullaby.

(Sings.) "Amazing Grace how sweet the sound that saved a wretch like me."

(Stops singing — beat.)

And then the state patrol and the sheriff come. I looked at her face and I knew she was at peace. She died there, by the side of the road right in my arms.

(Dinah realizes she's sitting on the floor, feels awkward and gets to her feet.)

Look at you. All that hair is all dried out.

(Dinah takes up a spray bottle and spritzes Sandy's hair that isn't in the rods.)

SANDY: What did the cops say?

DINAH: They couldn't been nicer. They took us into the police station in Beunie. There was a secretary there loaned me some clothes from her car. I was just covered in that girl's blood. They told us the girl tried half dozen times in the last couple of years to do herself in. Everyone agreed it was only a matter of time before she succeeded. The sheriff couldn't have been sweeter to Jack over his truck. Fifty-seven miles is all he had on it, and the front fender's all stowed in, and the windshield's shattered.

SANDY: That's incredible. I . . .

DINAH: I went over to Beunie day before yesterday. I wanted to take that nice secretary her clothes back. And I went over to visit that girl's mama. She's living in a mobile on the edge of town.

SANDY: Did she think you killed her daughter on purpose?

DINAH: Oh no. Not at all. She didn't say much. Just that her daughter — her name was Alison. Alison was supposed to be taking her medicine. Cause she was, you know, mental. And the mother couldn't always get her to take it. She tried it before — killing herself. Just a matter of time. That's what her mom said. Just a matter of time.

I sat with her for a while and then I said, "I wanted you to know that when your daughter passed on to the Lord she wasn't alone. I held her in my arms, and I know she was at peace."

SANDY: What'd the mother say?

DINAH: Nothing. She just lit a Lucky Strike. She smoked it down some, and she said, "Thank you for coming." I didn't know what else to say, so I left. Jack got the truck back from the body shop yesterday. Can't tell nothing was ever wrong with it.

SANDY: Well you know what I think?

DINAH: What's that, sugar?

SANDY: I think it's God's plan that you be there. Coulda' been some trucker who wouldn't know how to hold a poor dying creature to ease her fear.

DINAH: I hope that's true. I've wondered about it. Her eyes . . . Never mind. She's at peace now. Finally.

(Dinah continues to roll rods into Sandy's hair as the light fades.)

END OF PLAY

POETRY READING
by John Chandler

FIRST PERFORMANCE
January 1997

ORIGINAL CAST

Edna	Virginia Draper
Ronald Putzman	Jason Buckley
Justin	Malte Frid-Nielsen
Audience-at-the-Poetry Reading	Makaela Pollack, Johnny Davis, Kelly Hatcher, Steve "Spike" Wong, Avondina Wills
Directed by	Betty Dodge
Sets by	Donna Teague

CHARACTERS
EDNA
PUTZMAN
JUSTIN
UNNAMED YOUNG MAN
UNNAMED YOUNG WOMAN
VOICES OF RIDICULE FROM AUDIENCE
LAST ACTOR IN AUDIENCE

POETRY READING

In the middle of the stage is a podium and behind it a small table with a pitcher, a glass, and a vase with a rose. A middle-aged woman, with rimless glasses, dressed in a conservative dress, an academic, comes to the podium, blows into the microphone, smiles out at the audience.

WOMAN: Good evening. We are privileged to have tonight, Ronald Putzman, whose book, *Angels in the Jaws of Alligators,* has just come out. Poems from his book were previously published in *The Undercurrent Review, Fumigant International, Yardarm Press,* and *Second Door on Your Right.* Mr. Putzman's writing on subjects from caterpillars to body piercing has been hailed by numerous critics for its authenticity and daring. Mr. Putzman. *(As various people situated in the audience clap lightly a man walks to podium with a sheaf of papers in his hand, pours himself a glass of water, eyes his audience over the podium, clears his throat, takes another glass of water, then steps around the podium and pushes his glasses upward along his nose. Again he clears his throat, partly turns to retreat back to the other side of the podium, then turns toward the audience again and begins to speak.)*

PUTZMAN: I was about to thank Edna for that introduction, but I thought, that's just what is done at every poetry reading. And then I thought, fuck it, I'll just start reading my poetry, but that's also what an audience would expect. Something under control. Something that will conform to everyone's experience. A drab repetition of numerous past experiences. Well . . . *(He drinks again from his glass and smiles, looking directly at someone in the first row, a woman.)* . . . haven't I seen you at other readings? Berkeley? Palo Alto? We should talk about it after the reading, somewhere where we can concentrate. *(He looks at the whole audience, smiling.)* That wasn't serious. In the old days maybe, but not today. This young woman could haul me in front of some court or another for that — sexual harassment. *(He turns serious.)* The harassment I intend to commit tonight, human beings out there in the audience — and I don't dignify you or diminish you with the term "ladies and gentlemen" — is of a completely different nature. Could I have a volunteer from the audience?

(A young man puts up his hand.)

PUTZMAN: Yes, you there. Come on up. *(As the young man approaches the stage, Putzman continues talking.)* This is a poem without words. *(The young man has reached the stage.)* I name it 'The Moon.' Now what is your name?

JUSTIN: Justin.

PUTZMAN: *(Rapidly.)* Just in time? Just in jest? *(Smiles.)* Just in from the east coast? *(Pause, then rapidly.)* Just kidding, now Justin, turn your back and drop your pants, then bend . . .
(From audience, another voice.)
YOUNG MAN: For God's sake, man, show a little dignity.
PUTZMAN: *(Tapping the stunned Justin on the shoulder.)* Thanks, forget it. *(To audience.)* Now we're getting closer to what this evening is about. My first two selections, "Sexual Harassment" and "The Moon" are audience participation pieces, and come from vaudeville and from talk shows. Their impact depends on your feeling their inappropriateness, and I take the comment from the audience to be the highest praise. Show a little dignity is another way of saying, you violated the rules. Now this poem I am speaking right now, "Violating the Rules," is, like the first two poems, an introduction, a burrowing into the center of the horror of the evening. *(Grins and squints out at previous speaker.)* Tell me, Mister Dignity, what's your idea of a poem? Come on, I bet you know a favorite. Show us what dignity is. *(He takes a step forward and waves the man to his feet.)* Don't just sit on your dignity, speak up.
YOUNG MAN: *(Without spotlight on him.)* It's not my job to recite tonight. You're the reader. I just wish you would do it, and stop the tricks.
PUTZMAN: *(He has a beatific smile on his face.)* We're waiting, Mr. Know-It-All.
YOUNG MAN: *(Still in the dark.)* I don't know it all, I just appreciate beauty.
ANOTHER VOICE: Do it.
A DIFFERENT VOICE: Yes, say it.
(Murmurs of agreement, reminiscent of a revival, as Putzman reaches back, gets the rose, twirls it, making a show of sniffing it and being transported. From here until he tosses the rose away he should display it and gesture with it in a taunting way.) Yes, say it. Say it. *(One woman hums loudly the first line of "Amazing Grace" then a whole chorus of four or five people holds the last note.)*
YOUNG MAN: *(His voice emotional, nearly cracking from conflicting desires.)* No, I can't. Not here.
PUTZMAN: *(Breezy, becoming derisive.)* Saving it for church? Saving it for your wedding night? Let's have a hand for Mr. Dignity's offering. It's short, but to the point: No I can't, not here. Perhaps he was inspired by my earlier comments, in jest, to this lovely young woman near the front row. What the hell was that theater in New York, back in the late sixties or early seventies, where the play could go anywhere, and the actors sometimes ended up screwing the audience? Look, I want to tell you, if you're

inclined, just go on ahead and do it, during my performance. I always thought jazz accompanying readings was a little artificial. See, I brought half a dozen condoms, in case you get carried away. Remember what your mother told you, Don't go out into the rain without your rubbers on. Seriously. *(He stops and looks very sharply at the audience.)* Serious. For me a successful reading would be people writhing around in between rows of seats. And you know what their bodies would be exuding, what words I would accompany all that with? *(He steps again toward the front of the stage, comes from behind his podium. He points with free hand out toward where the man is sitting.)* I would be saying, over and over, 'Yes, yes I can. Here.' How did the angel taste to the alligator? Divine. Look around you. Lick your chops. This was my final poem — "Feeding Frenzy." Those of you who buy my book will notice that the pages are blank. You may interpret them any way you wish. You still out there, Mr. Dignity? Last chance for beauty. *(Pauses, leans toward the audience, his hands linked in a pious clasp.)* No? *(Tosses rose over his shoulder.)* Well, my next poem is, "I Am a Fraud."

> Hasn't that occurred to you
> yet? that I'm a fraud, or are you awed
> or bored (pronounced like Bawd)
> Or do you think I'm groovy?
> I bet you'd rather see a movie
> or stay in bed
> and get (or give) some head
> or share a luscious screw.

Amazing isn't it? I just thought that one up. I mean seriously, what dragged you here? And how do you know I'm who I'm supposed to be. I mean this gorgeous young woman here in the second row is the only one *I've* seen before, she's the only one who can vouch for me, and we haven't *known* each other. Do you know what I mean? Do you read your Bible? And even if I am Putzman the poet, does that dignify what I'm saying here? *(As he speaks the young woman he has been referring to rises, looks around the audience.)*

YOUNG WOMAN: I don't know what he's talking about. I've never been to a reading of his before.

PUTZMAN: She's lying. She's really my wife. She's a plant. We planned this, for her to say this at this point.

YOUNG WOMAN: That's a lie. I think you *are* a fraud.

(From this point the audience shows its impatience and outrage in murmurs and occasional louder comments of "fraud" while Putzman is speaking.)

PUTZMAN: Thank you. That concludes my poem, "I Am a Fraud," an interactive, audience engagement poem.

SOMEONE IN AUDIENCE: Liar.

PUTZMAN: May I speak for a few moments about theory.

SOMEONE ELSE IN THE AUDIENCE: Get off the stage.

PUTZMAN: One of the things we poets have difficulty with is the division between audience and poet, not to mention the difference between poetry of the page and poetry of the situation, not to mention the division between poetry and the average Joe . . .

SOMEONE IN AUDIENCE: *(In an authoritative voice.)* Not to mention the difference between you and a real poet.

(Putzman pauses but does not acknowledge in any way the heckling.)

PUTZMAN: . . . if I may use an old sexist name for the working person. I am a poet dedicated to breaking down barriers. A love poet. *(Derisive laughter from the audience.)* Not in the old sense of a man writing something ornate to a woman, no doubt trying to seduce her with high sounding words that she probably can't understand and is therefore flattered by. I mean availability poetry. I mean, if this . . . person out there in the second row, who may be my wife, would just listen to the whole production of this evening she would realize what I am saying to her. *(He looks toward her.)* I mean, I can't spell it out, I'd be liable, legally liable. I mean, I've dissolved the distance between us, don't you see. You're not reduced to someone who watches me pretend to know things, to be in contact with beauty when in reality ninety percent of the time I am a swine. I am showing you the whole me, and you are invited to respond. That is what I mean by interactive poetry. It's a lot like domestic disputes. It's REAL.

YOUNG WOMAN: It's not real. It's disgusting. He was right. *(She points toward the young man who spoke up earlier. The spotlight fixes on him and her. She smiles.)* I could tell by your voice that you really love things, that you feel them. When you couldn't bring yourself to speak in this . . . this . . . environment, I knew we were compatible.

PUTZMAN: *(Scornfully.)* Environment, compatible. You mean you read the same self-help books. Come on, Sally. Cut the crap. How many times can I take your leaving with another man during my readings?

YOUNG WOMAN: *(A little shaken, directs her next comment to the audience, looking around her.)* I'm not Sally, I'm not his wife, I've never seen him before tonight and I never intend to see him again. *(She takes a deep breath, eyes closed, looks back at the young man, resumes her smile. They get up from their seats, leave the auditorium together. All but one of the actors in the audience rise and leave after the new lovers.)*

PUTZMAN: *(Eyes closed, wringing his hands.)* Again it happens. *(He opens his eyes and stares at the audience.)* This is the life of a poet, sacrificing everything to one's work. Truth . . . truth will always be lonely.

LAST OF THE ACTORS IN AUDIENCE: *(Standing.)* Truth? *(Laughs.)* What the hell do you know about truth? I'm sick of these god damn things. You either can't follow what they're saying or they're just talking a lot of bullshit. I'm not taking this any more. *(Leaves in a huff.)*

PUTZMAN: *(In real pain, as though the words are dragging out of him.)* Emancipation. The title of the last poem is "Emancipation." *(He stares at the audience and is silent for a moment.)* It's hell being an interactive poet, you know? Angels in the Jaws of Alligators *(Spoken slowly, slowly.)*

I open my jaws —

Flight escapes.

Oh, this hunger, this hunger

For wings.

(He turns, begins to walk off stage. As he walks his body slumps increasingly over, until after the fourth step he is on all fours, crawling the last few feet.) *(Edna comes back out onto the stage, deftly picks up the discarded rose and replaces it in water, than walks to podium and smiles impassively into the darkness of the audience.)*

EDNA: Thank you, Mr. Putzman. Our next reader for the evening . . .

(Lights turn off suddenly.)

END OF PLAY

THE RAIN ARE FALLIN
by Richard Bennett

FIRST PERFORMANCE
January 1997

ORIGINAL CAST

Leona Peters . . . . .Dierdre Hamilton
Jules Solomon . . . . Robert Allen Johnson
Bessie Mae Fairburn . . . . Desiree Sales
Rafaello . . . . Oscar Davila
Directed by . . . . .Meg Herz Harlor
Sets by . . . . .Donna Teague

CHARACTERS

LEONA PETERS: a star, she has just completed her farewell performance, and is about to retire. She is a large and imposing black woman in her fifties, very articulate.

JULES SOLOMON: her husband and manager.

RAFAELLO: a famous Spanish tenor.

BESSIE MAE FAIRBURN: a tall and slightly awkward young black singer. She has a pronounced Southern way of speech that she continuously tries to correct.

SETTING

The dressing room of the world-renowned opera star, Soprano Leona Peters.

THE RAIN ARE FALLIN

Leona and Jules are in the dressing room. Leona has changed into evening dress for the farewell party. Her Aida costumes are hanging on the dressing screen.

LEONA: Tenors! Tenors! I could strangle that Rafaello. I'd leave him sealed up in the damn pyramid for all eternity. Stepping on my lines . . . three times! Did you hear how he cut me off?

JULES: I don't think anybody noticed. Certainly not the audience. They gave you three standing ovations. They shouted themselves hoarse. It was a magnificent farewell performance. Nothing like it in my experience.

LEONA: Oh, that was just for old times sake. But that little Spanish son of a bitch, breaking in on me like that! Thank God for retirement. No more tenors forever.

JULES: He was a very credible Omneris for such a little guy. Wonderful voice.

LEONA: You'd think he did it on purpose, the little rat. Oh, well it's over. If he comes to the party I'll throw him out the window.

JULES: He'll be there. Everybody will be there. Your farewell party — how could he miss it?

LEONA: I'll sit on him. That will serve him right, the little twit.

(The telephone rings. Jules answers.)

JULES: Miss Peters' room. Yes? Just a moment, please.

(Aside to Leona.) It's him.

LEONA: I won't talk to him. The nerve!

JULES: I'm sorry, but she can't come to the phone right now. Is there a message? I'll tell her, thank you. *(Covers the phone.)* He begs your forgiveness most humbly and wishes to see you.

LEONA: Tell him that if he ever shows his face I'll grind him into pate foie gras! Tell him . . .

JULES: *(Into phone.)* Madame says she'll be happy to see you at the party this evening. Ah. Bueno, see you then.

LEONA: Hard of hearing, are we?

JULES: Oh, by the way, there's a young woman who has been waiting to see you.

LEONA: She's not a tenor by any chance?

JULES: I don't think so. She was here earlier. Came all the way by bus from Mississippi.

LEONA: Mississippi! I forbid you to say that word in my presence. You know very well how I feel about that place.

JULES: Well, South of Tennessee then. I didn't want to bother you before the performance so I promised you'd see her after. It will only take a minute.

LEONA: Oh all right I'll talk to the young lady. Bring her in.

(Jules goes to the door and leads Bessie in. She is carrying a folded raincoat, slightly wet, which she nervously sets on a table.)

JULES: This is Miss Bessie Mae Fairburn.

LEONA: I'm delighted to meet you, Miss Fairburn.

BESSIE: Oh, thank you. I'm so happy to meet you.

LEONA: You've met my manager, Mr. Solomon?

BESSIE: Why yes, ma'am. We met earlier.

LEONA: Well, now. Did you enjoy the performance?

BESSIE: Oh, I didn't have any ticket, ma'am. I just waited outside. But I'm sure it must have been a thrillin' performance.

LEONA: *(Puzzled.)* So you came all the way from . . . down South, and you didn't get in to the opera. What a shame.

BESSIE: Well, I really just came to see you, ma'am.

LEONA: I see. Well, here I am, and it's a pleasure to meet you. Jules, do we have one of those pictures I could sign for the young lady?

BESSIE: Oh, that would be very nice, but I really came to ax . . . to ask you something. To ask a favor.

LEONA: Oh?

BESSIE: You see, I'm a singer, too.

LEONA: You are? *(Suspicious.)* And where do you sing, my dear?

BESSIE: Well, I sings mostly in the chorus at home . . . mostly sacred music. I mostly do the solo parts. I've learned some opera, too. I wants — I want to be like you. To sing in the opera.

LEONA: You do, mostly, do you? Well, Lord help you. I wish you well. It's hard work, Miss Fairburn. You have to be serious about it. You have to give up everything. Everything. Friends, family, love. There's no room for any of that. You need to be prepared to devote everything to music — Everything.

BESSIE: Oh I am, ma'am. I surely am. Only I thought, since you are retiring.

(Leona glares at Jules, who rolls his eyes.)

BESSIE: That you might . . .

LEONA: I might? I might what?

BESSIE: That you might be thinking of taking on a student.

LEONA: A student. Well, *(Glares menacingly at Jules.)* I don't know where you might have got such an idea in your head, Miss Fairburn. Taking a singing student is quite a serious responsibility. It would be the very last thing on my list right now. Jules and I are going to take a long vacation. We're going to travel, in Europe. Maybe around the world. I want to go to Milan and see something besides the inside of an opera house. I want to spend some time by myself with no deadlines, no rehearsals, and no tenors. No, I don't think that taking on a student is a good idea.

BESSIE: Oh, I'm sorry. I just thought, y'all being from Mississippi too.

LEONA: It happens that I have had my toes in that mud. But that's a long time ago. Sit down, Miss Fairburn, let me tell you what you need to do.

BESSIE: Yes, ma'am.

LEONA: *(Gently.)* Go back to Mississippi . . . on the very next bus. When you get there, get yourself into a junior college. Study language and speech. Study music theory. Study voice from the ground up. There are some scholarships available, even in Mississippi. Get your friends from the chorus to help with tuition. Work. Get a job if you have to. Wait tables. Music is hard work and it doesn't come overnight. But the opportunity is there, and if your voice is really as great as your friends think it is, you'll make it all right.

BESSIE: Oh. Thank you so much. You're so kind to take the time. *(She stands and picks up her coat, close to tears.)* Oh, I'm sorry. It's dripping on your table. The rain are fallin so . . . I mean it's raining so hard.

LEONA: Just a minute. *(She takes the coat and sets it back down, thinking.)* Miss Fairburn, would you just wait outside a minute. I want to talk to Jules. *(Bessie leaves silently, head down.)*

LEONA: *(To Jules.)* You put her up to this, didn't you?

JULES: Me? I'm innocent, my love.

LEONA: I know you better than that.

JULES: She's got a lot to learn.

LEONA: I used to talk like her, Jules. Did you know that? That's how I learned to say it. It all comes back. There we were in a little schoolhouse no bigger than this dressing room. The teacher wasn't much older than us. Just a little black girl barely able to spell . . . She wrote it on the board so we'd get it right: The rain are fallin. I haven't thought of that in years.

(There is a knock on the door. Jules gets up to see who it is. He comes back, worried.)

JULES: *(Whispering.)* It's Rafaello.

LEONA: It's all right. Let him in.

(Rafaello enters, carrying flowers which he thrusts at Leona.)

RAFAELLO: I had to see you to apologize. I'm so mortified. Your last performance and I ruined it for you. Please, I beg you to forgive me.

LEONA: There's nothing . . .

RAFAELLO: Oh, but I was terrible. My timing was all off. I kept coming in too soon.

LEONA: No Rafaello, it wasn't your fault. You tried to cover for me. We can fool the audience for a time, but we can't fool ourselves. No, it was me. It's no crime, I'm just getting older. I can't climb those scales so fast any more. You did your best to help me over it and I appreciate that.

That's why I have to step down, Rafaello. You notice it already. Pretty soon the whole world will notice it. I'm too proud to let that happen. It's time to let younger and stronger voices take over.

RAFAELLO: Oh, madam, what will we do without you? You are our brightest star. There will never be another your equal. I am devastated.

LEONA: Oh, there will be others. *(She looks at Bessie's coat.)* I can assure you of that. Rafaello, amore mio, you've been wonderful. I'll see you at the party later?

RAFAELLO: Of course, of course. My heart will be breaking, but I wouldn't miss it. *(Gives her a big embrace and departs.)* Hasta luego, my angel.

LEONA: Hasta luego.

(Rafaello leaves.)

JULES: Well, we should be getting over to the party.

LEONA: Jules, do something for me, will you?

JULES: Anything, of course.

LEONA: Go ahead to the party without me. I'll be along after a while.

JULES: But it's your party. Everybody will be waiting for you.

LEONA: Give them something to eat and drink and they won't even miss me. And I won't be long. Just something I have to do. And, Jules . . .

JULES: Yes.

LEONA: Thanks, Jules . . . Send our Miss Fairburn in, would you?

JULES: Hasta luego.

(Jules leaves, in a moment Bessie enters, still rather downcast.)

LEONA: Now then, Miss Fairburn. Bessie Mae, let's hear you sing.

BESSIE: *(Brightens.)* You mean, now?

LEONA: Yes, right now. Let's go see if we can find a piano somewhere. This is an opera house, after all. *(She picks up the coat and takes Bessie's arm.)* Don't forget your raincoat. *(Gently.)* The rain are fallin, it surely are.

(Leona and Bessie leave together.) (Curtain.)

END OF PLAY

RETROGRADE
by Doug Brook

FIRST PERFORMANCE
January 1999

ORIGINAL CAST
- John . . . . Christopher Sugarman
- Lynn . . . . Katryn Kinser
- Directed by . . . . John Howie Patterson
- Sets by . . . . Mark Hopkins

RETROGRADE

The setting is unimportant. Lynn and John are together onstage. There are several breaks that represent time gaps. These gaps should be portrayed by the actors in brief lapses, nothing fancier.

A retrograde is a musical construct, wherein a melody goes in a certain direction, then concludes by repeating itself exactly in reverse. This scene does the same thing. They go from hate to love to hate again. It is important to present the progressions distinctly, or it might make little sense.

LYNN: I really hate you.
JOHN: You're entitled to your wrong opinion.
LYNN: You see? How am I supposed to keep working with someone as irreverent and sarcastic as you?
JOHN: And somehow I'll again suffer through a partner who has no sense of humor when she's working.
LYNN: You're insufferable. No wonder you're not married.
JOHN: You're much too critical and absorbed in your perception of the world. No wonder you're divorced.
LYNN: Let's just get our work done.
   (Break.)
LYNN: I can't believe the time we had to put in tonight.
JOHN: I can.
LYNN: It's four-thirty already. The sun will rise in an hour or so.
JOHN: I tried to warn you.
LYNN: You're always so damned smart . . . I guess you're right. You did warn me.
JOHN: See? I can be right sometimes. The question is, can you stand it?
LYNN: I don't think so. But I guess I'll have to learn if we keep getting stuck working together.
   (Break.)
JOHN: Before you get all worked up about being stuck with me again, you should know that I requested it.
LYNN: Really? Why?
JOHN: Because of how you feel about me.
LYNN: You are such an ass! Why do you always have to do that?
JOHN: Okay. Seriously. We've worked well together. Even though we don't get along. Actually, especially when we didn't get along.
LYNN: Why are you so sure we get along now?
JOHN: I didn't say we do.

LYNN: Yes you did. You said "didn't" which implies it's no longer the case.

JOHN: Fine. But that's not what I meant. We seemed to take a small step toward being civil last time. Either way, somehow we seem to get results together.

LYNN: I suppose that's true. Somehow, as hard as you try to avoid it, we do some good work.

JOHN: Shall we get to work?

LYNN: After one question.

JOHN: Shoot.

LYNN: Is that the only reason you put in the request?

JOHN: I'm trying to be nice, but don't flatter yourself. You've heard what everyone says. I'm all business. If I haven't noticed anyone else around here why would I notice you?

LYNN: Because I'm better.

(Break.)

JOHN: What's with us? At the rate we're going we'll still be here when the morning staff arrives.

LYNN: It is something else, isn't it?

JOHN: What?

LYNN: You wouldn't admit it if you were at gunpoint, would you?

JOHN: Admit what?

LYNN: That you're attracted to me.

JOHN: You're right.

LYNN: I'm right that you're attracted to me, or that you'd never admit it?

JOHN: You decide. I'm too busy. Let me know when you've made up my mind.

(Break.)

LYNN: Well, it's four-thirty again.

JOHN: Yes, it is.

LYNN: Want to watch the sunrise with me? It's gorgeous from the twenty-eighth floor windows.

JOHN: Seen it.

LYNN: Why are you fighting me so much?

JOHN: You said before.

LYNN: So you are attracted to me.

JOHN: Maybe I'm referring to you saying that I'd never admit to it. You don't get it. Maybe there's nothing to admit to. Why would I admit to something that's not true?

LYNN: You're so impossible.

JOHN: Isn't that why you're attracted to me?

(Break.)

LYNN: It's been a slow week.

JOHN: For you, perhaps.

LYNN: You want to do dinner this weekend?

JOHN: I'm impressed. Even with all the noise of the women's movement, rare is the time you actually find a woman asking a man out.

LYNN: You're dodging.

JOHN: Though I read in the paper that it happened once last week to an unsuspecting law clerk in Boise.

LYNN: You're being very difficult.

JOHN: He was asked out by a junior partner, no less.

LYNN: You're avoiding the question.

JOHN: It's not exactly driving you out the door.

LYNN: The only reason I want to have dinner with you is I want to see if you can stop sounding like a jerk for twenty minutes if your mouth has food in it.

JOHN: I chew loudly.

LYNN: That figures.

JOHN: I doubt it would last more than ten minutes.

LYNN: I heard that about you.

JOHN: Maybe it's a question of being motivated enough by my company.

LYNN: *(Starts out.)* You're so sure of yourself . . .

JOHN: Eight-thirty. My place. I know you know where I live.

LYNN: And why would you assume that?

JOHN: Because the drawer with the personnel files is closed.

LYNN: I'm sorry. I'd assume that it's always closed.

JOHN: You would assume that. Which is why I left it slightly open earlier, in case you got curious.

(Break.)

LYNN: This is the first minute we've been alone all week. I wanted you to know that I really enjoyed last Friday night.

JOHN: I thought we weren't going to discuss "us" at work.

LYNN: No one's around.

JOHN: Okay. I'm sorry. Let's start again.

LYNN: I really enjoyed last Friday night.

JOHN: I could tell.

LYNN: Is that all you have to say?

JOHN: Couldn't you tell that I did?

LYNN: Yes.

JOHN: So you already know the answer. Why repeat the obvious.

LYNN: It's nice to hear sometimes.
JOHN: Eight tonight. I'll tell you all about it. Your place this time?
(Break.)
LYNN: Well, that went better than I thought.
JOHN: So you weren't fired?
LYNN: No. Neither of us will be. As long as our work doesn't suffer, he doesn't mind us having a relationship. Apparently there was a betting pool on whether we'd ever get together.
JOHN: The liabilities of being two single people in a company full of old married couples.
LYNN: He's actually trying to take credit for setting us up by forcing us to work together.
JOHN: A true manager. Coming in after the fact and taking credit where it isn't due.
LYNN: Stacy won a hundred dollars. You're not going through all this just to get twenty percent of her cut, are you?
JOHN: Of course not.
LYNN: Good.
JOHN: I'm getting thirty-five percent.
LYNN: That's okay. I'm getting forty percent of Bill's two hundred dollar take.
JOHN: Hey, I was kidding. You were too, right? Weren't you?
LYNN: So, did you bring the file with you?
(Break.)
JOHN: Have you heard the latest betting pool? How soon until we're engaged.
LYNN: I know. Chris bet one hundred on New Year's Eve.
JOHN: You sold out.
LYNN: He promised me forty percent.
JOHN: Well, you'll have to propose to me, then. Unless of course I beat you to it, say for fifty percent of a bet on Thanksgiving.
LYNN: Why Thanksgiving?
JOHN: It's before your New Year's Eve bet, we have the next day off, and I get double or nothing if it's outside with a beautiful view of the skyline.
(Break.)
LYNN: Do you have those graphs done yet?
JOHN: You really are getting impatient in your old age.
LYNN: And you're getting impertinent.
JOHN: Look, I'm working as fast as I can.
LYNN: You used to work faster.

JOHN: That's because I used to be trying to minimize the amount of time I had to spend in the same room as you.

LYNN: Why did you stop?

JOHN: Because I never seem to be anywhere without you anymore, so why try?

(Break.)

LYNN: Has anyone spoken to you today?

JOHN: Avoiding me like I have malaria. You?

LYNN: Nope.

JOHN: Think they're upset?

LYNN: Why should they be? It's just their betting pool that was ruined. I'm the one who didn't get proposed to.

(Break.)

JOHN: There. Another project wrapped.

LYNN: Do you remember the last time we watched the sun rise on the twenty-eighth floor?

JOHN: Yes.

LYNN: Would you like to again?

JOHN: Not today.

LYNN: What's going wrong?

JOHN: I don't know. Things just feel different.

LYNN: What do we do about it?

JOHN: We keep going. We see what happens. You're the one who always believed in fate.

LYNN: Ah, yes. Fate. The other, only slightly less profane four letter f-word.

(Break.)

JOHN: I haven't seen you around as much lately in the office.

LYNN: That bothers you?

JOHN: Yes.

LYNN: Wow, you admitted to something openly. It must really bother you.

JOHN: I want to try and make things work, too, you know.

LYNN: You're the one who wanted to hide our relationship in the office.

JOHN: I thought we got past that.

LYNN: I was just getting used to the idea.

JOHN: I don't believe it.

LYNN: What we have here is a failure to communicate. Maybe if you weren't so flippant and nonchalant I'd know what you're thinking more.

JOHN: Maybe if you wouldn't sit there and wait to see if I did what you wanted, while you intentionally avoid giving me a hint as to what that may be so I'll magically figure it out for myself, I'd have a chance at satisfying your needs in our relationship which, believe it or not, is what I've always wanted to do.

LYNN: Wow. I didn't realize you ever stopped to think about my needs.

JOHN: That's not fair.

LYNN: You're right. It's not fair to expect that you'd think you ever need to stop to satisfy me since you finish faster than it takes for you to roll over and go to sleep.

(Break.)

LYNN: It's nice to be working on a project together again.

JOHN: It would be if you'd stop trying to fix our lives long enough to fix our statistics.

LYNN: I'm sorry.

JOHN: No you're not really. You're just being agreeable to make peace.

LYNN: You can have your wrong opinion. But if that's how you feel, I'll stop.

JOHN: Fine.

LYNN: You know what I'm thinking?

JOHN: That we worked better together when we hated each other.

LYNN: Love and hate are closely related emotions.

JOHN: You and your cereal box philosophy.

LYNN: God I hate you.

JOHN: That's probably why you broke up with me.

LYNN: At least that way me might get some work done.

JOHN: Well, then let's get it done. I don't want to deal with anything else right now.

(Break.)

LYNN: Let's just get our work done.

JOHN: You're much too critical and absorbed in your perception of the world. No wonder you're divorced.

LYNN: You're insufferable. No wonder you're not married.

JOHN: And somehow I'll again suffer through a partner who has no sense of humor when she's working.

LYNN: How am I supposed to keep working with someone as irreverent and sarcastic as you?

JOHN: You're entitled to your wrong opinion.

LYNN: I really hate you.

(Blackout.)

END OF PLAY

SAN FRANCISCO FEVER
by Anne Adams
(suggested by a short story, *Roman Fever*, by Edith Wharton)

FIRST PERFORMANCE
January 1999

ORIGINAL CAST

Angela Throckmorton . . . . .Billie Harris
Eunice Hoskins . . . . .Jean Weisz
Directed by . . . . .Leonard Maestas
Sets by . . . . .Mark Hopkins

CHARACTERS

ANGELA THROCKMORTON: Mid-seventies, widow of Walter Throckmorton, former U.S. Ambassador to Rome, Paris, Special Envoy to Moscow, Beijing, etc. Expensively dressed, coat with fur collar.

EUNICE HOSKINS: Mid-seventies, widow of Robert Hoskins, former principal of high school in which Eunice taught English until her retirement. Sensibly, plainly dressed.

TIME
The present.

PLACE
Outdoor terrace tea garden on top of fashionable hotel in San Francisco with view of Golden Gate Park.

SAN FRANCISCO FEVER

At rise, Angela and Eunice are standing at the parapet, looking towards the park.

ANGELA: Golden Gate Park. That should bring back memories.
EUNICE: It's so different now.
ANGELA: But the Begonia Gardens are still there. You should remember them.
EUNICE: It was a memorable trip!
   (Beat.)
   You must miss Walter a lot.
ANGELA: Yes . . . Very much.
   (Beat.)
   The sun is getting low . . . We should finish our tea.
   (They return to their table. Eunice gets knitting out of bag.)
ANGELA: That was an awfully nice letter of condolence you wrote.
EUNICE: I wanted to write. It was such a shock when I read the obituary in *Newsweek*. *(Pause.)* You didn't know my Robert had passed away, too. *(Pause.)* I don't think you ever met him.
ANGELA: No. I wish I had known him. He must have been a very nice man.
EUNICE: Yes. Yes, he was.
   (Beat.)
   I felt I owed myself a trip.
ANGELA: I'm glad you came this way.
EUNICE: You said to call if I ever did.
   (Beat.)
   I've been able to keep up with you and Walter through the newspapers. What an exciting life: important people, exotic places, dazzling receptions. I wonder you could keep up . . . with him.
ANGELA: I managed, dear. They even called me his "right hand man."
EUNICE: His right hand . . . man?
   (Silence.)
EUNICE: *(Continued.)* My life hasn't changed much. I still have my volunteer work, book club, prize begonias . . .
ANGELA: Ah, begonias . . . Maybe it was here in San Francisco that you began to . . . like them.
   (Beat.)
   But you must not have a very pleasant memory of our trip out here.
EUNICE: Oh, yes . . . yes. It was an event — it was very important for me.

ANGELA: But it ended so badly.
(Beat.)
I've always felt a big guilty . . .
EUNICE: Oh no! You couldn't help it — my getting so sick and having to go home.
ANGELA: But you must have been . . . disappointed.
EUNICE: I suppose I was. San Francisco was such an exciting place during the war. All the sailors . . .
ANGELA: Do you remember the ride out from Chicago? Three nights on the train with those rowdy sailors? *(Eunice smiles.)* I was surprised when you flirted with them. Especially the one we called "the Octopus." It would have horrified mother! She never would have let me go on the trip if you hadn't come with me. *(Imitates mother.)* "You are not going alone on the train to San Francisco. You must go with some good responsible person. Perhaps Eunice Banks. She seems such a nice girl." She remembered you from the North Shore Country Day School.
EUNICE: I felt a little like a paid companion.
ANGELA: Mother thought you were "worthy."
EUNICE: You must have hated me!
ANGELA: Oh no. You turned out to be more interesting than I thought.
(Long pause.)
You know, no one had any idea you and Robert were serious. You hardly spoke of him on our trip together.
EUNICE: Everything was undecided.
ANGELA: But right after our trip, you were married — in Grand Rapids! And you didn't come home . . . for years. Just . . . disappeared.
EUNICE: Robert got a teaching job in Grand Rapids right away.
ANGELA: And you taught English . . . ?
EUNICE: Thirty-five years. I started when Jason was in first grade.
ANGELA: Ah, Jason! What a marvelous career he's gone on to! Please, I mean this in the most admiring way . . . I always wondered how two such exemplary people produced someone as dynamic as Jason. Another smash Broadway play! The last time we were in New York, we caught the opening of "The Wrath of the Borgias." We couldn't get near him afterwards. It was like a mob scene from Julius Caesar!
(Beat.)
Our Paul always seemed so much less . . . vivid.
EUNICE: A son of Walter's should be . . . vivid!

ANGELA: Well, if I were an invalid, I'd certainly rather be in Paul's hands. I always wanted a brilliant son . . . and got a saint instead.

EUNICE: *(Keeps on knitting.)* Jason did bring some excitement into our lives . . . *(Angela walks again to the parapet and looks out over city.)*

ANGELA: *(Pause.)* It's beautiful at dusk.

(Eunice puts her knitting in her lap.)

EUNICE: It was so long ago . . .

ANGELA: I haven't forgotten.

(Beat.)

You even flirted with *Walter*, though he and I were already engaged. *(Long pause.)* He did look handsome in his naval officer's uniform!

EUNICE: He was a good-looking man.

ANGELA: He seemed flattered when you kept looking at him in that restaurant in Fishermen's Wharf. I admit I was a bit jealous!

(Beat.)

You didn't pay any attention to the ensign he brought.

(Eunice ostentatiously doesn't respond.)

ANGELA: You were full of surprises on that trip — going out by yourself just after dark to Golden Gate Park — even though you had a 'delicate throat.'

EUNICE: It was such a beautiful night.

ANGELA: "I'm going to see the moon rise" — so you said.

EUNICE: Goodness! My very words.

ANGELA: People said it was that expedition that caused your illness — your fever.

EUNICE: Is that what you told them?

ANGELA: Well, you were always thought of as being so prudent.

EUNICE: And that's what *you* thought . . . until that night?

ANGELA: Mother held you up so . . .

(Beat.)

It showed how superficial *she* was!

EUNICE: . . . Perhaps everybody was . . . in those days.

ANGELA: Yes. Perhaps it's just as well they didn't look under the surface.

(Long pause.)

There is something . . . that's been on my conscience all these years.

(Eunice stares at Angela.)

ANGELA: I know why you went!

(Long silence.)

ANGELA: Why you went out into the park that night!

EUNICE: To see the moon rise — by the begonias . . .

ANGELA: Begonias! You went to meet Walter!

(Eunice gasps.)

ANGELA: Yes, Walter! Not only that, but I can repeat every word of the letter that took you there:

"My darling. I must see you alone. Come to Golden Gate Park right after dark tomorrow. I'll meet you by the Begonia Gardens."

Signed,
Only your,
Walter

(Pause.)

ANGELA: Now, dear. You needn't blush. Walter and I never spoke of your little escapade.

EUNICE: You must have! How could you know? *(Pause.)* I burned the letter.

ANGELA: Yes. You would, naturally — you're so prudent.

(Beat.)

And, if you burnt the letter, you're wondering how on earth I know what was in it. That's it, isn't it?

(No answer.)

ANGELA: Well my dear, I know what was in that letter because . . . I wrote it!

EUNICE: *You* wrote it?

ANGELA: Yes. I wrote it.

(Silence.)

EUNICE: It was the only letter I ever had from him. . .

ANGELA: I wrote it. Yes, I wrote it! *(Pause.)* I was the girl he was engaged to. Did you happen to remember that?

EUNICE: I'm not trying to excuse myself.

ANGELA: And still you went.

EUNICE: Still I went.

ANGELA: I knew you were in love with Walter — I was afraid; afraid of you, of your quiet ways, your sweetness . . . afraid Walter was beginning to be attracted to you too.

(No reply.)

ANGELA: *(Beat.)* I wanted you to feel humiliated — rejected! *(Pause.)* And mad at *him*, too! I was in a blind fury when I wrote that letter!

(Beat.)

I don't know why I'm telling you now.

EUNICE: You've always hated me!

(Pause.)

ANGELA: Of course I never thought you'd get so sick you'd have to go home . . .

EUNICE: . . . the only letter I had . . .

ANGELA: Ah! You still care for him! All these years you've been living on that letter — treasuring the mere memory of its ashes!
(Beat.)
You tried your best to get him away from me, didn't you! But you failed! And I kept him! That's all.

EUNICE: Yes. That's all.

ANGELA: I wish now I hadn't told you. *(Pause.)* It all happened so long ago, as you say; I had no reason to think you'd ever taken it seriously.
(Beat.)
As soon as you could get out of bed your mother rushed you off to marry Robert Hoskins. *(Pause.)* People wondered at its being done so quickly but I thought I knew. You did it out of *pique* — to be able to say you got married ahead of Walter and me. Girls have such silly reasons for doing the most serious things.

EUNICE: Sometimes they do . . .

ANGELA: Girls in love are ferocious. I remember laughing to myself all that evening at the idea that you were waiting around there in the dark, dodging out of sight, listening for every sound.
(Beat.)
But I wasn't completely heartless. Of course I was upset when I heard you were so ill after . . . waiting and waiting.

EUNICE: But I didn't wait. *(Pause.)*
He was there.

ANGELA: Walter?

EUNICE: But of course he was there.

ANGELA: How did he know you'd be there?

EUNICE: I answered the letter. I told him I'd be there. So he came.

ANGELA: Oh God — you answered! I never thought of your answering . . .

EUNICE: It's odd you never thought of it, if you wrote the letter.

ANGELA: I was blind with rage.

EUNICE: *(Rises, gathers up knitting.)* . . . I'm sorry for you.

ANGELA: I don't know why you should be sorry for me!

EUNICE: Because I didn't have to wait that night.

ANGELA: Yes. I oughtn't to begrudge that to you, I suppose. After all, I had everything. I had him for thirty-five years, and you had nothing but that one letter that he didn't write.
(Silence.)

EUNICE: *(Starts to leave, then turns and looks at Angela.)* But I had Jason.
(Long, stark silence.)

ANGELA: *(Rises, shivers and draws fur around her shoulders.)* It is getting cold. We should go in.
(She follows Eunice out.)
(Curtain.)

END OF PLAY

SIMÓN MALDONADO'S EPIPHANY
by Juan Duarte

FIRST PERFORMANCE
January 1997

ORIGINAL CAST

Simón . . . . Oscar Davila
Nacho/Priest . . . . Jaime Avelar Guzman
La Diosa . . . . Teresa Marie
Guard . . . . Avondina Wills
Doctor . . . . Malte Frid-Nielsen
Directed by . . . . Leonard Maestas
Sets by . . . . Donna Teague

CHARACTERS

SIMÓN: A Mexican man in his late twenties, early thirties, not fat or thin, not handsome or homely. He wears an orange prison jumpsuit. His manner is alternately frenetic and nervously jerky then cool, street-wise and deliberately casual as he moves about, sits and talks to the priest.

PRIEST: A Mexican man, same age as Simón, in priestly garb. His face is sad, almost tearful. His movements are nervous. He is fearful and apprehensive, glancing toward the door repeatedly, even walking to the door and peering out through the glass, as if to call for someone to come, then walking around the room with his back to the walls, fingering a small prayer book and a rosary. He crosses himself now and then, avoiding eye contact with Simón.

GUARD: Big black man, fiftyish, with a blank expressionless face but his eyes dart about the room, avoiding eye contact with both Simón and the Priest.

A DOCTOR: Man in white lab coat, with stethoscope.

OFF STAGE VOICE: Resonant, low-pitched woman's voice with echo effect.

THE SCENE

A stark, bare, windowless room painted a sickly light green containing only a rectangular steel fold-up table and two steel folding chairs. The wall at stage right has a heavy door (steel or wood) with a 12"x18" wire glass view panel in upper center. A dim orange-yellow light comes through. The entire action occurs in this room.

SIMÓN MALDONADO'S EPIPHANY

Stage is in total darkness as voice is heard.

VOICE: He murdered me and burned down my Santeria. *(Pause.)* Now he waits to die. *(Low laugh.)* At one minute after midnight tonight *(Long pause.)*, he comes to ME!
(Tableau: As voice ceases, lights slowly start to illuminate the room. Simón is seated at the table, arms out to the sides, hands gripping the table edge. The priest is standing stock still, head bowed. Lights get brighter and suddenly come full on, in a flash. At this moment Simón starts to speak and the priest starts pacing.)

SIMÓN: . . . and I sent for you because the gringo chaplain here pisses me off and because you're from the Barrio like me. But I gotta tell you! I never believed all that crap we got in catechism. *(Looks over at Priest who is nervously shifting from one foot to the other. Priest shakes his head no and begins pacing.)* Sit down, Nacho! Hey, ese, I hope you understand but I can't call you *(Sarcastically.)* "PADRECITO." Shit, Nacho — we grew up like brothers, ese. We raised hell together! Didn't we? Didn't we — until your Mama sent you to the seminary so you wouldn't wind up in "juvy" like me, remember? Remember you and her wanted me to go to the seminary with you? *(Starts to express anger more and more.)* You were no better than me *(Mocking.)* PADRECITO! *(Priest jerks away and goes to the door for the first time and peers out.)*
(Simón continues, rising from chair violently and strides about the room flailing his arms and shouting.)

SIMÓN: But I didn't cop out and be a Jesus freak like you! Sure I fucked up *(Stalks priest who tries to avoid facing him.)* but maybe you did too, Nacho. All your prayers never got you that piece of Yolanda's ass you wanted so bad, did it?

PRIEST: Simón! I never, NEVER wanted to be with Yolanda! We were like brothers — you're right, Simón. Yolanda gave herself to all the other vatos in the barrio — you knew that! But you wanted her all to yourself. We were only fourteen and she was already eighteen and all the vatos had had her, Simón. How many of them did you beat up? And you even made me help, remember? You made me hold Jose Cano down while you broke his nose — and I pretended not to see when you kicked his *(Short pause then rushing the word.)* balls and I didn't snitch when you *(Pause.)* — when,

God forgive me, when *WE* beat Pablo Cruz so bad, although I only held him for you — that he went into a coma and then he *DIED*, Simón! *(Crosses himself over and over, then continues.)* God knows that I repent for that and all my other sins and HE forgives me. *(Priest hesitates.)* But I don't know if I can forgive *myself!* I pray for them all. I pray for you, Simón. I even pray for Yolanda!

SIMÓN: For Yolanda's *ass* you prayed, Padrecito! *(Exploding with guilt and anger.)* Well, *I* didn't have to pray for it, Nacho! She *gave* it to me! Lots of times! So maybe you never did hard time in fucking jails — but you never got any of Yolanda's ass neither! *(Here, Simón's anger is spent. His body sags and he slumps down in a chair and stares at his hands. Not looking at Priest, who has hurried to the door again, looking anxious through the panel, he mutters.)* Aw, hell, Nacho — forget it!

PRIEST: *(At door, looking back over right shoulder, but down, not at Simón.)* It's — it's all right Simón. But I need to give you the last rites. That's why I'm here. That's why you sent for me, isn't it? Repent and pray with me and God will . . . *(Voice trails off as he tries to catch Simón's words.)*

SIMÓN: *(Softly, low-pitched, talking to himself.)* . . . maybe if I'd gone to the seminario with Nacho instead of hanging out in the Santerias . . . *(Thought trails off, then, louder but still low-voiced.)* You ever go to a Santeria, Nacho? *(Priest shakes his head no, vigorously.)* No, I didn't think so.

(Simón continues in a low voice.) It's weird in those places, ese! And the weird brujos and brujas who run them. Some look like wrinkled old mummies — and others look like their skin is made of dried shit and they *stink* like it! But the weirdest was La Diosa. Can you believe that ugly old bitch calling herself The Goddess?! That fuckin' bruja tried to drive me crazy! *(Voice pitch rises.)* She tried to *make* me, man! There in her Goddamn place where there were other ugly things, like dried-up fish and animal skins hanging from hooks. And on a shelf there was a big glass jar and inside was floating a BABY'S HEAD, Nacho! I shit you not, ese! A baby's head with yellow eyes looking at me! And — and — on a table there were all these bultos — some wrapped in burlap, some in plastic bags — bundles for putting the curse on somebody and for making a woman go for you. That's what I was after in there — so I could get Yolanda not to fuck nobody but me! But La Diosa laughed at me with her big brown snaggle-teeth and tried to grab my balls! *(Breathing hard and rapidly now.)* That's when I hit her, ese. *Hit!* And *hit!* And then with my knife. . . *(Hitting and stabbing motions, then drops hands down to his crotch, head*

up, eyes closed, pelvis thrusting orgasmically, after which a long pause, then he resumes pacing, wiping hands on his front as if hands were bloody.)

SIMÓN: *(In an almost casual voice.)* I almost did go nuts in there, ese. The dumbshit lawyer they gave me tried to make me say I *was* nuts at the time. *(Starts striding, voice rising, fiercely shaking a finger "no"!)* But I wasn't nuts when I killed that bitch bruja! I was cool, calm and collected after I hit her the first time. Because I knew I was doing a good thing, man. She tried to put a curse on me. But I got *her* before she got me!

(Priest goes to door second time, fearful, now.)

SIMÓN: *(The Priest's quick movement seems to remind Simón of the Priest's words.)* Repent? Repent? For what! It was self-defense, ese! *(Voice gets shrill and trembly.)* I oughta get a *medal* for it instead!

(Tableau: At this point, lights dim and action-freeze on stage. Off stage voice begins.)

VOICE: Simón. *(Long pause.)* Look behind you. *(Simón, who has been facing stage rear, starts a slow-motion turn, and finally is facing audience, eyes focused above their heads.)* Do you see those two doors? *(Simón nods dumbly, lone spotlight on his face only.)* One leads to heaven and one leads to HELL! Which one do you choose, Simón? *(Simón slowly raises a shaky hand and points.)* At exactly 12:01 tonight you'll know if you chose right, Simón. *(Lights up full stage and action resumes.)*

SIMÓN: *(Still staring over audience's heads, hands clasped at breast.)* Nacho, I'm going to heaven. I know which is the right door, ese. *(Turns toward Priest who starts to back away toward door.)* God forgives every sinner. Isn't that what we learned in catechism? Isn't that what you just said?

PRIEST: Simón, God only forgives if . . .

SIMÓN: He forgives *ME* because I got rid of the bruja, ese! *(Pause. Then he smiles a ghastly smile, staring at the Priest.)* Who knows, ese, maybe I'll soon be seated at the right hand of God. *(Leans toward Priest.)* I'll put in a good word for you, Nacho.

PRIEST: *(Hurries to door, taps at glass and begins to cross himself over and over.)* May God have mercy on your soul, Simón Maldonado. *(Voice cracks. Guard's face appears in glass viewing panel. There is the sound of keys, the door opens and the Priest rushes out. The guard closes and re-locks the door. Simón now sits in chair facing audience, hands still clasped at breast, eyes focused above their heads.)*

(Tableau: Lights dim — no action on stage.)

VOICE: Simón! *(No response.)* Those doors? They don't lead to hell, Simón, or to heaven, either. *(Long pause. then, in a coy sexy tone.)* Simón, they lead to *ME*. *(Pause.)* I'm waiting, Simón! *(Lights up to harshest, brightest.)* *(There is the sound of keys again, the door opens and the guard enters carrying a hospital gown followed by a white-coated doctor wearing a stethoscope and carrying a clipboard. They stand in the doorway. Guard looks away back down the corridor. The doctor looks down at the clipboard then slowly raises thick-lensed, bespectacled eyes up and focuses on Simón, who has not moved, still staring over audience heads. Pause.)*

SIMÓN: *(Softly.)* Padre. *(His eyes slowly roll to his left, to the guard and to his executioner. Then screams:)* PADRECITO!
(Lights go out. Blackness.)

END OF PLAY

SLINGIN' HASH AT THE LOWLIFE BAR AND GRILL
by Susan Forrest

FIRST PERFORMANCE
January 1997

ORIGINAL CAST

Paul/Dancer . . . . .Jack Lawton
Carol/Dancer . . . . .Kelly Hatcher
Receptionist/Angie . . . . .Virginia Draper
Blondie/Betty . . . . .Marjorie Young
Uptight Man/Dave . . . . .Steve "Spike" Wong
Beautiful . . . . .Hope Nicora
Man in Cap/Chauffeur . . . . .Lawrence Thompson
Directed by . . . . .Jim Clark
Sets by . . . . .Donna Teague

CHARACTERS (Seven Actors)
RECEPTIONIST/ANGIE
CAROL
PAUL
BEAUTIFUL
UPTIGHT MAN/DAVE
MAN IN CAP/BLUE-EYED BOB/CHAUFFEUR
BLONDIE/BETTY

SETTING
An unemployment office in a small city.

TIME
Mid-morning.

SLINGIN' HASH AT THE LOWLIFE BAR & GRILL

Scene 1

> *An unemployment office. Seven chairs and three tables line the room. A number-dispenser sits on reception desk at one end of the room. There are two exits: behind the desk leading to the inner offices, and the street exit at opposite end of the room. The receptionist is on the phone for most of the scene. She will talk for a while, hang up, the phone will ring softly again, she'll pick it up, repeat. Seated around the room are: Carol and Paul, Uptight Man, Man in Cap (baseball cap pulled down over his forehead, will doze through scene) and his wife, Blondie.*
> *Carol sits, staring straight ahead. Paul watches for a while before speaking.*

PAUL: Don't worry. You qualify. You'll get unemployment for sure.

CAROL: Oh, God, I hope so . . . but it's still not enough to pay for the rent, let alone daycare. I just *have* to find another job!

PAUL: I'll help you find free daycare, Carol. And you will find another job. I mean, just look at what you've accomplished in a year. You're off the streets, you're clean and sober, you gave birth to a healthy baby, and you've held down an office job for 12 months! I'm so proud of you. *(He puts his arm around her.)*

CAROL: And I've spent every day for two weeks looking for another filing clerk job. My rent is $450 a month, Paul. *(Looks at him.)* Oh, I'm sorry. I don't mean to drag you down with me.

PAUL: How could you drag me down . . . I love you, sis. Look, maybe I could help you. I could drop one of my classes and give you $10 a week out of my tips.

CAROL: Paul, you're an actor, for God's sake. Actors never have any money. No, I have to find a way to do it by myself.

PAUL: I'll find a way to help you, Carol, I will. I swear I will.

> *(An old woman enters, carrying a big shoulder bag and holding a soup spoon. She walks to the desk, gets a number, stuffs it in a pocket. Coming to the room's center, she tosses the spoon deftly back and forth between her hands.)*

BEAUTIFUL: Pretty good, eh? That's a little trick I picked up in the Yukon, slingin' hash at the Lowlife Bar and Grill. Jeez, it seems like so long ago . . . twelve years . . . twelve years of my life wasted away in that freezin' hellhole. Why, you practically had to spread your legs every time a produce truck blew into town, it was *that* hard to find fresh vegetables in the Yukon. Gawd, I'll never forget —

UPTIGHT MAN: Madam, could we please watch your language? And while we're at it, we might lower our voice a —

BEAUTIFUL: *(Crosses to him, sits down beside him.)* I'll bet *we're* asking why I sacrificed twelve years of my youth at the Lowlife? *(He shakes his head 'no' furiously.)* Because I *owned* the bloody joint, that's why! When my ma died, you see, I had nothin'. Nothin'! She left me $2500, so I decided to go out in the world and make somethin' of myself. Moved up north and bought me a bar for $2000. Then I staked a fool gold claim with the remainin' $500. Two years later I put the place up for sale. Jeez, it was ten years before anyone bought it. Some yuppies from Saskatoon hot to open the 'First Espresso House in the Yukon.' Hah! If it wasn't *me* who was sellin' the place, I'da told them: "Kids, this is the Yukon. How the hell do you think you're gonna get fresh milk after your first week is up? *(Gets up, directing questions around the room.)* Let's see ... uh, from *wolf* milk? No, wait, how about *caribou* cream? Or ... or ... maybe you could whip up some ... *bear butter!*" *(Sits beside Paul.)* Yeah, that's what I'da said: "How about some *bear butter* to spread on some of those ... uh ... those *cappuccino* cookies you're gonna make outta them *penguin eggs?*" *(Blondie smiles and nods furiously at everything Beautiful says, thinking her extremely wise. Everyone laughs except Uptight Man. To Paul and Carol ...)*

BEAUTIFUL: Say, you look like a nice couple. Fallen on bad times, have you?

PAUL: *(Embarrassed because everyone's looking.)* Well, no ... I mean, not me. My sister was laid off.

BEAUTIFUL: Aw, Jeez, I'm real sorry to hear that, honey. Did somebody 'downsize' you?

CAROL: Why yes, that's exactly what happened.

BEAUTIFUL: Bad luck, kid. *(She reaches in front of Paul to pat Carol's knee. Paul shrinks back, involuntarily.)* What about your husband? Does he work?

CAROL: Oh, I'm ... uh ... on my own. It's my baby I'm worried about, not me ... and the apartment. I don't want to end up on the street. *(She cries silently, Paul puts his arm around her.)*

BEAUTIFUL: Fuckers! *(Gets up abruptly, walks around the room again.)* Jeez, the words they use these days! Downsizing. Why? Because words like 'downsizing' make it easier for them executives to sleep at night! Downsizing! As meaningless as all them bloodless New Age words they use these days. *(Pointing to Uptight Man, who is self-conscious.)* Let's say you're the boss. You say, "We're terribly sorry, we're downsizing, restructuring the company. So we must let you go." *(To Carol.)* And you say very politely, "Oh, that's all right, sir. My Inner Child is upset, and I sure wish I knew where my Guardian Angel was right now, but the Goddess within me says I'm going to be just fine!" Twenty years ago, the boss woulda said, "You're laid off. Sorry." And you woulda said, "Yeah, well thanks, sir. And by the way, I saw your wife kissing the security guard in the parking lot last night!" *(Everybody laughs except the Uptight Man.)*

BEAUTIFUL: *(Sitting beside Paul again.)* Sorry to go off like that, kids. Sometimes I get a little carried away with myself.

CAROL: Oh, that's okay. I haven't laughed in a week. It feels good.

BEAUTIFUL: So what're your names, kids?

CAROL: Carol.

PAUL: Paul.

BEAUTIFUL: Beautiful.

PAUL: Thank you.

BEAUTIFUL: What? Oh, no . . . no, that's my name. Beautiful.

PAUL: *(Laughing.)* Well, pleased to meet you, beautiful. *(Paul shakes her hand.)*

BEAUTIFUL: Bet I'm the oldest woman you ever said *that* to.

CAROL: I like your name.

BEAUTIFUL: Nickname, really. My real name is Mary Smith. Bet you're wonderin' how —

RECEPTIONIST: *(Loudly, waking Man in Cap.)* Number . . . *(Carol, Man in Cap, and Uptight Man all look down at their stubs, start to rise out of their seats.)* . . . Number Two Hundred and Sixty-Four. *(All sit back, disappointed, except Man in Cap, who goes to reception desk.)* All right, someone can see you now, sir. Just go through the door here, pass four doors, turn right, then walk to the end of that hall, turn right again, pass seven offices, turn left, and go into the sixth office on your right. That's Miss Steven's office, Room 1803.

BEAUTIFUL: *(Looking across to Blondie.)* As I was saying, bet you're wonderin' how I got the name Beautiful, right? *(Blondie nods eagerly.)* Well, I'll tell you. It was given to me by the most interestin' man I ever met, on the night of the Grand Re-opening of the Lowlife Bar and Grill . . . *(Blackout.)*

Scene 2

The Lowlife Bar and Grill. The reception desk has been rotated and is now a bar. A shelf full of liquor bottles and glasses has been added behind the bar. Tables and chairs are re-arranged upstage bar style, with space for a dance floor. Upbeat '60s country music plays, continuing through the scene. Drunken Couple (actors who played Carol and Paul) are holding each other up on the dance floor, swaying to the music. Betty (Blondie) leans against the bar, drinking beer with the lecherous Dave (Uptight Man). He whispers in her ear from time to time, and will occasionally grab her bottom. When he does this, Betty will laugh and push him away. Angie (Receptionist), the waitress, enters from kitchen (behind bar) with a plate of fries and a bottle of ketchup. She sets them down in front of Dave and Betty.

ANGIE: There you go, Dave. You can enjoy these fries while they're still hot if you can keep your hands off Betty for long enough.
BETTY: *(Laughing as Dave covers the fries with ketchup and dives into them.)* They can't be any hotter than he is! Thanks, Angie. They smell great!
(A younger and more vivacious Beautiful comes out of the kitchen. After cooking all day, she's exhausted. She wipes her hands on her apron.)
ANGIE: Hey everyone! If you haven't met her yet, say hello to Mary, our new owner.
(Betty and Dave say 'hi.' The dancers mutter and wave languidly.)
BEAUTIFUL: Hi, there. Jeez! It's good to get out of the kitchen. But it was a pretty good crowd for the first day, wouldn't you say, Angie?
(A big man swaggers into the restaurant (previously Man in Cap). He has an extra eye in the middle of his forehead. As Beautiful stares in shock, he turns to nod at the others in the restaurant. The dancing couple waves.)
BETTY/DAVE/ANGIE: Hi, Bob.
BOB: How're you doin. *(Surveys the room.)* Hey, the place looks great! *(Turns to Beautiful, who jumps. Embarrassed, she grabs a cloth from behind the bar, starts wiping.)* You must be the lady responsible for all this.
BEAUTIFUL: Uh . . . why, yes . . . yes, I am. Well, with the help of Angie here, of course.
BOB: Nice job. I see you didn't change the name, though.
BEAUTIFUL: Why change the name when the clientele hasn't changed since 1890?
(Music stops. Everyone freezes, gawking at Mary, who doesn't realize she has insulted Bob. No one insults Bob and gets away with it. Pause.)
BOB: *(Suddenly, he laughs loudly. Everybody relaxes, music resumes.)* Well, well,

she's not only beautiful but she's got a sense of humor. Angie, how about pourin' me a Jack Daniels.

ANGIE: Sure thing, Bob.

(She gets a bottle and glass from the shelf, pours a drink while he watches, then hands it to him. Beautiful has been staring at Bob's third eye again, thinking he hasn't noticed.)

BOB: *(Slamming his glass down.)* Okay, Beautiful, let's get things straightened out, then maybe we can be friends. They call me Bob, Blue-Eyed Bob. Two brown eyes beautifully balanced by this blue one here. *(Leaning forward so she can get a real good look. Beautiful shrinks back.)* Lovely, ain't it?

BEAUTIFUL: *(Awkward.)* Uh, well . . . yes, it is, I . . . I've heard about it.

BOB: What'd you hear? That I've got three eyes or that some people around here still call me a 'Cyclops'? *(Looks around the bar.)* You want to tell me who they are?

(Music stops. Everyone freezes, including Beautiful, who is scared stiff.)

BEAUTIFUL: Well, uh . . . you see . . . uh, they don't exactly call you a . . . a . . . cy — Okay, maybe they do. But no, I *don't* want to tell you who they are.

BOB: Well don't worry about it, Beautiful. If it doesn't bother me, why should it bother you? At least you didn't faint like all the others.

(Music continues. Everything goes back to normal.)

BEAUTIFUL: *(Bravely calling his bluff.)* Well, I guess I'm just not the faintin' kind. And since it doesn't bother you, can I ask you a question? Since you've got *three* eyes instead of just *one*, shouldn't they call you a 'Triclops'?

(Music stops. Everyone freezes, watching. Bob stares at Beautiful for a long time. She stares right back. Pause. Finally, he picks up his glass, downs the whiskey in one gulp, slams it down again.)

BOB: You closed Sundays? *(Beautiful nods.)* You like meat loaf with gravy and mashed potatoes? *(She nods again.)* Then why don't you come over to my place for dinner Sunday night, Beautiful?

BEAUTIFUL: *(With a sexy smile.)* Why, I can't think of anything I'd rather do, Bob.

BOB: *(Getting up.)* Good. Two miles south of here on Roaring River Road . . . big old green house. My parents built it when they moved here from Chicago with their funny-looking baby. But personally, I think three eyes are better than one, don't you? Six o'clock okay?

BEAUTIFUL: Six o'clock is fine.

BOB: *(Crossing to exit.)* Good. See you then, uh . . . What's your name, anyway?

BEAUTIFUL: Just call me Beautiful.

(Blackout.)

Scene 3

Unemployment Insurance Office. Same people as before (without Man in Cap). Receptionist is on the phone. Everyone is watching Beautiful and smiling, including Uptight Man.

CAROL: So then what happened? Did you and Bob become . . . you know . . . close? *(Pause.)* Oh, I'm sorry. I didn't mean to ask such a personal question.
UPTIGHT MAN: *(Smiling.)* What do you want to bet she's going to tell us anyway?
BEAUTIFUL: *(To Blondie.)* Think I should tell them, honey? *(Blondie nods furiously.)* Okay, I will. Blue-eyed Bob was the best lover I ever had. But it sure took me a long time to get used to looking at him while we were in the throes of passion. Two eyes closed and one big blue eye staring and winking at me. You know, he always swore he couldn't see out of that one, but I never really knew if –
RECEPTIONIST: *(Loudly.)* Number . . . *(Carol, and Uptight Man look down at their number stubs, start to rise out of their seats.)* . . . Number Two Hundred and Sixty-Five. *(Carol sits back. Uptight Man goes to reception desk.)* All right, someone can see you now, sir. Just go through the door here, turn left, go up one flight of stairs, turn left, walk to the end of the hall, turn left again, pass nine offices, turn left, and go into the second office on your right. That's Mr. Brimley's office, Room 2117.
(Carol looks down at her stub, then at Paul. She is starting to worry again. Paul ruffles her hair in a brotherly way. Beautiful watches, smiling. She grabs her purse, rummages through it, pulls out a wallet and a pen, opens it.)
BEAUTIFUL: What's your last name, honey?
PAUL: *(Answering for Carol, who is too confused.)* It's Pearson, P-e-a-r-s-o-n.
BEAUTIFUL: *(Writes. Finishing, she rips out a check, hands it to Carol.)* Here's a little something to tide you over while you look for another job, honey. And don't worry, you'll find one soon. *(Carol and Paul stare at it, dumbfounded.)*
(A big man with a mustache and wearing a chauffeur's hat and jacket enters the room, spots Beautiful.)
CHAUFFEUR: We better get goin' now, Beautiful. You have to be at the dentist's office in fifteen minutes, remember?
BEAUTIFUL: *(Jumps up, grabs her bag.)* Oh, yeah. Gotta keep these old teeth in shape. Jeez, it was nice meetin' you all. *(Shakes hands with Paul and Carol,*

still in shock. Then she goes to Blondie, shakes her hand.) Bye, Blondie. I didn't get to know you, but you sure seem like a pleasant girl. *(Speechless, Blondie smiles and nods. Beautiful exits, followed by the Chauffeur.)*

CAROL: *(Running to door.)* Wait, Mister, wait! *(The Chauffeur comes back.)* Uh . . . Beautiful gave me this check, and . . . well, could you please give it back to her? I can't accept it, it's far too much.

CHAUFFEUR: Now why would I want to do that, ma'am?

CAROL: But it's for *Ten Thousand Dollars!*

CHAUFFEUR: Then you must need it. You see, sometimes Beautiful likes to help people. She knows what it is to be down and out. Besides, it would hurt her if you gave it back to her, so you just keep it. She's got millions . . . made a killing on a $500 investment in a gold mine a few years back. Good luck, ma'am.

(He turns to leave again. Blondie jumps up.)

BLONDIE: Wait, sir! *(The Chauffeur turns to her.)* I was wondering if . . . well, would you mind if I asked you your name?

CHAUFFEUR: So she's been talking about me, has she? Well, ma'am, the name's Bob, Blue-Eyed Bob.

(Bob takes off his cap, exposing his eye, sweeps the cap through the air to his chest, and takes a deep bow.)

(Blackout.)

(In darkness: a bloodcurdling SCREAM is followed by a THUD.)

END OF PLAY

SNACK TIME
by Eric Elliot

FIRST PERFORMANCE
January 2001

ORIGINAL CAST
    Woman . . . . .Janine Theodore
    Coyote . . . . Jim Eckhart
    Satan . . . . .Brian Trybom
    Directed by . . . . .Sarah Albertson
    Sets by . . . . .William "Skip" Epperson

SNACK TIME

Lights up on a desert.
Enter the Woman, dressed in khaki shorts and a flannel shirt, carrying a backpack. She is badly sunburnt.

WOMAN: Hello! Hello! Can anybody hear me? Oh God! *(She takes off her pack and pulls a water bottle out of it. There is only a tiny amount left.)* No sense in saving it. *(She drinks the water and throws away the bottle.)* Well, that's it. What a stupid way to die. I wonder how long it will take?
(Enter Coyote, dressed in jeans, cowboy boots and a flannel shirt. A coyote mask covers his head, a tail protrudes from his jeans.)
COYOTE: You must be lost.
WOMAN: *(Screams in surprise.)* Aahh!
COYOTE: *(Surprised by the Woman's scream, screams.)* Aaahhh!
WOMAN: I must be hallucinating!
COYOTE: Jeez! You scared me. I thought maybe a monster was sneaking up on me. They do that, sometimes.
WOMAN: You — You're a coyote!
COYOTE: I'm not *a* coyote, I'm *the* Coyote!
(The Woman just stares at him.)
COYOTE: You know — The Trickster. The one who scattered the stars across the sky. *(Beat.)* Oh come on! I'm the guy who stole fire from the gods for you ungrateful hairless monkeys!
WOMAN: You can't be real. I don't believe this.
COYOTE: *(In a hurt tone.)* I don't believe you haven't heard of me.
WOMAN: Sorry.
COYOTE: Ah, that's OK, it's not your fault, it's the schools now days . . . say, you got anything to eat? It smells like there's something in your bag.
WOMAN: Uh, well, I think I've got a couple of granola bars left. *(She digs around in her pack and pulls out two bars.)* You really are talking?
COYOTE: No, I'm not.
WOMAN: What? But you are!
COYOTE: Yeah, I am, but if you knew the answer, why'd you ask? Is this all you've got?
WOMAN: I've been out here for four days! I've run out of everything!
COYOTE: *(Unwraps bar and starts eating it.)* Well, I can see why you saved these for last; they're disgusting! What are you doing out here anyway?

WOMAN: This was my boyfriend's idea. I don't go for the New Age stuff much, but he's totally into it. He arranged this . . .
COYOTE: Where is he? Does he have any food on him?
WOMAN: He's back in Seattle. His jerk of a boss came up with a bunch of work for him at the last moment. He did it on purpose too, because the last time I visited John at work, Mr. Slime-Bag patted me on the ass and propositioned me! As if! I don't care how much gold jewelry he wears, he's fifty, fat and bald! I told him if he touched me again I'd Mace him. He *knew* we'd planned this trip; he just did it to get revenge. John spent a lot of money on this trip and it wasn't refundable, so he insisted I go without him.
COYOTE: Oh. *(Coyote unwraps the second bar and begins to eat it.)* This stuff is really terrible.
WOMAN: You want terrible? *(The Woman pulls a brochure out of her backpack and holds it out to Coyote.)* An authentic "Native-American Spirit-Quest." This "Once-in-a-Lifetime Mystical Experience" turned out to be the most miserable camping trip I've ever been on! It's a furnace out here in the daytime, and it's *freezing* out here at night! Everything's poisonous or has spikes on it, and I didn't even get a tent! Now I'm talking to . . . I *think* I'm talking to . . . I wonder if heatstroke makes you see things?
COYOTE: *(Looks curiously at the brochure.)* Adam Red Horse? Adam Red Horse is running this scam? He's as crooked as a dog's hind leg! Used to sell "Sacred" Zuni fetish figures at the rest stop at the top of Oak Creek Canyon. Had 'em made in Tijuana — plastic. You can't blame him, though. Everybody needs a few tricks to get along. There's a lot of skinny honest people around. Now, Adam Red Horse, he's sure not starving! I think his jeans have a forty-eight inch waist. Yeah, he's pretty tricky, but what does he get from leaving some tourist out here with no food?
WOMAN: I was only going to be out here for three days. I was supposed to hike back to the highway and meet him yesterday, but I got turned around somehow. The cheap compass he gave me didn't work, and now I'm lost and out of water . . . *and* food.
(Coyote waves the last bit of the granola bar in a "cheers" gesture.)
WOMAN: I'm afraid I'm going to die out here.
COYOTE: Lots of people do. *(Coyote bends down and picks up a small bone and sniffs at it.)* See? Rabbit.
WOMAN: Ugh! Listen, if you're not a hallucination . . .
(Enter Satan. He is dressed in a business suit. He has horns and a barbed tail. His skin, his tie and his socks are bright red.)
WOMAN: *(Sees Satan and screams.)* Aahh!

COYOTE: *(Surprised by the Woman's scream, again, screams.)* Aaahhh! Damn! Quit doing that!

SATAN: Jonathan Sykes! I have come for your soul!

WOMAN: Oh no! I *am* seeing things!

COYOTE: Well, if you don't like seeing things, try closing your eyes.

SATAN: *(Looks around.)* Where is Jonathan Sykes?

WOMAN: John? He — he couldn't come. He had to work.

SATAN: *(Satan pulls out an organizer and flips through it. He tucks it under one arm and pulls out a palm-pilot and punches a few buttons, then holds it out to The Woman.)* Look! Jonathan Sykes, Middle-of-Nowhere, Arizona, today, 2 P.M. Where is he?

WOMAN: He's at work. He couldn't come. You see, his . . .

SATAN: I can't believe this! *(He pulls out a cell phone and dials.)* Get me Asmodeus! No I don't want his voice-mail! *(Listens for a beat.)* I AM THE PRINCE OF DARKNESS, AND I . . . Oh, all right, I'll hold!

WOMAN: *(To Coyote.)* That's the Devil!

COYOTE: Oh, I like *that! The* Devil! And I'm just *a* coyote! Don't you think there are other devils?

SATAN: What do you mean, "the network's down"? I don't even have a description, how am I going to find . . . *(He slowly turns and looks at the Woman. He flips the cell phone shut.)*

WOMAN: What?

SATAN: You know Jonathan Sykes. Where is he?

WOMAN: At work. In Seattle.

SATAN: *(Puts away the phone and gets out the palm-pilot.)* Address?

WOMAN: You're kidding.

SATAN: DO I LOOK LIKE I'M KIDDING?

COYOTE: You *look* like you dressed for the wrong party. Those shoes aren't made for the desert, you know.

SATAN: Stay out of this, trickster.

WOMAN: Please, what do you want with Jonathan?

SATAN: *Address?*

WOMAN: I'm not telling you anything until you answer me.

SATAN: *(He glares at her for a moment and then holds out the palm-pilot to her.)* There! Everything is in order. Two weeks ago Jonathan Sykes performed an ancient ritual of summoning. Now, after a fortnight, his soul is mine! *(He chuckles.)* He didn't even ask for anything in return!

WOMAN: Wait a minute! I recognize this. It's just that New-Agey squiggly design he put up over his door for good luck. He got it out of "New Magick" magazine!

SATAN: Well, he must have made a little mistake when he copied it. What a shame. One should be very careful when one dabbles with the dark arts.

COYOTE: You're tellin' me. That time at Mishongnovi when I . . .

SATAN: Shut up!

COYOTE: *(To the Woman.)* Jeez! This guy has no manners. Are you going to lose your boyfriend to some goblin with latté stain on his tie? *(To Satan.)* Made you look.

WOMAN: *(To Satan.)* Please. It was an accident. John didn't now what he was doing.

SATAN: That makes no difference. *(He taps the palm-pilot.)* The accounts are out of balance. I am owed a soul.

WOMAN: Well, you're not going to get John's. I'm not going to tell you anything!

SATAN: You can't save him. As soon as those damned imbeciles in tech support get the network back up, I'll be able to update my data-base. *(Gestures with the palm-pilot.)*

SATAN: All you can do is delay me for a while. If you give me his address now, perhaps I won't be so hard on him. If not . . .

(While he is talking the Woman reaches into her backpack. She pulls out a small silver cylinder and sprays something into Satan's face while at the same time making a grab for his palm-pilot. Satan does not react or lose his grip on the palm-pilot.)

SATAN: What was *that* about?

WOMAN: Uh . . . Mace?

SATAN: How ridiculous. Perhaps you would care to try holy water?

WOMAN: How many women carry holy water around?

SATAN: You would be surprised. Now are you going to tell me how to find Jonathan Sykes?

WOMAN: No! I won't!

SATAN: Maybe I should take your soul instead. That way the ledger would be balanced and I wouldn't have to wait.

COYOTE: I think you should tell him.

WOMAN: What? But you said . . .

COYOTE: Hey, you gotta know when you're out-classed. If you go head-to-head with this guy, you're gonna lose.

WOMAN: Oh. *(Beat.)* All right. I guess I don't have much choice. *(She takes the palm-pilot and makes an entry, then hands it to Satan.)* There. He's got the corner office upstairs. Heavy guy, about fifty — going bald. Rolex, gold rings, you know the type.

SATAN: I certainly do. *(Looks at the palm-pilot.)* Zip code?

WOMAN: I don't know. Everybody in Seattle knows where it is. Just ask!

SATAN: Hmn. I'll be going now. Enjoy the — wasteland.

(Exit Satan.)

COYOTE: A suspicious person might think you didn't exactly tell him the truth.

WOMAN: Didn't somebody say, "Everybody needs a few tricks to get along"?

COYOTE: It must have been a very smart person who said that. Well, I gotta be going.

WOMAN: Wait! I'm still lost! Can you lead me out of here?

COYOTE: I don't have time; I've gotta scrounge up something to eat.

WOMAN: You ingrate! I gave you food.

COYOTE: That crap? I could barely choke it down!

WOMAN: It was the best I had!

COYOTE: Well, you should try the dumpster behind the truckstop on Highway 89. Sometimes you can find half a fried chicken! Extra crispy.

WOMAN: I don't know where . . . *(Beat.)* Hey, that's a good idea!

COYOTE: It is?

WOMAN: Yes, that sounds really good. Nice juicy chicken. Crunchy skin, just dripping with grease! Mmm-mn!

COYOTE: Yeah! That *is* a good idea.

WOMAN: Why don't we go there now? I'll buy us *two* chickens!

COYOTE: And fry-bread?

WOMAN: All the fry-bread you want! Now, which way is it?

COYOTE: See those rocks over there? It's just behind them . . . You could hear the traffic if you didn't have such stubby little ears. Only half a mile.

(The Woman turns and gives him a withering look.)

COYOTE: *What?*

(Lights out.)

END OF PLAY

SOUP
by John Howie Patterson

FIRST PERFORMANCE
January 1998

ORIGINAL CAST
    Brian . . . . .Jay Kensinger
    Dad . . . . .Richard McKenzie
    Directed by . . . . .Jean Weisz
    Sets by . . . . .Mark Hopkins

CHARACTERS
DAD: A man in his sixties.
BRIAN: His son, twenties.

SETTING
The living room and kitchen of Dad's messy apartment.

SOUP

Setting: The living room and adjacent kitchen of a small messy apartment. Upstage left is the kitchen. A good seventy-five percent of all the counter and stovetop area is covered with dishes, silver, and miscellaneous paper. The living room, with a couch and TV, isn't much better. Ironically, a vacuum cleaner stands next to the couch, indicating the apartment residents perhaps had the intention to clean at some point, but never followed through. A dining table stands on the edge of the living room, right next to the kitchen. Stage right is a doorway leading out of the apartment.

At rise: Dad, in his mid-sixties, dressed casually with a cooking apron on, sadly stirs a pot of soup in the kitchen. Brian enters from a room adjoining the living room carrying an old, yellowed pillow. He lays the pillow down on the dining room table.

BRIAN: You can almost hear an echo in here.
DAD: Sad, isn't it?
BRIAN: In a way.
DAD: Got time for the soup?
BRIAN: Better not. Mickey's Mom is whipping up something for us at the house.
DAD: I was kind of hoping we'd have a little time — before you — but that's okay, if you want to get going. I'll just put some in a container — you can take it with you.
(Dad pathetically puts some soup in a plastic container. Brian watches him silently.)
So — is there anything — nothing you need — that I can —
BRIAN: Got it covered, Dad.
DAD: How about the finance department?
BRIAN: That's what the job's for.
DAD: Well yeah, but that first paycheck is still several weeks —
BRIAN: I'm living there rent free remember? Until I get on my feet.
(Dad is taking a long time to serve the soup. Brian looks at his watch. Dad looks up at Brian, sees his impatience and quickly finishes serving it.)
DAD: *(Handing it over the counter to Brian.)* There you go. You'll probably get — oh — three bowls out of that.
BRIAN: Thanks.
DAD: You want more? Bigger container? You could freeze some. Have it for weeks if you want it. I could —
BRIAN: Dad — I gotta go.

(Silence.)

DAD: Yeah.

BRIAN: You're mad aren't you?

DAD: No, no —

BRIAN: Dad.

DAD: Well it is all kind of sudden and —

BRIAN: What's sudden about it?

DAD: I just — I'm surprised, that's all.

(Moving away from Brian, Dad starts to pick up the apartment.)

So soon. A little notice would've been nice.

BRIAN: What — so you could find someone else to rent the room? You knew I was leaving eventually.

(Dad doesn't answer. He continues to pick up the room.)

There you go again.

DAD: What?

BRIAN: You're not even listening.

DAD: I'm listening.

BRIAN: No you're not.

DAD: I can listen and clean at the same time.

(Dad stops cleaning, looks at Brian.)

Is that why you're leaving? Cause I don't listen?

BRIAN: I didn't even want to get into this. Good-bye.

(Brian starts going toward the front door.)

DAD: *(Picking up the pillow.)* You forgot your pillow.

BRIAN: Keep it.

DAD: No, no, you keep it. It's —

BRIAN: All right, fine. You want me to take the pillow, I'll take the pillow.

(Brian tries to take the pillow but his father grips it tightly.)

DAD: This is your college pillow.

BRIAN: You want me to frame it? Right next to my diploma?

(Dad is silent for a moment.)

DAD: I didn't keep you here you know. I never held you back. I've always wanted the best for you. And your brothers. And I always said you know, whenever you wanted to go, that I had no feeling whatsoever.

BRIAN: So what's the problem now?

(Silence.)

Dad?

DAD: Just go.

BRIAN: Dad —

DAD: The problem now is — you don't have money, you don't have a job —
BRIAN: I do have a job.
DAD: Minimum wage. That's not a job.
BRIAN: It's almost twice minimum wage.
DAD: Won't be enough to live on.
BRIAN: Maybe not the way you live.
   (Silence.)
DAD: What's that supposed to mean?
BRIAN: Nothing.
DAD: Listen — when I retired, I did it comfortably. I thought ahead. If I want to buy cars, take trips —
BRIAN: It won't last forever.
DAD: That's my business.
BRIAN: *(Looking around the room.)* This place is a sty.
DAD: Well thanks. We can add that to the list of things I did wrong. I didn't listen, I didn't clean — *(Motioning around the room.)* Hell, half of this crap is yours —
BRIAN: Hell it is.
DAD: Least you could do is help me pick up before you —
BRIAN: Whoa. Wait a minute here. I am not a slob. I made — a constant and concerted effort to keep this place clean — while I lived here. That is the truth. But if that's what you need to feel better. Fine. *(Brian starts picking things up around the room. He starts putting things into piles.)* This is yours, this is yours, this is yours. Oh, what's this? *(He examines an official looking piece of paper.)* No wonder you have such a hard time doing your taxes. All the important papers are scattered all over the floor.
DAD: *(Snatching the paper from Brian.)* Gimme that.
BRIAN: You're a slob, Dad, a first class slob. Face it.
   (Dad is silent. He sits, looking at the pillow.)
DAD: We drove across country with this thing didn't we? After you graduated.
BRIAN: Dad, you're the only person I know who can get sentimental over a pillow.
DAD: Well somebody has to.
BRIAN: I'm sorry I called you a slob.
DAD: No, you're right. I am a slob and I do need to keep this place up better and —
BRIAN: I didn't — I shouldn't — I shouldn't have said that.
DAD: Why not? If you meant it and it was the truth — so be it. Don't feel bad.

(Silence.)

BRIAN: But I want to.

DAD: *(Turning to look at Brian.)* What?

BRIAN: Feel bad.

(Beat.)

I want to feel bad. That's the point. I want to feel whatever I'm feeling. Try it all out without you —

DAD: Meddling.

BRIAN: Finishing my sentences.

DAD: Sorry.

BRIAN: Giving advice. Comforting me. Making it easy for me.

DAD: You want to fuck up on your own.

BRIAN: Exactly.

DAD: So who's stopping you?

BRIAN: Nobody. Nobody except me.

DAD: And me apparently.

BRIAN: No. Not you. Not exactly. It was never you, Dad. Maybe you made it a little harder by being so —

DAD: Hospitable?

BRIAN: Yeah. Maybe I would've been better off if you had just cut me loose after graduation.

(Beat.)

But I'm not blaming you. *(Brian touches his Dad on the arm.)* I've enjoyed living here. I've enjoyed our time together. *(Dad grabs Brian's wrist and squeezes it.)*

DAD: We've had some great times haven't we?

BRIAN: Yeah. And there'll be more. Don't worry.

DAD: *(Standing up and hugging Brian.)* All right then. Get the hell out of here. Go set the world on fire.

BRIAN: Thanks, Dad. And seriously, I'd be glad to help you organize in here sometime if —

DAD: Don't worry. I'll hire a maid. A maid who does taxes on the side.

BRIAN: *(Picking up the soup.)* I'll call you. *(Moving toward the front door.)* Maybe we can do lunch next week.

DAD: Maybe.

(Beat.)

Say hello to Mickey for me.

BRIAN: *(Opening the front door.)* Yeah. I will.
   (Beat.)
   Bye.
DAD: Bye.
   (Brian starts to leave. He stops.)
BRIAN: Dad?
DAD: Yeah?
BRIAN: I love you.
DAD: I love you too.
   (Brian exits. Dad stands quietly near the front door for a moment, then ambles into the living room. He surveys the messy room, then picks up a trash bag that's lying on the floor. He slowly starts cleaning up, putting everything he wants to save onto the couch and everything he wants to throw out into the garbage bag. Once he has the floor clear, he grabs the vacuum and unwinds its cord. On his way to plug it in behind the kitchen table, he notices Brian's pillow on the table. He picks it up and holds it sadly for a moment, undecided about what to do with it. He holds it up against the wall to see how it looks. Sadly, he pulls it down from the wall and grabs the plastic garbage bag. He holds the pillow over the plastic bag for a moment, as if saying good-bye. Then he drops it in and seals up the bag. He then moves to the kitchen, scoops a large spoonful of soup out of the pot and puts it in his mouth.)
DAD: Not bad. Not bad at all.
   (Blackout.)

END OF PLAY

THERAPY IN THE PARK
by Doug Hanvey

FIRST PERFORMANCE
January 1996

ORIGINAL CAST

Lucinda	Mikki Adams
Bernie	John Holbert
Joseph	Avondina Wills
Marlissa	Meadow Davis
Dieter	Robert Berryessa
Directed by	Brian Spenser
Sets by	William "Skip" Epperson

TIME
11:50 A.M. on a warm and bright day.

SETTING
A park in the downtown of a medium to large city, surrounded by tall buildings. A park bench or two dominate the scene.

THERAPY IN THE PARK

As the lights come up, we see Lucinda, a woman in her late twenties to mid-thirties, sitting on a bench. She is wearing a very unattractive wig. A fancy department store shopping bag sits on the ground next to her feet. After a moment, Bernie, a man in his early to mid 30s, enters. He radiates anxiety and the feeling that he is under an inordinate amount of pressure. It soon becomes apparent that he wants to communicate with Lucinda, but lacks the nerve. After a short time of this desperate display of shyness, he makes a very loud groan, as if to attract attention, as he sits down next to her. She notes this public display of emotion and regards him silently for a moment.

LUCINDA: Hey, you OK?
BERNIE: *(Nervously.)* Oh, no, I wouldn't say that.
LUCINDA: Kind of stressed out, huh? This city can do that to you.
BERNIE: Yeah, I guess so.
(He turns to look at her for the first time.)
LUCINDA: *(Offering a hand.)* Lucinda.
BERNIE: *(Taking it.)* Uh, Bernie, hi. Hey, thanks for, you know, noticing me.
LUCINDA: *(Amused.)* How could I not?
BERNIE: You know, talking to me. It's something I've always wanted to be able to do. You know, to just go up and talk to anybody you see. Anybody that looks interesting. Someone you maybe find attractive and want to get to know. You know.
LUCINDA: Yeah, sure.
BERNIE: Actually, that's why I'm here. See, I made a bet with my therapist.
(She smiles.)
No, really. This is actually the end of my therapy hour, and I made a bet with Nick, my therapist, that in ten minutes flat I could talk to five different people down here in the park. Actually, *he* made the bet with me.
(Pause.)
That's only two minutes per person.
LUCINDA: Not exactly quality time.
BERNIE: Well, it's just for the practice.
LUCINDA: It *is* hard to meet people these days. *(Coyly.)* Especially members of the opposite sex. *(Pause.)* Is that . . . the eventual goal?
(Bernie nods.)
So you're looking for that special somebody, huh?
BERNIE: *(Embarrassed.)* It's not so much the talking, it's the getting going part.

The saying hello part. I'm kind of shy when it comes to that. *(Grimly.)* Anyway, Nick's on the ninth floor of number four hundred forty there watching me with two hundred power binoculars. *(Waves up at the building.)*

LUCINDA: Sometimes it helps me to meet people when I dress up like someone else, you know, wear a wig or something. I feel like a different person, kind of like I'm at a Halloween party or something. Then it's not so vulnerable trying to meet people.

BERNIE: Yeah.

(Pause.)

LUCINDA: Isn't it unethical for a therapist to make a bet with a client?

BERNIE: Oh, it's not for anything, really.

(She ponders this information for a moment, laughs.)

LUCINDA: Oh I get it. He bet you *could* do it, and you bet you *couldn't*. And now you're out to prove him wrong. *(Laughs again.)*

BERNIE: Well, no, not actually. He doesn't think I *can* do it. I mean, that's OK. He told me he *wants* to believe in me. But I think I know what he's up to. It's one of those advanced techniques. I think it's supposed to make me angry enough to get me over my fear.

LUCINDA: So you're pissed, huh?

BERNIE: *(Blankly.)* Not really.

LUCINDA: So what's the bet?

BERNIE: Huh?

LUCINDA: What happens if you win?

BERNIE: Well, if I win, Nick won't ever pretend again he doesn't know me when we meet in public. See, that happened last week and, you know, I *really* didn't like it. But I don't think there's too much chance of me winning, 'cause I had to agree with him that it was unlikely I'd be able to do it.

LUCINDA: Not much of a bet.

BERNIE: No, I guess not. I mean, I'd like to be able to do it, I really would. I've wanted to my whole life. I'm just not sure I can.

LUCINDA: Well, look at it this way. We've been introduced. I mean, that's the worst part for you, right?

(Bernie nods.) (Shyly.)

I mean, you know, maybe we could go to lunch or something after the ten minutes is up. *(Getting no response, she continues on another tack.)* Look, you've only got four more people to meet. You know, *I'll* bet you you *can* do it.

BERNIE: Yeah?

LUCINDA: Sure. And this way, whatever happens, you'll win at least one bet. But this'll be a real bet. How about . . . loser buys lunch?
(She offers her hand, they shake.)
BERNIE: Well, sure. OK *(Brightens.)* Maybe I *can* do it.
LUCINDA: Sure you can. Meet you back here in . . .
(Bernie checks his watch.)
BERNIE: *(Grimly.)* . . . seven minutes.
(Lucinda walks off and Joseph walks on. They know and greet each other. Joseph is a large, rather dilapidated and scraggly, but seemingly happy man. He sits down on a bench. Bernie sits down next to him. Joseph turns to look at Bernie and then scoots a bit closer to him. Joseph rarely stops smiling throughout the following scene. He leans over in Bernie's direction.)
JOSEPH: Are you feeling . . . gay?
BERNIE: Oh, uh, I, um . . .
JOSEPH: Well, *are* you?
BERNIE: Gay? No, I don't think so. Well, once when I was in college I fooled around with . . .
JOSEPH: *(Interrupting.)* Not *queer*, man, *gay*. You're talking about queer. Gay isn't queer. Gay . . . is *gay*. You know, *happy*, man. Gay! Like old times.
BERNIE: *(Twitters.)* Oh, uh, sure, I guess I'm, uh, gay. *(Reflects; seriously.)* Well, maybe not so gay today. I'm under a great deal of pressure.
JOSEPH: Oh yeah?
BERNIE: Well, you see, it's not like *external* pressure. It is in a way, but it's a self-growth thing. *(With self-assurance.)* It's an advanced technique. Nice talking to you, but I've actually got to go now.
JOSEPH: But tell me about this, man. This is *interesting*.
BERNIE: *(Looks at watch.)* Yes, but you see I really don't have time. I've only got five minutes left and I've got people to meet. Three of them, actually.
JOSEPH: Let me tell you something, man.
BERNIE: *(Getting anxious.)* Yeah?
JOSEPH: Gay's where it's at, man. *Happy*. That's what turns people on, you know, makes you ap*proach*able. Hey, there's a chick, man. Be gay. Don't worry so much, man. Be gay. I'm gay. Go for it, man.
(Bernie can only nod.)
JOSEPH: And another thing, man.
(Bernie worriedly checks his watch.)
BERNIE: *(Leaving.)* Um, I better go meet this, uh, chick.
JOSEPH: Just remember man, gay!

THERAPY IN THE PARK

(*Bernie turns away and sees a pretty and vulnerable-looking young woman, Marlissa, coming slowly down the sidewalk, in full tennis regalia and carrying a tennis racquet — not properly, but drooping and swinging from the base of the handle. She appears to be somewhat distraught. Bernie gets the quick idea to mime swinging a tennis racquet: serve, forehand. He tries with difficulty to look "gay," smiling ingratiatingly. She goes up to him.*)

MARLISSA: (*Miserably.*) Oh, God, maybe *you* would understand.

BERNIE: (*Hopefully.*) Sure.

MARLISSA: The most *awful* thing just happened to me. I was just down at the courts, (*Motions.*) you know, and having the greatest time, and then, (*Almost starts to cry.*) you know how the balls have those numbers on them, like Wilson Six and Dunlop Three, so you don't get them mixed up with the other people's balls. Well, (*Starts to cry again but gets her control back.*) our ball went on the next court and I said, "Excuse me, could you get our ball, please." (*Speaking faster.*) And he said, "What kind," and I said "Dunlop Three," and he said: (*Very slowly and solemnly.*) "That's what we have." (*With a big out-breath.*) Oh God! And he, he (*Almost hysterical.*) couldn't figure out which was our ball. (*Weeping uncontrollably.*)

BERNIE: (*Disturbed and wants to help.*) God, I'm sorry.

MARLISSA: (*Over the top hysterical.*) And he didn't *care!* He didn't think it was important. But it *was.* It *was!* Was! Was! (*Has totally lost it now, continues to babble incoherently.*)

BERNIE: Oh God, yeah, sure . . . (*Checks watch.*) Look, I'm sorry, I'd really like to help, but I've, I've got to go, I'm, well, running late.

MARLISSA: (*Through muffled sobs.*) Go then! (*She starts to move on.*) Just go! You don't care either!

BERNIE: No I do, really! I just, it's kind of hard to explain.

MARLISSA: Go! Go!

(*Bernie now bears an expression that conveys guilt and anxiety simultaneously. As Marlissa walks off, he turns around as if to try to forget her and sees an older man, Dieter, place a fake pigeon on the ground. He then proceeds to "feed" the pigeon by throwing crumbs from a paper bag. Soon, after realizing the bag is just about empty, he turns it upside down to empty the remainder. Dieter has a strong, deep voice and thick German accent.*)

DIETER: Go on now, eat up! It's good bread! (*He notices Bernie watching him and eyes him back slightly suspiciously. Then, as if to make conversation . . .*) These birds! I come to feed them and do they eat? What do they want, Bratwurst?

(*Bernie is speechless. Finally he leans over and picks up the pigeon.*)

DIETER: Hey, hey! What are you doing?
(Bernie sets down the pigeon.)
BERNIE: This is a fake pigeon.
DIETER: You think this is real bread? *(Mutters obscenities in German as he stalks off.)*
(Pause.)
BERNIE: Shoot! Where'd everybody go? That's only four people. *(Looks at his watch.)* Two more minutes.
(Bernie looks up at Nick's building and waves, with a quick nervous smile. He walks a little farther and sees a woman on a bench. In reality, it is Lucinda, but she has taken off her wig, and now we see her real (and much more attractive) hair. She is wearing sunglasses and is very pretty. He does not recognize her though discerning audience members may by noticing the same shopping bag, purse, etc. He sits down next to her, thinking maybe he's actually going to be able to do it. Checks his watch again. Tries to think of something to say.)
BERNIE: Um . . .
LUCINDA: *(With a thick Southern accent.)* Oh, I just love it when a man is brave enough to come right up and talk to me.
BERNIE: Oh, well . . .
LUCINDA: It's just so manly. *(Looking him over.)* Hey, you're kind of cute.
BERNIE: Oh, thanks. Well. *(Checks his watch.)* Time's up. *(Smiles.)* Hey, what do you know?
LUCINDA: *(Coyly.)* Have we run out of time?
BERNIE: Oh, no. *(Realizing she's quite attractive.)* Not at all.
LUCINDA: *(Speaking slowly while taking off her sunglasses; near the end of the sentence her accent disappears without a trace.)* Oh good, because I do *so* much enjoy talking to you.
BERNIE: Have we met?
(Lucinda takes the wig out of her bag and flops it on her head.)
Oh, Lucinda, it's you! *(Almost a monotone.)* Oh darn!
LUCINDA: What's wrong?
BERNIE: I was supposed to talk to five different people, but it's you again. That's still only four. And time's up. Shoot! I didn't do it. I lost the bet.
LUCINDA: Did you recognize me without the wig?
BERNIE: Well . . .
LUCINDA: No, you didn't. And do you think your friend did up there? I highly doubt it. I've been watching you, and there was no way I was going to lose our bet. So I'd have to say you did indeed talk to five people. Actually,

I think I can speak for most women when I say I'm *much* too complicated to be just one person.

BERNIE: Well . . .

LUCINDA: Now remember what I said about wearing a wig? Most guys are afraid of my looks. But . . . *(Twirls the wig around her head.)* . . . there's nothing like this for approachability. Now I've met you *twice!* And you know what? That means I won the bet. *(Takes the wig off.)* And so did you, actually.

BERNIE: So . . . that's your real hair?

LUCINDA: *(Again with the Southern accent.)* Oh, you bet, honey. *(Smiles.)*

BERNIE: Gosh . . . you were kind of here for the same reason.

LUCINDA: *(Embarrassed.)* Yeah. Well, guess it's time for lunch, huh? Congratulations! *(Offers her hand and they shake.)* You know, I'm feeling almost . . . gay! *(Bernie gives her a "you too?" look.)*

LUCINDA: Well now. He's a nice man! Hey, time for lunch. *(Lucinda dons her sunglasses. They link arms and begin to walk off.)* Does this mean you're cured now?

(Bernie gives a quick wave and thumbs-up back toward Nick as they exit.)

END OF PLAY

TURNING INTO MOTHER
by Elaine Clark McCarthy

FIRST PERFORMANCE
January 1996

ORIGINAL CAST
- Lavinia .... Joy Wiggins
- Jan .... Patti Fitchen
- Flower .... Susan Myer
- Jeff .... Casey Wood
- Directed by .... Clifford Henderson
- Sets by .... William "Skip" Epperson

TURNING INTO MOTHER

Setting: A large living room, the lair of an old hippie in a crumbling stately house. Furniture draped with shawls; books, candles, etc. all over the place. In the center of the upstage wall is a fireplace. Above the fireplace a large frame surrounds the "portrait" of Lavinia, in reality a small stage-within-a-stage just big enough for the actress to pose stiffly in a brocaded armchair, her ankles primly crossed, frowning slightly, hands folded. Every hair is neatly tucked into her bun, her brooch is perfectly straight, her skirt covers her knees. She's about seventy. In front of the fireplace stands the same brocaded armchair. It has become a bit shabby and is mostly hidden by a tartan shawl.

At rise: Jan, a woman of about sixty, sits playing solitaire. She cultivates the appearance of a madwoman: too much jewelry, frothy clothing, etc.

JAN: Damn. It's not going to come out.

LAVINIA: If at first you don't succeeed, try, try again.

JAN: Still bringing me up? Be quiet, or I'll put the blanket over you.

LAVINIA: If you'd grow up, I wouldn't need to go on raising you.

   (Jan moves some of the cards around, continues the game. After a few moves she claps her hands and stands up.)

JAN: Hah! That's thirteen in a row. An omen.

LAVINIA: It doesn't count if you cheat.

JAN: What do you care? You're dead.

LAVINIA: If I'm dead, who are you talking to?

   (The doorbell rings. Immediately, Flower and Jeff enter. Flower is twenty-eight, dressed in a stylish little suit, carrying a briefcase. Jeff has an equally buttoned-up appearance.)

FLOWER: Mother?

JAN: Darling! Welcome home!

   (She dashes to her daughter, hugs her dramatically.)

JAN: And this must be Jeff! Son!

   (She gives him an equally enthusiastic hug.)

JEFF: Pleased to meet you.

JAN: You're perfect for each other; I can feel it! Just like a pair of bookends!

JEFF: I told you she'd like me. Flo thought you wouldn't like me!

JAN: Oh, she gets some odd ideas sometimes; you have to make allowances. It skips a generation, you know.

JEFF: Does it? I thought women were supposed to turn into their mothers.

JAN: I wish.

LAVINIA: No you don't. I've tried and tried, but you never wanted to be like me a bit!

JAN: Don't just stand there, Flower. Come sit! Tell me about the wedding plans; I want to hear every detail!

JEFF: Flower?

FLOWER: Flo, mother; please.

JAN: I think you should have a dozen tiny little girls, each with a different color dress. They could *throw* matching petals all during the ceremony; wouldn't that be nice?

FLOWER: Actually, Mom, everything's already planned . . .

JEFF: Did she call you 'Flower'?

LAVINIA: You've put your foot in it the first minute! Why don't you ever listen to me?

JAN: I don't see why she wants to be called 'Flo.' It sounds like someone's maiden aunt!

FLOWER: I had it changed in court the day I turned eighteen. It's been ten years since anybody called me 'Flower,' but she still "forgets."

JEFF: I kind of like it.

FLOWER: I bet I was the only kid in the whole course of western civilization whose mother named her after a skunk!

JEFF: "Flower." It suits you, hon.

JAN: At least I didn't name you 'Bambi'!

FLOWER: Oh, god; here we go again. I knew this was a mistake.

JAN: A Flo by any other name would smell as sweet.

FLOWER: She's going to ruin everything!

LAVINIA: I warn you, if you don't start acting respectable, you're going to spoil this for her. Nobody wants to marry a girl whose mother is . . . peculiar.

JAN: I only . . . Oh, all right. I'll call you "Flo," Flo. It feels like calling you "grandma," but I suppose I'll get used to it.

FLOWER: It's not just that. I'd sort of forgotten . . .

JAN: I'm not surprised; you haven't been here for months!

FLOWER: . . . how you dress. We'll have to get you something respectable to wear; you can't come to my wedding looking like that.

JAN: You don't like it?

LAVINIA: Buy the blue suit, I said, but would you listen? Oh, no! You had to have your own way, as usual.

JEFF: I don't know, it's got panache. Maybe with a crown of ivy instead of the baseball cap . . .

FLOWER: I saw a lovely grey suit the other day at Saks. I'll have them send it. I'm sure it'll fit beautifully.

JEFF: Grey, sweetheart?

FLOWER: Why not? It's no use pretending she's going to *act* normal, but at least she doesn't have to look like a leftover medium from "Blithe Spirit."

JAN: I suppose I could dress it up with a few scarves . . .

JEFF: I don't know, Flo; I see her in red, myself. I've always wanted a mother-in-law in a flaming red dress.

FLOWER: You never told me that!

JEFF: You're so . . . understated yourself, sugar, I didn't think there was a snowflake's chance.

LAVINIA: Red! Everyone will think you're a scarlet woman!

JAN: I do have my velvet Ms. Santa thingy from Christmas . . .

FLOWER: Oh, my God! What next?

JEFF: Sounds great! That'll wake the pastor up!

LAVINIA: You know, I don't think this young man is quite the thing. He's got some very odd ideas.

FLOWER: I've never seen you in anything red, Jeff.

JEFF: She always forgets about my boxer shorts. Get a load of this!

(He starts to unfasten his pants.)

FLOWER: Jeff, for Heaven's sake!

LAVINIA: For heaven's sake stop him, Janice! Somebody might be looking in the window!

JAN: Dear boy, when Flow . . . I mean, Flo . . . when Flo told me she was bringing home an accountant, I really feared the worst.

JEFF: The way I see it, Mother Calender, there's no need to tell people what they don't want to know.

JAN: Call me Jan, darling. Do you like red and purple together? So many people . . .

FLOWER: Dearest, could I talk to you a minute?

(Flower doesn't wait for Jeff to answer, but jerks him aside.)

JEFF: Sweet, your mother was . . .

FLOWER: Jeffrey Doyle, I've been trying to keep clear of her . . . her *craziness* all my life. If you think for one minute . . .

(Her voice sinks to inaudibility; the two continue to talk.)

LAVINIA: I must say, I wouldn't have expected Flower to bring home such a very *unsuitable* young man.

JAN: He'll absolutely be the making of her! The answer to a mother's prayer.

(Lavinia is about to reply hotly, but stops herself and thinks furiously for a moment.)

LAVINIA: You know, dear, perhaps he's right about the dress. I believe the red thingy would look nice.

JAN: You're joking, mother! You hate that outfit.

LAVINIA: You'd look like a corpse in grey, dear.

JAN: You would know.

LAVINIA: I don't see how. You buried me in an orange caftan! It wasn't even my own dress.

JAN: It was the best you'd looked in years!

(Jeff and Flower's discussion heats up.)

FLOWER: But I don't *want* people to know I come from a long line of lunatics!

LAVINIA: "A long line"? Ungrateful brat!

JEFF: I never realized you were so . . . so repressed!

FLOWER: Wanting a normal life is not 'repressed'!

LAVINIA: I was her role model, and this is the thanks I get! You go ahead and wear the Ms. Santa thingy, Janice. Serve her right!

JAN: Well, I never thought I'd see the day you'd take my side, even dead.

LAVINIA: How can you say that? I've always only ever wanted what was best for you, you must know that.

JAN: Only you wanted it to be *your* idea of best.

LAVINIA: Isn't it fortunate that at this time of crisis, our ideas should finally match!

JAN: Fortunate! I think it's damn suspicious. You're just egging me on so they'll break up. Death has made you devious, Mother!

LAVINIA: How could she be happy with a man like that? Not that she deserves to be happy.

JAN: He's just what she needs, Mother! He'll wake her up! Flo! Flo, dear, I've changed my mind. I'll wear your grey suit and behave myself, I promise.

FLOWER: At this point, Mother, I'm not at all sure there's going to *be* a wedding.

LAVINIA: He's too much like you! She'll be fighting him all her life. You've got to stop trying to mold her, Janice. Show a little restraint!

JAN: Stop trying to mold her? What's this all about? You're dead and you're still working on me!

LAVINIA: That's different.

JAN: I'm not going to stand by and watch her lose someone who's so perfect for her; not if I can help it!

LAVINIA: There's nothing you can do!

JAN: We'll see about that. Stop fighting, you two; just cut it out this minute!

FLOWER: No, mother. If we're this different, it's none too soon to find out.

JAN: It's not that you're different. It's *her* evil influence!

FLOWER: Grandma's? What are you talking about?

JAN: She's been filling my head with ideas, pushing me to cause a rift by insisting on the red dress.

JEFF: I think you should maybe sit down, Mother Calender.

FLOWER: Really, Mother, get a grip. You're letting your imagination run away with you.

JAN: She won't let me alone; yakking day and night. I haven't slept in days.

LAVINIA: She's never going to believe that! She always had to wear earplugs to bed because your snoring shook the whole house.

JEFF: What does she say?

JAN: Oh, this and that. How everybody thinks I'm crazy.

FLOWER: Nobody thinks you're crazy, Mother. Just a bit . . . eccentric.

JAN: Go ahead, ask her. "Barking," she'll say. Go on.

JEFF: Do you think we should send for a doctor?

JAN: A doctor? Goodness, can't a woman talk to her mother without everybody getting into a tizz?

JEFF: Has she ever mentioned this before?

FLOWER: No, never. I always thought she was crazy, but there was no indication she was actually *insane*.

JEFF: Don't worry, Mother Calender; it's going to be all right.

FLOWER: Can you hear me, Momma?

JAN: Certainly I can hear you. Do you imagine I can hear my mother talking to me because I've gone *deaf*?

LAVINIA: What are you up to, Janice?

JAN: I don't suppose Flow . . . Flo . . . will be able to cope with me all by herself. I'll probably need constant attention. Round the clock, I wouldn't be surprised. Just until I recover, of course.

FLOWER: *(To Jeff.)* There's something a bit too convenient about all this.

JEFF: Convenient? It's positively inspired! Don't you worry about a thing, Mother Calender; I'll be right there to lend a hand. *(He gives Jan a huge wink.)*

JAN: Ahhh.

JEFF: Tell her you love her, Flo. Maybe that'll help.

FLOWER: Of course I love her! But I'm not going to *be* her no matter what kind of stunt she pulls!

JEFF: I should hope not! You're perfect the way you are.

FLOWER: Even in a biege suit?

JEFF: As long as you don't abandon those scarlet silk underpants.

FLOWER: All right, I know when I'm beat. Go ahead and wear a red dress to the wedding, Momma. Wear anything you want.

LAVINIA: Scarlet underpants! Janice! Talk to your daughter! What if she gets knocked down in the street!

JAN: She's right, dear. You will be careful in traffic, I hope? Mother and I don't want you to get hurt.

LAVINIA: That isn't what I meant!

JAN: She's at it again, Jeff. Could you just grab that blanket?

JEFF: Blanket?

JAN: Put it over the picture, dear; it's what I do when she gets on my nerves. There's a ladder behind the sofa. That's right.
(Jan leans back in the armchair with a satisfied smile, as Jeff gets the ladder out.)

LAVINIA: Go ahead, cover me up. You know I'll still be here, underneath. You can't silence a mother as easily as that. The Rock of Gibraltar's clay by comparison. I'll be here when the Eiffel Tower has turned to rust, watching over you, guiding you, advising you, keeping you from making horrible mistakes . . .
(Jeff mounts the ladder with the blanket. When he reaches the top and flings it over the picture frame, we
Fade to black.)

END OF PLAY

UNDERPANTS
by Wilma Marcus Chandler

FIRST PERFORMANCE
January 2000

ORIGINAL CAST

Twyla . . . . .Kristen Vaughn
Kitty . . . . Meg Herz Harlor
Art . . . . Frank Borovich
Directed by . . . . .Karen Schaumberg
Sets by . . . . .Dohn Grube

CHARACTERS

TWYLA: A shopper, over forty, well-dressed, carrying many shopping bags. She's been at it a good part of the afternoon.

KITTY: A woman in her late thirties; baggy jeans, a loose tee-shirt. No purse. Average height, average weight, average looks. Nice gold wedding ring. No diamonds.

ART: Kitty's husband. Early forties. Very conservatively dressed. Polyester pants, shirt, white socks, Hush Puppy shoes, plastic pen protector in shirt pocket. Very visible wedding band.

SETTING

The lingerie section of a mid-priced department store. Late afternoon.

SET

A long double-row of ladies underpants. The top row is composed of pastel colors arranged by size. The bottom row is the same but the colors are much richer and the styles are more flamboyant . . . lace, thongs, etc. in bright reds, purples, lime green, etc.

For the top row, a shopper might comfortably stand, but to reach the lower rack one has to squat down to inspect the merchandise.

In the distance is a sign (or another rack) indicating bras and slips.

There are three frilly, flower-covered chairs for the customers to use. They are near the panties rack.

UNDERPANTS

At rise: The panties rack is lit with a strange, altar-like glow as though it were a shrine. Distant drums are heard, like a ritual in some primitive village is in progress. Twyla enters from the audience. Kitty and Art are already on stage browsing through the panties department, but because it is dim on stage we do not see them immediately. As Twyla delivers her opening monologue she will progress from the audience area, where she will speak to a few people in the audience as though they, too, were shoppers, to the stage. The lights will become brighter and the music will subtly change from drumming to Musak as befits a one-cut-above-bargain-basement department store.

TWYLA: I love to shop, I *know* everyone doesn't, but *I* do. I can just get lost in all the choices and then when I finally decide — I decide!! It's like a good workout, you know? My husband hates it, but I don't think it's the actual shopping, but the *choosing* that wears him out. Doubt. Doubt. *(Laughs.)* It's a sad thing to see people fall by the wayside from self-doubt! Go for the burn, I say!!
(Beat.)
It wasn't always fun, though. I've had to really work at it. My most vivid memory as a child is of shopping with my Mother for school clothes every Fall. I must have been about eleven or twelve . . . very self-conscious, wanting to look just right all the time. My friend Myra Hirsch had a dress for every day of the school year . . . I'm not joking . . . her closets were amazing!! . . . Anyway, I mostly wore my cousin Edith's hand-me-downs, but that was okay because she had lovely taste in clothes and fairly free rein in choosing what she would buy each year . . . except for that kelly green camel's hair coat which I had to wear for *five winters* until my piano teacher finally said something to my parents about how my wrists were sticking out and getting very chilled and later in life that might cause arthritis . . .
(Beat.)
Anyway, my mother would take me to "The City" to shop. We'd go on the train and would plan to shop all day looking for sales, having lunch . . . in theory it was always a spectacular event . . . but this one time stands out because it was sort of a turning point for me. *(Beat . . . she is up on the stage by now.)*
The first store we go to is having all these post-summer sales and my mother finds a two-piece gray and fuschia checkered seersucker suit . . . sport top and dirndl skirt — hideous!!! She asks me if I like it. I believe it is an

innocent question and I say NO!! but she looks at the price tag and says, "Let's hold on to it for a while" and she starts carrying it around the store while I look at Ship n' Shore blouses and Lanz dresses. Finally, after a few minutes she announces that the gray is my new school outfit. Her voice was very calm, as I recall, "Either this or nothing." Slap. Slap. I could see my whole year stretched out before me. I literally had NO new clothes. I began to calculate. Is it better to get something new and hate it or wear all of last year's stuff?

(Beat . . . she has sunk into one of the flowered chairs . . . put all her bundles on another.)

(Now she notices Art and Kitty for the first time and will become more and more distracted by them as she concludes her monologue.)

I would have behaved differently now. Now I don't care what anyone thinks. I took the outfit just to have something new, and I wore it and lived in shame all that fall . . . every other Monday, and I always felt disgusting. No one ever said anything against it, but I felt such shame, both for the way I looked in it and for giving in to her.

Ah, well, that was years ago.

(Beat.)

Then there was the time I was a vegetarian . . . *(She starts to be distracted by Kitty and Art.)* It was at one of those family reunions . . . *(She stops as their conversation becomes the focus of attention.)*

KITTY: *(Browsing at the top row of panties.)* What do you think of the pink ones? I love this color!

ART: *(Ignoring her and deeply engrossed in his own work.)* Look down here at these. *(He holds up a pair of dark purple thong panties.)* What do you think of these?

KITTY: *(Not looking.)* Ummmmmmmmmm. *(She continues the search through the pastels.)*

ART: Look down here, will 'ya. There's some really good ones.

KITTY: *(Still holding the pink ones she squats down to the lower rack.)* These are cute. *(Holds up green pair.)* Do you like this green or is it kind of sickening?

ART: *(Takes the green ones and considers her question seriously and thoughtfully.)* No. I like them. Let's hang on to these.

KITTY: *(More looking.)* Do you like the red? *(She pulls out two pair of bikini undies.)* These look HUGE, but I like *these*, though . . . *(Puts one pair back.)* Kinda festive.

ART: Yeah. Let's take those, too. Put 'em on the pile.

(*He takes the green and red panties and puts them on a nearby chair with several others that have been previously selected. It should look as though they have been choosing for quite a while and are narrowing down their choices.*)

KITTY: I can't take them all.

ART: Well. We'll see. We'll decide.

KITTY: Tell me which you like the best. Oh! Look at these!! (*She's back at the pastels . . . holding up yellow and lavendar.*)

TWYLA: (*Tearing herself away from watching them.*) Being a vegetarian was my revenge. It wasn't too long ago I'd come home to family reunions and she'd cook a big roast beef and preside over it and everyone would ooh and aah and pass their plates in a meat frenzy and when I'd refuse she'd get enraged and say, "Are you implying that I wasn't a good mother?"

And my Dad would tell her to be quiet and pass the potatoes and my husband would look at all of us as though we were from some small village in the Gulag.

ART: Let's make two piles. The good ones and the great ones. Then we'll decide.

KITTY: Good idea. I love the lavendar ones and do you like this white lace trim?

TWYLA: (*More and more involved in Kitty and Art.*) Talk about the Gulag . . . (*She sort of indicates them with a small gesture.*)

ART: It's okay. I like these the best. (*He holds up a pair of black satin thong panties . . . very skimpy — kind of swaying them on the hanger to show how they move . . . but with great seriousness. This is not a frivolous affair for Art.*) (*Twyla is now intrigued by this conversation which began, for her, as just background sounds and has now fully engaged her attention. She has begun to just eavesdrop but as the scene continues she flat-out stares at them.*)

ART: I also like the gray ones. They're unusual. (*He holds up another sort of thong panty.*)

KITTY: Art?

ART: Yeah?

KITTY: Honey? I hate to tell you again, but thongs are very uncomfortable. I really don't like wearing them.

ART: (*Unfazed.*) Well . . . oh, I really like these. (*Yet another pair of thongs.*)

KITTY: I hate to burst your bubble, Hon, but I don't like them.

(*Twyla is listening carefully now . . . rapt attention.*)

ART: Sometimes we have to compromise. I compromise a lot.

KITTY: Maybe a couple of each kind. (*She's not placating, she's very straightforward.*) Which ones should I get?

TWYLA: (*Who can't believe her eyes and ears.*) Excuse me . . .

(*They do not realize she is addressing them.*)

ART: Okay. Let's go over the "great ones" pile, first.
TWYLA: *(Determined to get into this.)* Excuse me . . .
(Kitty and Art both turn to look at her.)
Uh . . . do you have the time?
KITTY: Oh, sure. It's *(Looks at watch.)* four thirty-five.
ART: *(Looks at his watch.)* I have four twenty-nine. You must be fast, Honey.
KITTY: Oh, well, it's around four-thirty. Fuchsia? *(Holds up fuchsia briefs to Art.)*
ART: Too big, don't you think? For you?
TWYLA: *(Still determined to get the true story on this couple.)* Excuse me . . .
ART: Yes?
KITTY: Yes?
TWYLA: I know it's none of my business. But I'm quite taken with how you and your husband share such an interest in your underwear shopping. I don't think I've ever seen anything like it. I know my husband wouldn't even walk into the store with me much less recognize lavendar from fuchsia. I'm sorry . . . I don't want to seem nosy or a bother but I'm quite amazed. *(She is very embarrassed but bumbles on.)* I'm quite drawn into . . . I mean, I'm kind of . . .
ART: Well we do most things together.
KITTY: No decision is too small.
ART: Come on, Kitty . . . make your decisions.
KITTY: Well, how about *(She selects four pair from the pile.)*
ART: Yes. Good. And then, two more for good behaviour. *(Laughs.)*
KITTY: Okay. *(She laughs, too.)* One of these *(The pastel briefs.)* and one of these. *(The black thong.)*
ART: *(To Twyla.)* Everything is compromise! Bye now. Happy shopping. *(To Kitty.)* Now . . . let's go look at bras.
(They go off to other part of store.)
TWYLA: *(Left alone in the flower-covered chair.)* That's disgusting! It's too weird!! *(She sits staring out as though hit by a truck. Silence. Her face and body go through several changes . . . disbelief, smirking, dismissal of the whole thing, then finally sadness . . .)* It wasn't a joke. It wasn't even a chore. *(Gets up. Goes to audience.)* Does your husband help you pick out underpants? Do you even want him to? *(Goes back to rack . . . starts browsing, picking up different panties.)* They probably clean house together on Saturdays. He does the laundry . . . different piles for white, dark . . . she freezes the meals for the upcoming week in little Tupperware thingees . . . They drink Sanka and splurge occasionally on Folgers. Everything works on schedule for them I bet . . . but their nights . . . *(She softens.)* I can imagine

they shower in their pink and blue bathroom and with their clothes off they are sleek . . . exotic maybe . . . he puts on a silk robe and she puts on the panties-of-the-night . . . everything turns kind of sumptuous . . . *(Her face is filled with sadness.)* Who would ever know? *(She bumps into one of the chairs . . . her shopping bags fall . . . things get messy.)*
(In the distance the drums begin . . . very softly.) Damn! *(She is holding two different kinds of panties in her hand as she bumps into the chair.)*
(Puts them back in the wrong place . . . takes out more . . . returns them incorrectly . . . she is visibly upset . . .)
Now I don't know which ones I should get.
They upset me.
Why do I have to make these choices by myself. I hate this.
(Goes to audience.)
Which ones should I get?
Tell me what looks good.
What looks sexy?
Oh, shit.
Why am I asking you?
(Puts everything back . . . again in the wrong places.)
I know I said I love shopping . . .
(She stops . . . laughs.)
So there must be some "at home" feeling about all this . . .
all the products spread out . . . choices . . .
sending a welcome . . .
(Looks at Kitty and Art in the distance, buying bras.)
It's a beautiful thing. *(Lights start to fade on them.)*
(Sits down.)
(Looks at her watch which she has been wearing all the time.)
Uh oh. I better get home.
(Drums a bit louder.)
(She rises . . . gathers her bundles, pulls herself up to the same jaunty stance she had upon entering and exits through the audience.)
(Lights glow on a very messed up panties rack while the drums play on.)
(Blackout.)

END OF PLAY

ZEN GRAVY
by Sharon Bandy

FIRST PERFORMANCE
January 1998

ORIGINAL CAST

Margaret ....Patti Fitchen
Grace .... Irene Teagarden
Betsy .... Sharon Bandy
Directed by ....Bonnie Ronzio
Sets by ....Mark Hopkins

ZEN GRAVY

ACT I
SCENE 1

> *Time: the present. A kitchen in suburbia. Two women stand over a stove. One, Margaret, is in her mid-forties, wearing all black, stretch pants, turtleneck, and exotic jewelry. She is frequently rude and condescending, but, in her own way, vulnerable. Her sister, Grace, is in her late thirties. She is dressed in frumpier clothing and an apron, and has spent the bulk of her life trying to please Margaret and her late mother.*

MARGARET: Gravy is like a strange dog, Grace. It senses fear.

GRACE: Funny. *(Pause.)* I wish I could remember what Mama said to do with the flour. Always pour it in before the drippings? Or always put it in last? *Always* something.

MARGARET: You've either got the gravy gene or you don't. Mama had. And I sure as hell don't. Give me that spoon. Forget the spoon . . .
(Margaret digs through the kitchen drawer.)
You should be using a whisk anyway. Do you even have a goddamned whisk? I know Mama did.

GRACE: Margaret, SIT DOWN.

MARGARET: Well, I don't know why you've got to get so snippy all of a sudden. I was just trying to help.

GRACE: Thank you, but I'm doing just fine.

MARGARET: Fine, then. *(Silence.)* What time did you tell Betsy to come over?

GRACE: Around two, I told her. She should be here shortly. She's bringing rolls and pie. Such a sweet girl. Too bad about her and Rick. I always thought they got along so well. Never heard any yelling. Their lawn always looked so nice.

MARGARET: What the hell does a nice lawn have to do with a happy marriage?

GRACE: All I'm saying is that everything looked so perfect over there . . . That's all I'm saying, Margaret. Can you try not to bite my head off every time I open my mouth? It is Thanksgiving, after all! *(Throws big clump of flour in gravy pan.)* Oh no, it's going to be lumpy. All these lumps. Now, I remember! Mama said, "Always sprinkle the flour into the grease." Oh well — looks like we'll just have lumpy gravy.

MARGARET: You're fighting it too much, dear. Be one with the gravy.

GRACE: I really don't have time for your Zen-speak right now, Margaret. If you haven't noticed, I'm trying to get Thanksgiving dinner on the table.

MARGARET: You really should try it. It might bring a little peace into your life. You're so angry. Back in my yoga days I could meditate for four hours straight without . . .

GRACE: If you will remember, your yoga days were followed by physical-therapy-slash-chiropractor days, and you still walk with a limp, SO DON'T ZEN ME!

MARGARET: I just want you to relax a little Grace, dear. If you close your eyes while you stir you can feel the energy of the gravy. Be one with it.

GRACE: I am one with it, Margaret. *(Throws spoon to the floor.)* I am lumpy, slowly thickening, and a blotchy shade of beige — I *AM* the God-damned gravy!

MARGARET: Sit down, dear. You're taking this much too hard.

GRACE: Look at us, Margaret. Here we are, two divorced women, waiting for a soon-to-be-divorced third to join our club, for a pathetic Thanksgiving dinner. We're not even a family anymore. Can't you see that? This is all pretend. We have no kids, never had a father to speak of, and now we have no mother on top of it. All we have is each other. And we're so different, it's as if we're not related at all. I bet if we met each other, I mean, if we weren't sisters, we wouldn't want to spend a minute together. Not one minute . . .

(Doorbell rings.)

GRACE: *(Continues.)* Come on in, Betsy. Door's open . . .

(Grace goes to stove to tend to gravy. Betsy enters briskly. She carries a basket of dinner rolls and a pastry box with a pie in it. She is Texas-southern, in her early thirties, perkily dressed with lots of makeup and well-tended hair.)

BETSY: Oh my goodness, what a glorious smell. There's nothing quite like the smell of Thanksgiving turkey. I'm sorry I'm a little late. Did I miss anything? It really was so nice of you to invite me over. I think we're going to have a great time, don't you? I wasn't sure how I was going to feel about today, you know. What with Rick just two miles away at his folks . . . without me. But I feel fine. Really, I feel just fine.

(Margaret looks at Betsy.)

BETSY: No, really . . .

MARGARET: Well great, then. We WILL have a good time. I think I'll put on some music.

BETSY: Oh, music sounds like a good idea. I've been listening to a lot more music. You know, since Rick left. The house just seems so empty, so quiet. I really am fond of the older stuff, the . . .

(Margaret goes to the stereo and turns it on. Sitar music wafts painfully and

loudly in the air, interrupting Betsy's rambling. Grace reacts by grabbing a bottle of aspirin and cupping her hand under the sink to catch water. Margaret reacts by going back to the stereo and turning the music off abruptly.)

GRACE: It really is nice of you to join us today. I imagine you're wishing you were down in Texas with your family?

BETSY: Oh no, not really. We never celebrated Thanksgiving like y'all do. My Daddy'd usually barbecue up a big ol' batch of ribs and we'd stuff ourselves silly. Mama's a terrible cook, so she saved face by not having to cook a traditional dinner, and people thought we were eccentric — Mama likes that . . . people thinking she's eccentric.

GRACE: So does Margaret.

MARGARET: Humpff.

BETSY: Oh, I don't think you're eccentric at all, Margaret. You dress a little different, sure, but you're really nice and you do normal things, drive a normal car, eat normal food I imagine, *(Nervous laugh.)* I guess I'll see soon enough . . .

GRACE: We're almost ready to eat. Margaret has set a lovely table, and I think the turkey is almost . . .

(Telephone rings. Margaret and Grace look at each other, as if to ask, 'who could that be?' Grace moves to answer the phone.)

GRACE: *(Continues.)* I won't be a minute. *(On phone.)* Hello. Yes, this is the Doyle residence, who is this? Yes, this is Grace. Who is this? *(Pause.)* Who? Oh my God.

(Grace drops the phone. Margaret picks it up.)

MARGARET: Hello, this is Margaret Doyle. May I help you? Who? No shit?! *(Pause.)* Well, Mr. Doyle, it was kind of you to call after — let's see — how long has it been? Oh yes, thirty-five years, but we're not interested . . . Mother? She's not interested either . . . She's dead.

(Margaret slams down phone.)

GRACE: You hung up on him? Did you get a number? I wanted to talk to him.

MARGARET: Oh sure, you really looked like you wanted to talk to him when you threw the phone down.

GRACE: I dropped it! It was a shock, that's all, and then you . . . you went and hung up on him. *(Close to tears.)*

BETSY: I'm afraid I'll have to agree with Grace here. She did drop the phone. Definitely a drop, not a throw. Shouldn't we be eating soon?

MARGARET: What would you have to say to that man, Grace? What? Come on over? We're having a warm family Thanksgiving with turkey and stuffing and lumpy gravy — we're just missing a family? Love to have ya? Huh? Is that what you were going to say?

BETSY: Grace dear, don't cry, Margaret doesn't mean what she's saying. I'd guess you're just a little shocked that's all.

GRACE: Margaret, calm down. We all should calm down. We've just got to think this through, that's all. What if he calls back? What'll we do? We need a plan.

MARGARET: What if he calls back? Are you serious?! Let's see . . . I'm forty-one now . . . carry the two . . . I'll be seventy-seven when he calls back. I'll worry about it then!

(Blackout.)

SCENE 2

One hour later, same kitchen, dirty dishes piled up, meal is over.

BETSY: That was a marvelous meal, really marvelous. Much better than anything I could have done, and way better than Rick's mom's meals by a long shot. She's one of those experimenters . . . you know what I mean? Always throwing an exotic ingredient into the stuffing, like mandarin oranges, or, one year, she puts cranberries IN the stuffing, and everything turns this disgusting shade of pink. Pink stuffing, just oozing out of the turkey's . . . you know . . . cavity. Rick was the only one who would eat it. Rick would eat dog shit if his mother put it on a plate for him. *(Pause, looks around, a little embarrassed.)* I'm sorry. I guess I got a little carried away there. Great meal, though, delicious, really.

MARGARET: Betsy, you DO talk a great deal, don't you.

GRACE: Margaret!

MARGARET: Well, she does. I'm only stating a fact. I find it endearing though. She's managed all through dinner to keep us off the subject of our wayward father.

BETSY: I was only trying . . . Yes, I guess I DO talk too much. It's just what I do, talk and talk and talk. Rick always said that about me. Always needed me to listen to every single goddamned word he said, but wouldn't listen to me one lick. I'm sorry. *(Pause.)* I talk so I don't have to think, especially today. I only wanted to get through today without crying.

(Betsy begins to cry.)

GRACE: Now, Betsy, don't let her get to you. You spend enough time over here and eventually you'll develop a pretty thick skin. You'll find that she says what she wants, when she wants, and to hell with manners. Just ignore her. We all do. *(She looks around as if expecting to see their dead mother somewhere.)* I mean . . . I do.

MARGARET: Yes, just ignore me, dear. Now . . . Back to the question of the man who called earlier. What do YOU think we should do if he calls back?

GRACE: Well, I don't know.

MARGARET: Do you really think there is anything he could say that could make you want him in your life at this point?

GRACE: That's what I need to think about.

MARGARET: I just hope, for your sake, that if he calls back I am not the one answering the phone, because I'll tell you, I'll do exactly the same thing, hang up!

GRACE: Well I'm glad you are so on top of it. I, however, am not sure what I'll do when he calls back. I just feel like I have so many questions, not the least of which is why did you leave us?

MARGARET: I can answer that one. He left because he was a coward. He left because he didn't want two kids and a wife that got too old too fast.

GRACE: Oh Margaret . . .

MARGARET: He left because he didn't want to stay and work and come home at night and be a part of something so dull as a middle class family, living in a middle class town, living a middle class existence.

GRACE: He couldn't be all bad.

MARGARET: His problem was that he wanted to be extraordinary, I imagine. *(Laughs bitterly.)* Perhaps that's where I get it. Only he was . . . I mean IS, a bastard!

BETSY: Well, those were hard times back then, weren't they? Hard to make a living, support a family. I'm not making excuses for him or anything. I mean I didn't even know your father. I'm just saying it was probably difficult, that's all.

GRACE: There had to have been some good things. Tell me, Margaret. You knew him. You got to grow up a little when he was around. I don't even remember him. All I know of him is that picture Mama kept in her slip drawer. I'd sneak in and look at it when she went out for groceries. I used to talk to him, to his picture. I'd tell him what I'd done in school, who I had a crush on. I did that until I was about fourteen. Then one day, the picture wasn't there. I guess Mama just finally gave up on him.

MARGARET: Mama never gave up on him, Grace.

GRACE: You've got to tell me something. Give me one memory, anything.

MARGARET: OK, here's a memory for you. He was tall and had dark brown hair that he slicked back with Brylcream. He was handsome, I think. I remember going to the State Fair in Sacramento when I was about nine. You would've been too young to remember that. He took me on any ride I pointed to, and Mama was happy and we were a real family. He was a great father. When he came home from work . . . when he still had work . . . he'd toss me up in the air and call me his little mushroom. I don't know why, but that was his name for me.

GRACE: Why didn't you tell me this before? No one ever talked about any good times. No one ever really talked about him at all. Why didn't you say anything. Why did you let me go on thinking he was just a total shit?

MARGARET: Don't you get it?! The good times just make all the rest so much worse. How can I believe we were ever really happy? If he could just up and leave us like that he couldn't have possibly loved us. The good times don't mean anything. Can't you see that?! He didn't care, don't you get it, Grace?!

BETSY: I get it. I know exactly what you mean.

MARGARET: See, even Betsy gets it. Remember, she's the one with the perfect lawn and the husband who just up and left her. You don't hear her sitting here telling us how she loved the smell of him when he came in the house smelling like fresh cut grass. You don't hear her telling us about the redwood deck he built her last summer so she could show off her prize orchids. It's too hard to remember the good times, for Christ's sake.

BETSY: She's right, you know. I keep thinking that later I'll appreciate those little things Rick did for me . . . the things that made me love him in the first place. But I can't bear to think about them now.

GRACE: I just wanted to know him. That's all. He was never a father to me, not that I can remember. I guess that's why I don't hold it against him as much. I don't know what he should have been or could have been or was, so I expect so much less. I guess I always expect less. It makes sense now though, I guess.

(Telephone rings. The three women stare at one another. Long pause. Margaret moves toward the phone which continues to ring. She places her hand on the receiver. Grace shakes her head no. Phone stops ringing eventually. Slow Fade.)

END OF PLAY

COPYRIGHT STATEMENTS

ANCESTOR by Sam Patterson © Copyright 1995, by Sam Patterson. Reprinted by permission of the author. All inquiries should be addressed to Sam Patterson, 2286 7th Avenue, Santa Cruz, CA 95062.

APRIL SHOWERS by Philip Slater © Copyright 1999, by Philip Slater. Reprinted by permission of the author. All inquiries should be addressed to Philip Slater, 125 Tree Frog Lane, Santa Cruz, CA 95062.

ASHES by Claire Braz-Valentine © Copyright 1997, by Claire Braz-Valentine. Reprinted by permission of the author. All inquiries should be addressed to Claire Braz-Valentine, 4160 Jade St. #3, Capitola, CA 95010, or by e-mail at CBrazvalen@aol.com.

THE ATOMIC PINEAPPLE by David A. Sullivan © Copyright 2000, by David A. Sullivan. Reprinted by permission of the author. All inquiries should be addressed to David A. Sullivan, English Department, Cabrillo College, 6500 Soquel Drive, Aptos, CA 95003 or by e-mail at dasulliv@cabrillo.cc.ca.us.

DINNER by Richard Markgraf © Copyright 1999, by Richard Markgraf. Reprinted by permission of the author. All inquiries should be addressed to the author, 1830 Avenida Del Mundo, Coronado, CA 92118.

ETAINE AND ETAIRE by Karen Villeneuve © Copyright 1997, by Karen Villeneuve. Reprinted by permission of the author. All inquiries should be addressed to Karen Villeneuve, c/o Actors Theatre, 1001 Center Street, Santa Cruz, CA 95060.

FRIED CHICKEN, HOT OR COLD by Ann MacGregor Gibb © Copyright 1997, by Ann MacGregor Gibb. Reprinted by permission of the author. All inquiries should be addressed to Ann M. Gibb, 150 Atherly Lane, Santa Cruz, CA 95060.

HABITS by Steve "Spike" Wong © Copyright 1996, by Steven G. Wong. Reprinted by permission of the author. All inquiries should be addressed to Steve "Spike" Wong, 3410 Putter Drive, Soquel, CA 95073.

THE HARD CEL by Philip Pearce © Copyright 1999. Reprinted by permission of the author. All inquiries should be addressed to the author, 1037 Olympic Lane, Seaside, CA 93955.

ID by Kyle Wood © Copyright 2000. Reprinted by permission of the author. All inquiries should be addressed to the author, 211 Stockton Avenue, #7, Capitola, CA 95010.

LOVE AND DEATH by Kathryn Chetkovich © Copyright 1999, by Kathryn

Chetkovich. Reprinted by permission of the author. All inquiries should be addressed to Kathryn Chetkovich, P.O. Box 1500, Boulder Creek, CA 95006.

MATCHING COLORS by Edith F. Cooper © Copyright 1997, by Edith F. Cooper. Reprinted by permission of the author. All inquiries should be addressed to Tom Cooper, 304 Concord Drive, Menlo Park, CA 94025.

MRS. SCHEINBAUM by Frank Hilmes © Copyright 1999, by Frank Hilmes. Reprinted by permission of the author. All inquiries should be addressed to Frank Hilmes, 305 Elan Village Lane, #327, San Jose, CA 95134.

MY HIGHER POWER by Melissa Klein © Copyright 2000. Reprinted by permission of the author. All inquiries should be addressed to the author, 1616 Longfellow Street, N.W., Washington, D.C. 20011.

NOCTURNE, WITH APPLES by Scott Munson © Copyright 2000, by Scott Munson. Reprinted by permission of the author. All inquiries should be addressed to Scott Munson, 2252 Fairhill Lane, San Jose, CA 95125.

PARCHEESIED by John Howie Patterson © Copyright 1994, by John Howie Patterson. Reprinted by permission of the author. All inquiries should be addressed to John Howie Patterson, P.O. Box 791, Capitola, CA 95010 or by e-mail at jopat@aol.com.

PAY PHONE by Wilma Marcus Chandler © Copyright 1997, by Wilma Chandler. Reprinted by permission of the author. All inquiries should be addressed to Marie Winfield, 885 35th Avenue, Santa Cruz, CA 95062.

THE PERM by Dale Elizabeth Attias © Copyright 2000, by Dale Elizabeth Attias. Reprinted by permission of the author. All inquiries should be addressed to Elizabeth Land, 103 Camino Pacifico, Aptos, CA 95003.

POETRY READING by John Chandler © Copyright 1997, by John Chandler. Reprinted by permission of the author. All inquiries should be addressed to Marie Winfield, 885 35th Avenue, Santa Cruz, CA 95062 or by e-mail at jochandl@aol.com.

THE RAIN ARE FALLIN by Richard M. Bennett © Copyright 1997, by Richard M. Bennett. Reprinted by permission of the author. All inquiries should be addressed to Richard M. Bennett, 229 Pestana Ave., Santa Cruz, CA 95065.

RETROGRADE by Doug Brook © Copyright 1998, by Doug Brook. Reprinted by permission of the author. All inquiries should be addressed to Doug Brook, P.O. Box 130307, Birmingham, AL 35213 or e-mail at carfax@concentric. net.

SAN FRANCISCO FEVER by Anne Adams © Copyright 1999, by Anne Adams. Reprinted by permission of the author. All inquiries should be addressed to Anne Adams, 1400 Olive Springs Rd., Soquel, CA 95073.

SIMÓN MALDONADO'S EPIPHANY by Juan Duarte © Copyright 1997, by Juan Duarte. Reprinted by permission of the author. All inquiries should be addressed to Juan Duarte, P.O. Box 35, Loma Mar, CA 94021.

SLINGIN' HASH AT THE LOWLIFE BAR AND GRILL by Susan Forrest © Copyright 1998, by Susan Forrest. Reprinted by permission of the author. All inquiries should be addressed to Susan Forrest, 2116 West Cliff Drive, Santa Cruz, CA 05060 or by e-mail at sforrest@scruznet.com.

SNACK TIME by Eric Elliot © Copyright 2000, by Eric Elliot. Reprinted by permission of the author. All inquiries should be addressed to the author, 1165 So. 8th St., San Jose, CA 95112.

SOUP by John Howie Patterson © Copyright 1996, by John Howie Patterson. Reprinted by permission of the author. All inquiries should be addressed to John Howie Patterson, P.O. Box 791, Capitola, CA 95010 or by e-mail at jopat@aol.com.

THERAPY IN THE PARK by Doug Hanvey © Copyright 1995, by Doug Hanvey. Reprinted by permission of the author. All inquiries should be addressed to Doug Hanvey, 425 N. Hillsdale, Bloomington, IN 47408.

TURNING INTO MOTHER by Elaine Clark McCarthy © Copyright 1995, by Elaine Clark McCarthy. Reprinted by permission of the author. All inquiries should be addressed to Elaine McCarthy, 640 E. Fifth, Watsonville, CA 95076.

UNDERPANTS by Wilma Marcus Chandler © Copyright 1999, by Wilma Chandler. Reprinted by permission of the author. All inquiries should be addressed to Marie Winfield, 885 35th Avenue, Santa Cruz, CA 95062.

ZEN GRAVY by Sharon Bandy © Copyright 1997, by Sharon Bandy. Reprinted by permission of the author. All inquiries should be addressed to Sharon Bandy, 1030 Can Tex Drive, Sewanee, TN 37375.

JOHN HOWIE PATTERSON is an award-winning playwright, teacher of playwriting, and Manager of the Santa Cruz Actors' Theatre. For three years he ran the Playwrights' Workshop at Actors' Theatre, helping to nurture a whole new generation of Santa Cruz playwrights. His produced plays include *Lie of the Beholder, Ain't Goin' Nowhere,* and *Ubu Bandit*, an homage to Alfred Jarry's *Ubu Roi*. He was educated at Northwestern University and has taught playwriting at the University of California at Santa Cruz.

WILMA MARCUS CHANDLER is a director, actor, and choreographer in the Monterey and San Francisco Bay area. For many years she has directed the Theater Arts program at Cabrillo College in Santa Cruz and has been an innovator in both teaching and producing performing arts courses and workshops. She was the co-coordinator of the National Festival of Women's Theater and the Louden Nelson Reading Series in Santa Cruz. She has directed and performed for many theater companies, including The Black Repertory Theater in Oakland and the Bear Republic Theater and has taught at the University of Iowa and the University of California at Santa Cruz. She lives in the Santa Cruz mountains with her husband, the novelist and playwright, John Chandler.

704